Vincent J. Knapp

State University of New York College
Potsdam

Europe in the Era of Social Transformation

1700-Present

PRENTICE-HALL, INC., ENGLEWOOD CLIFFS, NEW JERSEY

Library of Congress Cataloging in Publication Data

KNAPP, VINCENT J (date)
 Europe in the era of social transformation 1700-
present.

  Bibliography: p.
  Includes index.
  1. Europe—Social conditions. 2. Europe—Economic
conditions. 3. Social classes—Europe—History.
I. Title.
HN373.K48   309.1'4   75-14244
ISBN 0-13-291971-0
ISBN 0-13-291948-6 pbk.

© *1976 by Prentice-Hall, Inc., Englewood Cliffs, New Jersey*

PRINTED IN THE UNITED STATES OF AMERICA

10 9 8 7 6 5 4 3 2 1

PRENTICE-HALL INTERNATIONAL, INC., LONDON
PRENTICE-HALL OF AUSTRALIA, PTY. LTD., SYDNEY
PRENTICE-HALL OF CANADA, LTD., TORONTO
PRENTICE-HALL OF INDIA PRIVATE LIMITED, NEW DELHI
PRENTICE-HALL OF JAPAN, INC., TOKYO
PRENTICE-HALL OF SOUTHEAST ASIA (PTE.) LTD., SINGAPORE

To Janice, Derek,
Colin, and Kyle

It is moments of violent emotion and excitement that endure longest in the human mind. Events of everyday life gradually fade from the memory or become blurred in the haze of time. One can discern the same process of selection in recorded history, the memory of mankind. The tale of wars and revolution, of man's violent deeds and passions, of his greed for power, fills many pages in the history books. Little account is taken of day-to-day life. The simple ordinary things are passed by or, at most, remembered as curiosities.

Introduction to B. H. Slicher van Bath,
The Agrarian History of Western Europe,
A.D. 500–1850

I think it could be plausibly argued that changes of diet are more important than changes of dynasty.

George Orwell,
The Road to Wigan Pier

In every civilization of the past, bar none . . . . [there] was always a lousy standard of living.

Miles Perkins,
Surplus Marketing Administrator,
U.S. Department of Agriculture

Contents

Introduction

Europe entered the eighteenth century impoverished, undernourished, and undeveloped, the majority of its populace consigned to lives of toil with little reward and even less opportunity. Because up to now history has been devoted largely to the study of political and intellectual currents—and thus to the lives and activities of a tiny minority, the elite—only recently has enough factual material accumulated to begin to illustrate the nature of life for most people in the eighteenth century. The discoveries of the last fifteen years in the areas of social and economic history have helped finally to illuminate the role of the masses. For the very first time, we are now able to look beyond the activities of those of wealth, leisure and education to what 95 percent of the population did with its time and energies.

This relatively new area of endeavor has come to be known as the "new social history," and its focus is radically different. What it attempts to do is examine the way of life and the standard of living of the many through the vehicle of social classes. In this sense, the new social history could be described as sociology teaching by previous example. It depends on sociological categories. It investigates the past in terms of upward or downward mobility, by means of levels of consumption, or in reference to continuity or change. It sees society, either the static society of the eighteenth century or the more dynamic society that followed, through the eyes of the various social classes of those ages.

The term that we use for all of this, the new social history, has one obvious limitation; alone, it does not describe the driving force behind much of the research now being undertaken in its name. For in addition to the interest in classes, there is almost a compulsion to discover exactly how people lived in previous ages. Never before has a branch of history been so preoccupied by economics or, to be more specific, with the standard of living of earlier decades and centuries.

A discussion of class and an examination of the European standard of living will dominate this particular book, an exercise in the new history. This means that the focus will be almost exclusively on social and economic developments, omitting many of the great political and intellectual trends of the last three centuries. We will look closely at the millions of Europeans who tilled the soil, engaged in crafts, and manned the shops. In this sense, social history is more democratically oriented, and far broader in compass than the elitist focus of the traditional discipline.

This does not mean, of course, that the elite can be neglected. Elites not only dominated agricultural society, they have taken on a commanding role in industrial society as well. The loss of Europe's aristocratic class to social and economic forces it could neither really understand nor control did not mean that society was then left without an elite. Actually, the passage from one stage of economic development to another was matched by the decline of an older elite, the aristocracy, and the emergence of a new one—the upper middle class, the Establishment.

The movement of these elitist elements within society was a signal that Europe was about to undergo, in the nineteenth century, a great age of change. Eighteenth-century society—rural, underfed, poor, static, and in so many ways unyielding—was a mirror of the past. Its aristocratic character, its emphasis on agriculture, its inability to feed itself went back more than a dozen centuries. By the eighteenth century, Europe was destitute. More than half the children were dead by the age of six, average life expectancy was no more than half what it is today in modern India, and up to 20 percent of women in their fertile years might expect to die in childbirth. This was an age when the majority of men were disabled by disease and malnutrition. Even in "prosperous"

England, with perhaps Europe's richest supply of food, it has been estimated that up to half the population could work with only marginal efficiency because they were either mentally or physically debilitated by malnutrition.

We now know that the source of Europe's lingering poverty was her backward agriculture. Agriculture is, of course, one of the most neglected fields of history; perhaps the prediction of one social historian that the potato will eventually become more important than the French Revolution will someday come true. The primary problem for Europe, and the cause of much of her backwardness, was her overdependence on grain. Indeed, Western man, and in particular the European, entered the nineteenth century as a grain eater. Far from being "the staff of life," grain is one of the least nutritious foods known to man, lacking in protein and overall vitamin content—indeed unfortunate for a population that ate bread three times a day and between 75 to 85 percent of the time.

This last fact illustrates one of the concerns of social history. Once below the level of the aristocracy and the upper middle class in the eighteenth century, a whole new set of concerns appears. Not politics and ideas but bread moved the mass of artisans and peasants. During the French Revolution, the focus of masters, journeymen, and apprentices in the city of Paris was not upon the great overriding political and moral issues, it was upon the habit that regulated their days and the income that sustained their weeks. The same was true of the peasant proprietor, the middle peasant, and the landless peasant, who made up a full 85 percent of the population. Their lives were dominated by social and economic custom, and what social history tries to do is to see them as they actually were.

The static and impoverished society of the eighteenth century would eventually give way to the greatest economic force history has ever known, industrialization. Industrialization transformed Europe's economy and its social order. It was in the long run an unqualified benefit, for it raised life expectancy from twenty-eight years in the eighteenth century to seventy-six today. But the short-run effects of the Industrial Revolution were not always so obvious, especially for the social classes that lost out as a result of economic and technological change. The process of industrialization ruined the older classes in society—the aristocracy, the artisans, and the peasantry. The dispossessed Russian aristocrat in Chekov's *Cherry Orchard*, the tramping artisan in search of work in England, or the bankrupt and evicted peasant in Germany and Ireland were scenes that were repeated innumerable times during a century characterized by both social decline and social advance.

The majority, however, benefitted from industrialization. The older view of a society dislocated by industrial poverty or cultural shock is no longer a viable interpretation. For if the Industrial Revolution alienated some socially and economically, it improved and uplifted far more. The older interpretation can be sustained only if one does not take into account the poverty and degradation of the peasantry in rural Europe, the social group from which the factory working class was to spring. Men lived close to their own filth and very often that of their animals. They ate inadequate diets, watched their children die, and lived in a single room. What changed all that, and the statistics to prove it mount continuously, was the Industrial Revolution.

Right from the beginning, the Industrial Revolution created a new society based on certain specific skills. It rewarded the new upper middle class elite generously, either in the form of profit for those who contributed capital or in the form of salaries for those who possessed managerial ability. But, unlike agricultural society, industrial society rewarded a much larger proportion of the population. It expanded the size of the professional element. It benefitted the shopkeeper who dispersed the products of industry and the clerks and accountants who kept money and goods moving. It granted all sorts of financial rewards to the skilled and semiskilled factory worker whose technical knowledge was of vital importance to the whole industrial process. It even benefitted those in agriculture whose talents helped to increase the food supply.

The period of transition in European society produced a multitude of changes. The standard of living rose perceptibly; the population shifted from the countryside to the city; and the process of social mobility broke apart a static society and created the phenomenon of upward mobility for the majority. The change that nineteenth-century men saw all around them was identified as progress, and it was thought by some that change, intense change, would last forever. But before 1914, older values based on principles such as heredity and social stratification began to reassert themselves as Europe's age of transition from an agricultural to an industrial society came to an end. Then came the two world wars, wasting life and churning up society once more, adding another generation of change to the two that had already taken place.

Postwar Europe after 1945 was a different place. One of the most backward areas of the globe had been transformed into one of the most advanced. Many of the problems of the past—crime, alcoholism, infant mortality, childbirth mortality, bacterial diseases, illiteracy, poverty, malnutrition, and lack of longevity—had all been eliminated or reduced to relative insignificance. Perhaps the reason why they were gone was a simple one; perhaps, as the German social critic Ferdinand Lassalle once remarked, it was all one great big "stomach problem," and the stomach problem, the great economic issues, had now been solved. Whatever the reason, Europe emerged from World War II a much more settled society. The social classes created by industrialization had now been formed and were being staffed more or less on a hereditary basis. And the products created by industrialization along with the redistribution of wealth imposed by governments raised the standard of living for all as never before.

This last point exemplifies the kind of change that took place in Europe during the era of social and economic transformation. Society is still concerned, concerned about pollution, the impact of affluence, and the growth of its cities, but somehow these concerns are different from those of the past. Lacking the life and death importance of previous problems, they seem less intense. They are different from the question of whether your child would survive the first year of life, whether drought would destroy the meager yield of your 5-acre plot, or whether you would die an early death from cholera or consumption. Psychological concerns have replaced the physical concerns of the past. The event that produced this change was the Industrial Revolution, and the purpose of this book is to look at the social and economic consequences of that truly momentous event.

Acknowledgments

I would like to thank certain individuals for assistance that I received in the preparation of this essay. My first thank you goes to Jeanne Dittmar who secured a great deal of the material for this book for me on inter-library loan. I am also indebted to Elizabeth Isenberg, whose knowledge of both nutrition and biology was most helpful to me, and to Phil LaHaye who continually enhanced my knowledge of plant growth and development. Any errors that I may have made in the area of human or plant biology are my own and not theirs.

I would also like to thank my typist, Clare King, my proofreader, Ed Alfonsin, and my wife, Janice, for her patience. All of them helped along the way.

Part One

The Social Classes
of the
Old Reġime
1715-1848

European society in the eighteenth century was as stratified as it had been in the fifteenth; it was overwhelmingly a static society, one that can be described by the German word, *Stände*. By definition *Stände* means the existence of a society within which the various social classes have found a more or less permanent place. In the eighteenth century, the great majority of men might expect to live and die at the same social level as the one in which they were born. Much has been made of the attempt by middle class elements to penetrate the aristocracy, but considered against the background of the entire society, this upward movement by a few is a marginal experience, one that hardly disturbed the tenor of Europe's pre-1789 way of life known as the Old Regime.

At the top of this rather fossilized social order was the European aristocracy, which was divided into two very distinct groups. Far and away the more powerful and the most influential were the great magnates, whose enormous wealth in land had long since permitted them to emerge as the true social, political, and economic leaders of their time. Below them, in a society in which birth was obviously the major social distinction, were the more numerous aristocrats of the time, the members of the lesser nobility. The lesser nobility, with only a portion of the resources commanded by the great magnates, usually played a smaller role in leading society and did so inevitably at a local rather than at a national level, the level at which the great magnates operated.

Eighteenth-century European society was a classic society, subdivided into distinct aristocratic, middle class, and lower class elements. The relatively limited middle class was, like the aristocracy, a divided class. The upper reaches of the middle class, which along with the upper levels of the aristocracy represented yet another economic elite, ranged in membership from business to the professions. Within the upper middle class, bankers and merchants came to personify the type of wealth and prestige that some men, at least, could acquire even if they had not been born into the aristocracy. Far below the upper middle class, both economically and socially, stood the lower middle class. By virtue of the fact its members owned, employed, and produced, even if only on a modest scale, they deserved to be called middle class. The two elements that composed this part of the middle class were the master artisans of the cities and the peasant proprietors, the peasant cultivators, of the countryside.

The privileged and productive elements who formed the separate levels of the aristocracy and the middle class did not together account for more than 15 percent of the population. The rest were the lower classes, whose inadequate incomes left nearly all to live well below the level of subsistence—that is, below the level at which there was enough food, clothing, and shelter to sustain life. Of those who lived in cities, groups such as journeymen and apprentices were more fortunate because they could, at least in good times, do well enough because of the city's higher material standard of living. The same was not true, however, of the urban poor, too often the destitute of rural society who migrated to the cities and who formed the most unfortunate element in urban society.

The vast majority of Europeans in this preindustrial society were not, of course, either aristocrats, merchants, shopkeepers, or town dwellers; a full three-quarters of the Continent's people were middle or landless peasants. They lived in poverty, scraping out less than a subsistence on tiny plots averaging 5 acres or as sharecroppers or laborers.

The Aristocracy of the Eighteenth Century

Out of a total population of 189 million in 1800, the aristocracy could claim only about 4 million members. At most, the number of great magnates never included more than five thousand families from Ireland to Russia. Although small in numbers, the upper reaches of the aristocracy held a superior position because of their vast landholdings (thousands of acres) and the wealth that they were able to derive from those holdings, usually in the form of rent. By contrast, the estates of the lesser nobility, who were far more numerous, were often less than a few hundred acres, and their incomes marginal in comparison.

The privileged position of the aristocracy was based upon birth, but inevitably it expressed itself in terms of certain social distinctions—rank, rights, duties, symbols, dress, diet, education, and often as not in terms of a certain attitude that led many to talk of an aristocratic bearing or mystique. That expression may have been nothing more than the aristocracy's own conviction that it alone was born to rule and to command:

Too often, the aristocracy idealized itself, as when in 1791 the Irish aristo-crat Edmund Burke described aristocracy as the possession of certain graces. He argued that to be an aristocrat meant

> To be bred in a place of estimation; to see nothing low and sordid from one's infancy; to be taught to respect one's self; to be habituated to the censorial inspection of the public eye; to look early to public opinion; to stand upon such elevated ground as to be enabled to take a larger view of the widespread and infinitely diversified combination of men and affairs in a large society; to have leisure to read, to reflect, to converse; to be enabled to draw the court and attention of the wise and learned wherever they are to be found; [and] to be habituated in the pursuit of honor and duty.[1]

Whether aristocrats ever achieved this ideal is debatable; it is not even sure that these were their goals, for the aristocracy sought to survive as a class at a time when the land was not an inexhaustible means of support. Because of primogeniture, which excluded all but the oldest son from inheritance, many younger sons of great magnates as well as the lesser nobility sought to augment their incomes from other sources. They did this by penetrating the military, the churches, and the bureaucracies. In fact, the growth of absolutism actually did much to help the aristoc-racy survive into the nineteenth century. The royal armies of the time, for example, perpetuated aristocratic wealth. A striking example is the French army under Louis XV, which supported 18 marshals, 226 lieuten-ant generals, 540 field marshals, 466 brigadiers and 24 army inspectors at salaries ranging between 10,000 and 12,000 livres a year.[2]

The Great Magnates

The size of the aristocracy varied from one country to another, numbering around 400,000 in France, 500,000 in Spain, and 300,000 in Hungary toward the end of the eighteenth century. No matter its size, the class was always dominated by a few hundred rich and well-to-do families. Their names were famous throughout Europe: the Newcastles

---

[1] Peter Viereck, ed., *Conservatism* (New York: Van Nostrand, 1956), p. 20.

[2] That is, between 2,000 and 2,400 eighteenth-century American dollars, at a time when the level of subsistence in France required an income of about 1,250 livres a year (about $250). The best way to understand the significance of incomes in the eighteenth century is to compare salaries to the minimum required at the time for subsistence. By doing this, one can more fully com-prehend just how much wealth 10,000 or 12,000 livres actually represented. For those who like such figures, 12,000 livres would be equivalent to about $24,000 in present-day purchasing power.

in England, the Lafayettes in France, the Schoenborns in Bohemia, the Manins in Italy, and the Esterhazys in Hungary. These aristocratic families commanded resources that not even bankers could approximate before 1800.

In western Europe, that is, in the area west of the Elbe, where feudalism had faded, rent from the lease of land was the magnates' primary source of revenue. Their wealth was often staggering. The great landowners of England included no more than four hundred families, yet together they owned about 23 percent of the cultivable land in England and Wales. These four hundred derived from their lands incomes of between £5,000 and £50,000.[3] On average, they owned estates ranging in size from 5,000 to 10,000 acres. Landholding in neighboring Ireland was just as lucrative for a relatively small number of absentee landowners who, between 1780 and 1815, were collectively able to increase their total rental income from £5 million a year to about £15 million. Characteristic of the Irish situation was the Fitzwilliam family, which managed to increase its annual income over three decades from £19,000 to £33,000.

The wealth of the Fitzwilliam family could easily be matched on both sides of the English Channel. In England, the duke of Newcastle could count on an income of £40,000 a year from estates in ten counties and landholdings in the city of London, while in France the marquis de Lafayette could count on a yearly annuity of about the same amount. In northern Italy, the general European pattern of large landed estates dominating the countryside also prevailed. In the republic of Venetia, where patrician families had taken on the characteristics of a ruling aristocracy, the Manins could claim landholdings in excess of 14,000 acres, while the Contarinis could claim estates adding up to 7,000 acres.

In eastern Europe, where feudalism and feudal practices continued to live on, giant estates also formed the basis for aristocratic power. Here, in places like East Prussia up to 1808, the aristocracy was the only element even permitted to own land, while in Austria ownership of the land was nearly an aristocratic monopoly in fact if not in law. In this part of Europe, the historic connection between ownership of the land and noble status was more than cemented by the continuation of the feudal system. Instead of rent, the nobility could depend upon labor and the sale of the produce of that labor as a free source of income. Here too, a small elite dominated the nobility. In Hungary, still very much feudal in 1846, there were 336,807 adult male nobles out of a total adult male population of 3.5 million, about 9 percent. Of that number, less than two hundred could be considered great magnates; they were the princes, counts, and barons, the great peers of the Hungarian realm. The greatest of them all

---

[3] The British pound was worth about 5 American dollars in the last part of the eighteenth century.

was Prince Esterhazy, who owned 29 estates, 160 market towns and 414 villages. His annual income in the first half of the nineteenth century has been set at between 800,000 and 1,700,000 florins.[4] He was followed by Baron von Sica, who owned 19 estates; Count Karolyi, who also had 19; and Count Szechenyi, who had 18. Together the forty-six leading families of Hungary owned more than 3,600 square miles of territory.

Wealth of these proportions, of course, meant that the upper 5 percent of the population owned 80 percent of the resources. The concentration of wealth so obvious in other parts of Europe was equally characteristic of Russia. In a country where serfdom sometimes bordered on slavery, a nobleman usually measured his wealth in terms of the number of male serfs he owned. In 1834, 1,453 serfowners, most of them great magnates, owned 3,556,959 adult male serfs. The average number of adult male serfs owned by each proprietor was 2,448 (plus their families). The Russian Ministry of the Interior in 1859 placed a total value of about 7.6 million rubles [5] on each one of these seigneurial properties.

This immense concentration of wealth did not benefit the countryside, largely because the upper reaches of the aristocracy had during the course of the seventeenth and eighteenth centuries became urbanized. With the single conspicuous exception of England, the higher nobility had almost everywhere taken residence in the cities and concentrated its huge purchasing power there, which explains why the cities were economically and culturally so much more advanced than the countryside in preindustrial Europe.

The movement to the cities was noticeable everywhere in Europe by the early part of the eighteenth century. In England, the great lords, while still resident in the countryside for part of the year, had long since established townhouses in the city of London. Ever since the time of Louis XIV, the higher nobility had been attracted to either Versailles or Paris, there to take advantage of the superior intellectual and cultural climate. Most of the major capitals had their resident aristocracy by the middle of the century, and even smaller provincial towns such as Aachen or Bordeaux could boast of a small, permanent residential group of aristocrats. The movement that began in western Europe was copied, as was so often the case, by eastern aristocrats, primarily great magnates. The German traveler and commentator Karl-Ludwig, Freiherr von Poellnitz, noticed the tendency of the great in Austria to leave the countryside for cities like Vienna and Prague. And the Swiss observer J. C. L. de Sismondi, speaking of the well-to-do members of the Italian aristocracy, declared, "The well-to-do of every province live in its principal city. Even though

---

[4] Between $400,000 and $850,000 a year.

[5] $35 million for each one of these estates.

their fortunes consist almost exclusively of land, they consume the income without paying the slightest attention to its cultivation and without so much as going to see it." [6]

The great magnates of Europe not only separated themselves from their agricultural tradition but spent lavishly in the cities, constructing edifices that were a testimony to their love of leisure and fondness for consumption. The London aristocracy was especially enamored of Neoclassical designs, and some of the more famous aristocratic houses, such as Bedford House, Burlington House, and Chesterfield House, were all built along semipalatial lines in the Neoclassical style. In the century after 1650, the French aristocracy began to build great houses, really chateaus, which were more often than not bucolic rather than urban in inspiration, in the heart of Paris. The aristocracy of eastern Europe was no less insistent upon displays of splendor. The wealthy Bohemian Kinsky family not only insisted upon a palatial setting just outside the Hofburg, the imperial palace in Vienna, but also employed one of Austria's most famous Baroque architects, Lukas von Hildebrandt, to supervise the construction of the Palais Kinsky. Needless to say, no expense either in design or materials was spared.

Even though the great magnates were geographically separated from the land in many parts of Europe, their incomes from their estates were protected both economically and legally. As absentee landholding among the richer members of the aristocracy became the rule, the job of supervising their vast holdings fell to middle class stewards and land agents. Trained in accounting and marketing, the more talented overseers were able to provide their distant employers with steady incomes from well-managed properties. There are numerous examples of enterprising estate managers who successfully compounded the wealth of their masters. Stewards for the Tron family, which owned a large estate in the area of Padua, supervised the regular employment of 177 persons plus the hiring of 183 agricultural workers on a part-time basis. They supervised land reclamation, agricultural improvements, the production of cereals and livestock, and marketing, all at a profit of 77 percent on investment for the Trons, resident in Venice, in the year 1750. Equally ingenious stewards were able to expand the income and profits of the Dudley estates in Staffordshire and Worcestershire by going beyond agriculture and engaging in industrial and mining enterprises.

Vast landholdings, whether well managed or not, were a necessary prop for the perpetuation of the established position of Europe's great aristocratic families. The great landed estates of the eighteenth century were protected by two common legal devices, primogeniture and

[6] Robert Forster and Elborg Forster, eds., *European Society in the Eighteenth Century* (New York: Harper & Row, 1969), p. 83.

entail. Primogeniture, which existed everywhere in Europe except Russia, guaranteed that land would pass intact from father to eldest son by means of inheritance. This was one technique by which the aristocracy prevented the subdivision of giant estates; entail was still another. Entail made it illegal to divide up or parcel out estate land for sale. If an estate was sold, it had to be purchased in its entirety, a procedure that effectively prevented the sale of large estates to anyone except the rich. Entail helped to maintain the integrity of the system of large estates and was especially vital to the higher reaches of the aristocracy in places like eastern Prussia, where 62 percent of the land was held in large estates, and Spain, where a contemporary estimated that one-third of the arable land was in the hands of the separate branches of four great ruling aristocratic houses.

The removal of the higher nobility from the countryside to the capital allowed it to play a role in national development that had previously been the monopoly of monarchy. Generally speaking, the aristocracy as a whole had confined itself traditionally to local matters, but in the eighteenth century purely provincial concerns became the prerogative of the lesser nobility when the higher nobility moved on to the national level and penetrated the military, the church, and the civil service. At the time of Marie Theresa's death in 1780, the Austrian government had almost 1,500 chamberlains; her father, the emperor Charles VI, created 300 of them in one year, 1709. The Kinsky family of Bohemia in a single generation provided Austria with a great chancellor; two ambassadors, one to England and one to France; and two army officers. Better than 20 percent of the Swedish aristocracy sitting in the House of Lords was employed by the Swedish government either as courtiers, that is, as advisors to the king, or as civil servants. In Spain, the higher nobility, there known as grandees, had long since formed the inner circle of advisors for the Spanish kings in Madrid.

The growth of bureaucracy under the absolute rulers of the eighteenth century had not only created tens of thousands of jobs, it had also at one point favored the middle class. This was no longer true by 1700; by that date the nobility was making its peace with monarchy and being amply rewarded. The model of an efficient bureaucracy was the somewhat austere service which Frederick William I and Frederick the Great had created in Prussia between 1713 and 1786. Prussia's form of aristocratic-bureaucratic absolutism tended necessarily to favor the great magnates over the lesser nobility and men of middle class origin, although ability and talent could and often did modify the influence of birth and status.

The royal armies of the eighteenth century were a natural outlet for the martial tradition of the European aristocracy. So strong was that tradition among the members of the aristocracy that they moved easily into the officer corps of the time. The French army is a prime example.

Two-thirds of the 13,000 officers serving on active duty in 1787 were of aristocratic birth, while almost all of the 1,100 generals in the French army were the sons of the higher nobility. Since all commissions had to be purchased, the provincial nobility stood little chance against the wealth of the great magnates in the battle for the higher ranks. Moreover, the size of the French officer corps was obviously padded in favor of the higher aristocracy, since the larger Prussian standing army of the 1780s did just as well with only 80 general officers. The military tradition was, of course, strong everywhere in Europe, and aristocratic officers dominated the armies of the three military monarchies of the time, Prussia, Russia, and Austria. One study of the Swedish aristocracy showed that three out of every four aristocrats, both titled and untitled, held military rank.

In the established churches of the day, especially in the hierarchy, the aristocracy again sought either sinecures or advancement in order to maintain its special position within society. The most famous illustration of this trend was France, where by 1789 every bishop, archbishop, and cardinal of the Gallican Church proved to be an aristocrat by birth. Both abbeys and bishoprics were a lucrative source of revenue in an age when the Church collected taxes in the form of the tithe. Prince Louis de Bourbon Condé could draw an income of 400,000 livres a year as titular head of four monasteries, unusual but understandable at a time when the French Church owned 20 percent of the country's land. Vast holdings of this type were, of course, characteristic of churches elsewhere, and provided the aristocracy with a monopoly on wealth and positions in the Church of England and to a lesser degree in the Catholic Church of Spain. Not all the great aristocratic families took advantage of their bishoprics; some of them, like the Circe and de Brienne families in France, were both progressive and reformist.

The aristocracy's dominance of national institutions gave substance to the claim that its members were the natural leaders of society. Along with that responsibility went a way of life that for the higher nobility, at least, would have to be regarded as sumptuous. Conspicuous consumption was a permanent feature of life at this level of the aristocracy, as was devotion to leisure. The banquets held at Versailles were notorious for their excesses; so were the spending sprees of the English aristocracy. The first Duke of Devonshire, for example, spent £1,000 on a single supper and masked ball in London. The Schoenbrunn Palace in Vienna was lavishly decorated in the baroque style that the aristocracy loved for its opulence. Schoenbrunn helped to set standards for Austria's great magnates, who willingly copied the dress, manners, and decorum that were displayed there. The wealth of the Russian aristocracy was recorded over and over again in the form of art objects, porcelains, cabinetry, furnishings, and furs.

But the aristocrat's leisure was too often filled by boring ceremony. The elaborate ritualistic dinners of the Spanish court, Versailles, and St. Petersburg's Winter Palace did much to distinguish one nobleman from another by means of seating plans, but little else. The stately minuets of the period were as highly formalized as the demands of fashion, the wigs, satins, knickers and laces that were all part of the aristocrat's prescribed attire. So ritualistic had behavior become by the eighteenth century that even fox hunting in places like England and game hunting for the Alpine aristocracy of Austria were formal occasions.

The aristocracy was literate and did, at least, have intellectual pretensions. Most aristocrats were educated privately. Those who were destined for more vigorous occupations such as the clergy or civil service might receive a university education, but one that usually set them apart, especially when eating and socializing, from the commoners. Many famous universities in Europe, including Oxford, Barcelona, Vienna, St. Petersburg, and especially German universities such as Halle and Frankfurt, prepared a growing number of aristocrats for government service. Whatever formal education the higher nobility received was rounded out by an expensive continental tour that was supposed to add the final touch of polish and experience.

Great magnates were also well-known patrons of letters and of the arts in the cities. Parisian salons were copied everywhere, as was aristocratic support for the theater and music. Haydn was initially subsidized by various Austrian aristocrats before he finally entered the service of Prince Esterhazy. Mozart's patron was the Prince-Archbishop of Salsburg, while one of Beethoven's most enthusiastic supporters was Prince Lichnowsky. The English aristocracy financed the painters Thomas Gainsborough and Joshua Reynolds, and lionized novelists such as Samuel Richardson. The theater, growing more sophisticated and satirical all the time, could not have survived in Paris without its aristocratic audiences.

The aristocracy was by no means immune from the diseases that took life so easily in the eighteenth century, yet the great magnates of the age did have enough energy to lead society. That energy was an outgrowth of a relatively advanced diet. At a time when the majority of men were grain eaters, the aristocracy had available to it food that might not necessarily have provided the best overall nutrition, but was nonetheless a good source of energy. Some foods were known almost exclusively to the upper reaches of society. This was particularly true of certain animal products, such as meat and poultry, and certain fruits and vegetables. The aristocracy was one of the few groups in society to have the B complex vitamins and vitamins A, C, D and E in their diets. Since vitamins must work in conjunction to be effective and since protein is vital for growth and stamina, it is clear that the aristocracy's dominance was in part based upon wealth and birth and in part on its unique exposure to some, but by no means all, of the forty nutrients needed for good health.

The Lesser Nobility

Although the lesser nobility numbered in the millions, its members occupied a definitely inferior position within aristocratic society. Cut off from the city, they remained, generally speaking, isolated from the world of the very rich and fashionable. After 1750 the lesser nobility finally sought to create its own style of life. Separated by income and distance from the great magnates, the provincial gentry could do little else than marry within its own ranks; marital alliances that would bridge the gap between the two aristocratic groups were rare.

The income range for the lesser nobility varied considerably. Some aristocrats, even though their estates were no more than a few hundred acres, were genuinely prosperous for long periods. This was true, for example, of both the gentry as a whole in England and the upper levels of the gentry in Hungary. A substantial minority of the gentry class survived not as a landed nobility but as part of the service aristocracy. This was particularly the case in Russia, where 83 percent of the aristocracy, mostly the lesser nobility, owned no land whatsoever. At the bottom levels not only did poverty threaten, but, even worse, many were faced with the prospect of becoming déclassé, that is, of losing their status. It was a threat that often became a reality for certain aristocratic families, the most famous being the French *hoberaux,* from which the term hobo derives, the poorest of the Spanish *hidalgos,* and the even more notorious Polish gentry, the *golota.*

Unlike the great magnates, most of whom could trace their ancestry back to the Middle Ages, the lesser nobility was not a true aristocracy in the medieval sense. Many of the lesser nobility had not descended from the knightly class of the Middle Ages, but were in fact the artificial creation of monarchy. The desire of monarchs like the French and Spanish Bourbons for loyal servants led them to raise thousands of upper middle class men to the level of the aristocracy. This process of ennoblement had helped to fill out the lower levels of the aristocracy, but it also created certain tensions. In France, a vital distinction was made socially between the higher nobility, the nobility of the sword, and the lesser nobility, the nobility of the robe, those who held aristocratic title not as a result of lineage but as a result of effort. De Chevigny's catechism for courtiers, published in 1706, made the following rather smug distinction:

Q. "What is nobility?"
A. "It is a quality which a prince bestows on one of his subjects for some outstanding achievement."
Q. "How many kinds of nobility are there?"
A. "Two, those of the sword and those of the robe."
Q. "Who are more esteemed?"
A. "Those of the sword . . . because their nobility was acquired only after frequent risks on their lives." [7]

If most of France's 58,000 noblemen in 1700 could not trace their lineage back to the Middle Ages, they often could trace their place in the aristocracy for at least three or four generations. As it turned out, this was plenty of time for the more illustrious members of the lesser nobility, the so-called high robe families, to become accepted. By and large, well-known robe families, such as the Berthiers, Caulets, and Amats, were also quite wealthy. Their original incomes were often swelled as they served as judges and magistrats, mostly in provincial cities, within the system of royal courts. Added wealth of a rather substantial nature fell to these men. High robe officials might expect to earn, on average, between 750 and 2,000 livres a year for fulfilling their judicial functions.[8] These incomes were considered just, primarily because the offices had to be purchased in the first place. They were valued because offices of this kind represented regular income, exemption from certain taxes, and social prestige for 2,000 high robe families.

The relative prosperity and high social position of the nobility of the robe in France could be matched by similar levels of the gentry elsewhere in Europe. The gentry was, in a certain sense, a second type of elite. Its survival, at least for some of its members, was both perpetuated and guaranteed by monarchy, but always at a less fortunate level than that of the great magnates. The English and Hungarian gentry represented yet another type of lesser nobility. In the main, they were country gentlemen, often of independent means, whose survival was not as directly dependent upon monarchy as was the service level of the gentry in places like France, Prussia, and Russia. It is true that the gentry in England and Hungary often served in the judiciary, representing the law in the countryside, just as the service aristocracy did in the provincial cities, but in England and Hungary it was often done on a voluntary rather than a compensatory basis.

As long as independent means guaranteed them a livelihood, as long as rent or labor provided them with a reasonable income, the rural gentry

---

[7] Chevigny, *Mémoires* (Paris: Colin, 1909), pp. 252–53.

[8] Again, the value of these incomes can best be gauged by an analysis of what a livre could buy in the first half of the century. Generally, a bottle of red wine cost a third of a livre; a large loaf of bread, one-fifteenth of a livre; and a kilogram of beef, one-tenth of a livre.

was content to remain aloof from government service, except in Russia, where state service was compulsory up to the time of Catherine the Great (1762–96). The vast majority of lesser landholders in England were able in the eighteenth century to hold their own and even prosper without government employment. The wealthiest gentry, about 700 or 800 families, could count on incomes of £3,000 to £5,000 a year, based on landholdings of 1,000 to 7,000 acres. The lower levels of the English gentry were not so well off. These 18,000 families had to get along on a few hundred acres and incomes that averaged about £1,000 a year—modest by aristocratic standards, advanced by the standards of general society. Still another representative group, the Hungarian gentry, presents a similar case of relative prosperity. The better-off members of the gentry were known as the middle nobility to distinguish them from other gentry who were either less well off or landless. Hungary's middle nobility, about 14,000 families, really represented the principle of aristocracy in the countryside in the eighteenth century, not the few hundred magnates above them or the 35,000 relatively poor members of the gentry who were aristocratic in name only.

When and if the land ceased to provide an adequate income, the lesser nobility moved into the service of monarchy as clerics in one of the national churches, as junior army officers (often in a provincial regiment), or into the civil service, there to compete somewhat unevenly with the great magnates. The lesser nobility was frequently to be found in the lower ranks of the Anglican, Catholic, and Orthodox hierarchies, the Lutheran churches being a major exception. Characteristically, a majority of the 36,000 active and reserve army officers serving under Louis XVI were found to be from the gentry. A higher and higher proportion of the Russian gentry was likewise drawn into the bureaucracy as the century wore on. Each September some 5,000 members of the Russian gentry trekked from their country estates to Moscow to put in nine months of customary bureaucratic service to the crown. This Moscow group was fairly typical of gentry all over Europe who were dependent upon administrative salaries as well as landed income for survival. Still another gentry element that found itself growing more and more dependent on monarchy was the Junkers of eastern Prussia. Originally knightly landlords, the Junker aristocracy characteristically dominated local matters, as the gentry did almost everywhere in Europe, through its control of the judiciary and through its manorial enterprises. Although prosperous on their estates, the Junkers began to penetrate the Prussian bureaucracy in the 1690s, establishing themselves rather firmly on a national scale. By the time of Frederick the Great, thousands of them had moved into the officer corps of the army and taken over senior positions in the bureaucracy. As it added to its monopoly of national wealth by means of governmental service, the Prussian Junker class, in alliance with monarchy, even began to take on the trappings of the higher nobility.

The fate of the gentry, then, varied from country to country, although almost everywhere a prosperous minority was to be found in every gentry class, along with poor cousins. The lone exception to this rule was England, where the entire gentry seemed somehow well off. Whether they belonged to the service aristocracy or were landed, or both, the gentry enjoyed a distinctive way of life. Unlike the great magnates, who translated their enormous social prestige and economic power into real political influence, the gentry was content to fill the lower levels of government or carry on with its more traditional role in rural Europe.

On the land, they lived essentially simple lives. Like the higher nobility, they were dependent for income upon rent, in cash or kind, from peasant tenants and sharecroppers in western Europe or upon servile labor in eastern Europe. Limited incomes forced many into a frugal, simple existence. Some groups, like the French nobility of the robe, still retained a measure of their bourgeois restraint; others, like the Junkers, had an old reputation for frugality. Still, the country gentlemen of the age did have their luxuries; they had manor houses and they drank, danced, hunted, and held lavish feasts on occasion. They too were devoted to luxury within the confines of their own class and resources.

The lesser nobility was not a particularly cultivated group. Education was limited; only those who entered government or church service received a university education. Except for members of the service aristocracy who had access to cities like Paris or Vienna, the gentry never really came into contact with the major cultural or intellectual trends of the time. Far removed from the urban seat of culture, the vast majority lived bucolic lives. The life of the Hungarian county squire in this age was rather typical. Often he owned two homes, one in the local village and one set a few miles out in the countryside. In his unpretentious house he often met with other members of the local aristocracy to determine policy for the county. At other times, he dispensed justice to his serfs. The middle nobility in Hungary lived well. On a continent where agricultural prosperity was often a matter of accident rather than design, the fertile Hungarian plain provided the aristocracy with an abundance of meat, fruits, and vegetables. Indeed, everywhere in Europe, the gentry ate well. Often paid in kind, that is in produce, it knew eggs, cheeses, poultry, and wheat, the cash crops the peasantry never touched.

The great magnates may have formed a closed caste in the eighteenth century, but the gentry did not. If French monarchs ceased after 1700 to raise merchants and bankers to the level of the gentry, their Spanish cousins continued to do so, as did the Romanovs, the Hohenzollerns, and the Habsburgs. Indeed, both the Irish and English peerage expanded significantly under George III, since the younger Pitt was evidently bent on combatting the old aristocracy with a new one. Those raised to the peerage met, however, a very uncertain future. The gentry was obviously a divided class. Some of its elements were sturdy and substantial, others just got by, and still others were destitute. In fact, a flaking-off process was already noticeable in the years after 1750. Perhaps the first indication that the Old Regime was moving toward social upheaval was the tendency of gentry elements to fall out of their class, to become déclassé.

A good portion of the class was in a state of flux, some rising, some declining. Because of their marginal incomes, many were caught in the inflationary spiral that began in 1750 with the growth of the European economy and has never ceased. The rate of inflation was only 2 percent, but even that was devastating at times. Even the prosperous English gentry felt the pinch, especially when inflation was coupled with a land tax that ate away at revenue. In France the gentry increasingly became the prisoner of custom, particularly in its dealings with the peasantry.

One of the characteristics of the rural economy in the eighteenth century was the long-term lease. Many peasants, both with and without land of their own, took out leases at fixed rents. Very often those rents were set at a certain sum for years and sometimes decades, which meant that members of the gentry had very often to get along on today's spiraling prices with yesterday's deflated rents. This economic bind, common to those with fixed incomes in an inflationary period, spelled disaster for many members of the lesser nobility. The system led many desperate gentry to try to force out of the peasants, already themselves often living a marginal existence, more of the remaining feudal dues which the peasantry traditionally owed to the aristocracy. The situation in the countryside, as the Marquis de Mirabeau noted, was changing; the great magnates were absent and the gentry grasping. The peasantry, meanwhile, was left to deal with either disinterested overseers or insecure country squires.

The tendency for unforeseen and unknown economic factors to eat away at certain unfortunate social groups is a constant. The higher nobility, of course, had the resources to overcome the mounting economic difficulties that were besetting the gentry. Government helped. The monarchs of the day created tens of thousands of jobs in government and in the military, but monarchs did not have the resources to create the hundreds of thousands that would have been needed if the aristocracy as a whole were going to be saved. Actually, government did save a portion of the gentry into the early nineteenth century, but it could not rescue a growing number, particularly in Russia. There, before the emancipation of the serfs in 1861, the lesser nobility, always without capital for investment, turned on its serfs, demanding more and more in the form of quitrents, money dues, and labor. It was during the eighteenth century that the term "rack-rents" came into common use; it referred to those moments when leases came due and the gentry suddenly doubled or tripled the rental price, a practice that became increasingly widespread through most of western Europe.

Many of these were long-term developments barely visible in the eighteenth century, more obvious by the nineteenth. They were a weathervane. To most men living in the eighteenth century, society seemed hardly disturbed. The economic effects of change were subtle and largely unobserved. Few men saw the loss of gentry status by some as an indication that larger changes might be imminent. Instead, society still seemed stratified, ruled by men who were members of one of three elite groups in the eighteenth century, magnates, gentry, and merchants.

2

The Rise
of the
Upper Middle Class

In the city, the two most powerful elites in the eighteenth century, the great magnates and the upper middle class, met and mingled, sometimes to the point of intermarriage. In an atmosphere where opportunities for earning wealth existed side by side with inheritance, it was almost inevitable that the higher reaches of the aristocracy would eventually blend with the well-to-do bankers of the time. For the great banking families of Europe, such as the Neckers of Switzerland, the Lavoisiers of France, the Boyds of England, and the Vandenyvers of the Netherlands, represented the epitome of upper middle class wealth in European society. There were, of course, other levels of this class, inevitably less prestigious and always commanding less income.

The largest number of individuals in the upper middle class were merchants, involved either in domestic trade or in the more lucrative, but always more dangerous, overseas trade. The more prosperous merchants of the time parlayed their wealth into the more genteel practice of banking, but most did not have the opportunity, for the European money market remained under the control of a few hundred banking families. Prior to the 1760s and 1770s, the only avenue to quick fortune was overseas trade. This was especially the case for the slave trade, in which profits from a single cargo could be 75,000 eighteenth-century American dollars. Toward the end of the century, a second and potentially even more profitable source of wealth loomed in the form of manufacturing. Investment in the process of mass production, particularly textiles through the domestic system, could bring windfall profits. A case in point was Johann von Schüle of Augsburg, who in a single decade anticipated the market for cotton and converted that foreknowledge into one of Germany's greatest fortunes and an aristocratic title.

Another group attached to the upper middle class in Europe's pre-industrial society was the professions. The professional element in upper middle class society kept its social status precariously. Stocked by the sons of merchants and bankers, and on certain occasions aristocrats, the professions were lacking in social prestige, even though it usually took wealth, position, and education to become a lawyer, judge, notary, educator, or physician. Somehow, the professions never seemed as manly to the highly elitist and socially conscious ruling groups of the time as the more respected aristocratic and business callings.

For long decades, the upper middle class was content to remain in its assigned place, always looking up to the aristocracy, trying to emulate it rather than seeking to overcome it. But as the wealth of the richest portions of the upper middle class increased, the desire for further social recognition became irrepressible. The prosperous within this class were buoyed along by a confidence that was the natural outgrowth of their wealth. For as commerce increased by 300 or 400 percent during the trading revival of the eighteenth century, so did profits. And profits were to embolden the upper middle class over the course of time, making it courageous enough ultimately to challenge the political and social position of the aristocracy sometimes by the threat of force, more often by means of persuasion.

The Commercial Middle Class

The economic system of the eighteenth century that was to lead to the world of high finance was commercial capitalism. At the center of that emerging and ever-expanding order stood Europe's banking system. The major banks of the time were located in the great commercial centers—London, Paris, Amsterdam, Hamburg, Frankfurt, Stockholm, Venice, Genoa, Madrid, Warsaw, and St. Petersburg. Here, with interest rates of about 10 percent, the great banking houses attracted the deposits of both the great magnates and the upper middle class. The result was always to draw money out of the countryside and the provinces and to concentrate it in the major metropolitan centers. There it was supervised by a handful of important bankers who compounded the wealth of the upper reaches of society by means of government loans and investment in commerce.

The two greatest money centers were London and Paris. Among the great financial families of London were those who were now linked to the English aristocracy by means of marriage. This is how the first contacts were made between the Duke of Bedford and the well-known London banker Josiah Child. Among those who could be mentioned here are Sir James Bateman, whose bourgeois family intermarried, as did Sir John Fryer himself, along with dozens of others during the first half of the eighteenth century. The English writer Daniel Defoe was in awe of these men; on one occasion he wrote, "Our merchants are princes, greater and richer, and more powerful than some sovereign princes." At yet another moment, he could not help contrasting the "immense wealth" of men "behind the counter" with the declining fortunes of some gentry and a number of "ancient families." [1]

By the last part of the seventeenth and the early eighteenth centuries, the wealthiest of the merchants were investing heavily in the Bank of England. All told there were more than 3,000 investors, but real power was in the hands of the bank's directors. In the early 1700s, they consisted of a small inner circle of merchant-bankers, men like Sir Peter Delmé, Sir Henry Furnese, Jacob Jacobsen and John Fauquier. By all accounts, Delmé was the leading spirit. In 1724, at a time when he was also Lord Mayor of London, Delmé held £118,358 in bank stock, £47,000 in East India stock, and over £122,000 in South Sea stock. [2] In addition to the great central bank, the Bank of England, London could boast of such banks as Barclay's (the family having originally made its fortune in linen) and Lloyd's (that family having acquired its wealth in the iron trade).

The Paris money market could almost always match the resources of London, but only because it was an international center for finance, serving the Continent. It too had banking families that rivaled the aristocracy in wealth and sometimes in prestige. Among those connected to finance and banking on a grand scale were the Lavoisiers, the de Francueils, the la Popelinieres, and the Labordes. The Labordes were closest to the upper reaches of the aristocracy, one of Laborde's daughters

---

[1] George Rudé, *Hanoverian London, 1714–1808* (London: Secker and Warburg, 1971), p. 52.

[2] A virtually unparalleled personal fortune of about 10 million American dollars in today's purchasing power.

having become the Countess de Noailles. Foreign bankers were also attracted to Paris because it was the principal market in all of Europe for government bonds. Bondholding, then, became the major source of income not only for French banks but for a number of Swiss, English, and Dutch concerns as well.

Other cities considered to have vital capital resources were Amsterdam, Stockholm, Hamburg, Venice, and St. Petersburg. Over the course of decades, each one of these centers produced its own indigenous financial aristocracy. The great German commercial center of Hamburg can be taken as representative of the rest. As elsewhere, growing commercial ventures soon led to the emergence of powerful banking families, interested in both finance and trade, families such as the Mercks, Rupertis, Gosslers, and de Chapeaurouges. The wealth of the de Chapeaurouges at the turn of the nineteenth century was indeed impressive, considering that it was accumulated in the carrying trade and not through more lucrative overseas ventures. By 1800, the head of the clan, Jean, had accumulated a personal fortune of some 400,000 marks and had another 365,000 marks invested in other enterprises.[3] Meanwhile the Rothschilds took the regular avenue to banking success by dealing all over the Continent, in indigo stored at Frankfurt, in private Dutch loans, and in the purchase of Austrian government bonds in Vienna.

The largest groups in the upper middle class were not the few banking families, but the more numerous merchants. Merchants were divided by the type of enterprise that they tended to follow. The merchant class in England and Holland was progressively involved in the highly profitable seaborne trade through the agency of either the English East India or Dutch West and East India companies. These giant joint-stock companies had their rivals, of course, in the French East and West India Companies and the Austrian Ostend East India Company. But the rivalry they offered was minimal, as the five thousand merchants controlling the three companies came close to monopolizing the colonial trade from their bases in London, Amsterdam, and Rotterdam. While a relatively small group of English and Dutch merchants were expanding their wealth through overseas trade, the remainder of the merchant element profited as wholesalers or retailers. Every European city, including those that were far from the major port facilities, had its representative group of traders. For example, a typical town of the eighteenth century was the French city of Orleans. In the 1780s, it had a population of about

---

[3] About 2 million dollars in current purchasing power. This figure, when compared to the accumulated wealth of some English banking families, probably represents a significant accumulation for any one individual on the Continent, where the principal source of wealth was wholesale or retail trade, not the more lucrative overseas trade.

40,000, of whom 1,000 men were listed as upper middle class. Some of them were engaged in the wholesale trade, others in providing the city's retail outlets, and still others in the professions. Wholesaling and retailing were frankly less profitable than overseas trade, but did provide tidy fortunes for merchants in such centers as Frankfurt, Madrid, and St. Petersburg. The distribution trades were, in point of fact, never as lucrative as the carrying trade, which is the real reason why fortunes on the Continent could never really match those of the merchant-princes of England and Holland.

The possibilities of accumulating fat yearly incomes within the merchant class depended on location. Wealth multiplied much faster in the great port cities than it did in the much more numerous provincial towns. In England, there were by the end of the eighteenth century a total of some 3,000 eminent merchants with incomes ranging from £1,500 to £10,000 a year. About half of them lived in London, the others in port towns such as Bristol and Liverpool. Actually, the number of truly well-to-do merchants in England had increased from 2,000 at the beginning of the century to 3,000 by 1800. Those that did enter the class, and the percentage of those experiencing social mobility was severely limited, usually rose from the higher reaches of the artisan class, in particular from the luxury trades. The chances for advancement that were possible in London were much less prevalent in the provincial towns. A striking illustration of rather restricted opportunity can be seen in the small German town of Weimar, in central Germany. In the 1770s, the town had a total population of about 6,000. Of this, a select group of about 150 individuals had incomes of over 600 talers.[4] This element was the local upper middle class of bankers, merchants, officials, and professional men whose yearly incomes were but a pale reflection of the wealth accumulating in the great port cities of Europe.

In an age when social mobility was limited by essentially static concepts of society, most died in the same social position in which they ᵒᵏ were born. Only the few experienced upward mobility and then only over a period of generations rather than during a single lifetime. The progress of the Trip family is illustrative of the process. By the eighteenth century, the Trips had added their names to the constellation of Dutch families noted for their material prosperity in the highly affluent upper middle class society of Amsterdam. The Trips now ranked with the DeWitts, Bickers, and Coymans among the rich and prosperous. But the process of admission had been a slow one, begun in the early seventeenth century. Over the course of generations, one after another of the family's leaders had expanded their fortune by astute business deals.

---

4 About $1,800 at a time when a family of five needed about $250 to live above the level of subsistence.

Starting in Dordrecht, Jacob Trip had first pushed the family into the iron trade, importing ore from France. Over decades, the family moved into the grain trade in Russia, became involved in the arms trade and the sale of merchant vessels, and finally ended up in the financial markets of Rotterdam and Amsterdam. Louis and Hendrick Trip capped their arrival in the higher reaches of Amsterdam's middle class society by building themselves a palace.

Outside of the capital accumulated by the aristocracy, all investment funds in the eighteenth century were in a real sense merchant capital. Some of it went into banking, but after 1750 new opportunities for investment began to appear. Almost everywhere in Europe merchant-manufacturers began to move in on the domestic system of production. With excess capital, merchants from Nottingham to Prague began to control and then take over the guild, or domestic, system of production. The moves were subtle. Initially, they purchased the raw materials, increasingly cotton, and then took control of marketing. In time, the merchant-manufacturers sought to set standards of production for the guilds under their control, and even to expand production into the countryside, where the guilds had no power. By 1800, the textile guilds of Europe were falling to the financial power of capital, losing one aspect after another of their independence to the new, aggressive merchant-manufacturers who were now hiring guildsmen as laborers. Eventually, of course, the merchant-manufacturers were to take over production completely, hiring a work force within a factory instead of following the older pattern of proceeding through the guilds.

The rise of merchant-manufacturers and later industrialists added a new peripheral group to the upper middle class, one that would become dominant over the course of time. New fortunes were now being made in manufacturing, occasionally before 1820 by machine production, but more often by means of controlling the labor force within the guilds. Throughout the great textile areas of northern England, northern and eastern France, southeastern Germany, Bohemia, Switzerland, and northern Italy, the guilds were falling under the sway of merchant-manufacturers. Their capital resources and ability to organize the various stages of textile production, raw materials, manufacturing, and marketing, simply overwhelmed the limited resources of small, independent master artisans who usually worked with a force of only about five men. They could hardly compete with corporations like Dixon and Company, which employed 3,500 rural and urban weavers in northern England, or J. M. Scheibler of Monschau, in the western part of Germany, an international corporation which hired more than 4,000 artisans as wage workers. Great fortunes were being amassed by merchant-manufacturers who were now

declining guilds

except in England and France, this process was very slowly worked out — indeed, much overlapping existed.

financing and controlling the domestic system by means of capital and middlemen. The von der Leyens in the city of Krefeld in southwestern Germany amassed a huge fortune by dominating the city's silk production. They did this by employing more than 3,000 masters and journeymen as wage workers. In another silk center, the French city of Lyons, some 750 merchants pooled their capital resources and by the 1830s had taken over silk production by depriving some 9,000 master artisans of their former economic independence.

While merchant capital was moving steadily into the area of domestic production, industrialists who owned their own factories and were concentrating labor and the various stages of production under a single roof were also making their appearance. Sometimes this was done with the help of machinery, sometimes not. Johann von Schüle, who operated in the German textile center of Augsburg, was characteristic of this emerging breed of Continental industrialists. Using raw cotton imported by the English East India Company, he established a factory in Augsburg in 1764. Employing a huge labor force of 3,500 individuals, he began to mass-produce cotton cloth without the help of machinery. With what amounted to a labor-intense industry, he captured the Central European market for cotton and transformed his own adventurous efforts into one of the largest fortunes in Germany. Machine production, beginning in the British Isles, also led to the enrichment of certain enterprising men. Among them was John Heathcoat, the founder of the machine-made lace industry, whose factories in the early 1800s in Tiverton, in Devon, and in St. Quentin, north of Paris, supplied both the English and Continental markets. Matching his ingenuity was the Marshall family of Leeds, specialists in the mechanized spinning of flax into linen cloth.

If the great magnates dominated national politics in alliance with the king, and the gentry provincial developments, the upper middle class was in control of urban development and policies. The ability of this class to retain control of urban government rested upon the principle of limiting participation in political life. Everywhere in Europe the franchise was reserved for those who paid the highest proportion of taxes. This device limited the electorate in eighteenth-century London, for example, to around 15 percent of the male population. At best, the right to vote was confined to the upper and lower levels of the middle class, a minority in the cities. The only places where the near-monopoly of the upper middle class in urban government were actually threatened were in the large and small capitals, such as Paris and St. Petersburg on the one hand and Weimar and Munich on the other. Here, the heads of government were often appointed aristocratic officials supervising an essentially bourgeois bureaucracy.

In most instances, however, the upper middle class was jealous of its entrenched local prerogatives and defended them stubbornly against the encroachments of central government. Business and professional elements were always ready to defend their elitist position. In France, both large and small towns fought off the tendency of absolutism to absorb their independence. Their defense was based upon a continuous effort to maintain their right to elect their own mayors, executive committees, and chief consuls to ensure local control. Inevitably, powerful local oligarchs, primarily from the business community, ran the government. In London, the directors of both the Bank of England and the East India Company were frequently mayors or in commanding positions on the city's common council. In the tiny German city of Weissenburg, in Franconia, local government was nothing more than a microcosm of London politics, with certain hereditary families like the Roths, Schnitzleins, and Oberdorfers dominating the town's ruling outer and inner councils, elected again by a limited franchise. It was the same in Frankfurt, where the only real political opposition came on those occasions when the heads of the guilds—the master artisans—refused to follow the lead of the upper middle class. The economic elite tended to prevail in the cities with, as a general rule, little interference from aristocratic administrators or the masters of the guilds.

The 250,000 families that comprised the upper middle class in Europe lived comfortably, only sometimes sumptuously. The impression the bourgeoisie gave was, in general, one of dependability and systematized effort, coupled with an inevitable dose of restraint. Prosperous bankers and merchants always held back; they were simply not given to either the frivolity or free-spending ways of the aristocracy, and the contrast was conspicuous. When Bertholdt Brockes, the son of a wealthy Hamburg merchant, made the grand tour, traveling from Venice to Rome to Paris to Antwerp, he did it with sobriety, avoiding gambling, women, and drink. His life was at all times characterized, he tells us, by a desire for "the most refined company," and an equally powerful inclination "not to waste my time." The lone excess he seems to have been capable of was an abiding interest in poetry.

Women from the higher reaches of the middle class gave off the same stolid and competent impression. Goethe's great-uncle, J. M. von Leon, himself from a wealthy Frankfurt merchant family, extolled the type when he declared,

> I see at the fair in Frankfurt a fine-looking merchant's wife sitting in her shop; she is superbly dressed, and gives orders to her servants like a princess; she knows how to greet persons of station, ordinary people and

the vulgar each according to worth and condition; she judges reasonably, and brings up her children well.

Of her husband, he says,

Her husband sits meanwhile in his office, makes decisions, disposes of thousands, and often deals with more people in an hour than others can manage to see in a day.[5]

No matter how they made their money, members of the class were held together by a similarity of outlook. Prior to industrialization, only the bankers could match the inherited wealth of the great magnates; merchants and manufacturers often had to be content with less. Still, despite the differences in riches, both groups thought along the same lines. Within Europe's static preindustrial society, the values of the upper middle class tended to be confined to that class. Only later, when with its accumulated wealth the upper middle class spearheaded the Industrial Revolution in the nineteenth century, would its special values percolate down through the remainder of society. In Europe's great agricultural age, the values they believed in were theirs alone. Directing the lives of those at the top of bourgeois society was the concept of work, the idea of logical, sustained effort over an extended period of time. The primary goal of the upper reaches of the middle class was the further accumulation of capital, and the only way to do this was to avoid the aristocratic tendency to squander wealth. The work ethic saturated upper middle class attitudes and led to long hours at business and a sober life style. Whether Max Weber's description of this way of life as Puritan is valid or not, it was by its very nature restrained and far different from that of the aristocracy.

Other values stressed by this class derived mostly from the emphasis on the concept of work. Education was vital, and the upper middle class penetrated the universities, usually in search of practical learning. The family was most commonly a tightly knit group, with women assuming a specialized role and children disciplined in preparation for an adulthood predicated upon emotional restraint and mercantile effort. The upper middle class believed in saving, because it could see, almost on a daily basis, the power that money could bring. Religion had its place, so long as it too blessed acquisition rather than piety.

The upper middle class was a second elite in European society,

5 R. R. Palmer, *The Age of Democratic Revolution*, 2 Vols. (Princeton, N.J.: Princeton University Press, 1959–62), I, 80.

not the equal of the great magnates in most circumstances but magnifying its wealth to the point where it stood economically above the gentry. In spite of a reputation for frugality, the upper middle class did not deny itself. It only spent in a different manner. Housing was often the best; the homes of bankers and merchants in Florence, Hamburg, and Paris all testify to this. Banquets were frequent. The business and professional element traveled extensively, either for commerce or for pleasure. Food, a form of luxury in this age, was plentiful. This class had probably the best diet available, and the greatest longevity, an average of fifty-two years.

Like the aristocracy, the upper middle class had available to it the type of diet needed for stamina. This included meat, which was largely consumed in the urban areas of Europe. In Paris around 1700, at a time when the average peasant was consuming 8 ounces of meat a year, urban dwellers were averaging 12 pounds apiece. But this statistic is not sufficiently revealing, for at the upper levels of urban society the rate of consumption was closer to 100 pounds per person. Moreover, port cities had fruits such as oranges, dates, and currants, unavailable elsewhere, and many cities knew vegetables such as peas, which were virtually unknown in rural Europe except for some areas of the English Midlands and northern Italy. In an age when exotic fruits and vegetables of this kind were known only to the aristocracy and upper middle class, food was indeed a form of conspicuous consumption.

As the wealth of this class increased, its members often sought to emulate those above, the aristocracy. This usually took the form of acquiring a title or an estate or both. But even here practicality reigned. Titles for the upper middle class were frequent enough, but the bourgeoisie sought them not only for social prestige, but for the exemptions and privileges that accompanied them. Around all the great European cities, landed estates were continually falling to the upper middle class— but a good 80 percent of the bank loans granted at the time had land as their collateral. Largely satisfied by their hereditary position within society in 1700, the upper middle class grew restive as the century wore on. Wealthy economically, but without political power at the national level and social prestige born of accomplishment, this powerful group grew increasingly discontented. It became less satisfied with aristocratic leadership and aristocratic trappings. Members of the upper middle class wanted the political power and social recognition they thought they deserved, prestige and influence commensurate with their own conception of themselves as the most productive and most dynamic element within society. What emboldened them and pushed them forward was their growing wealth.

The Growth
of Commercial Capitalism

The emergence of an industrial society in Europe in the nineteenth century was the direct result of two eighteenth-century developments, the availability of capital for investment, the consequence of expanding profits, and greater labor productivity, the natural result of an improving diet. There were only two great capital pools in existence by the year 1800, the wealth possessed by the great magnates and the upper middle class. That wealth literally financed the growth of industry. Its source lay in the growing sophistication of commercial capitalism, a product of eighteenth-century developments. For it was in that century that commercial capitalism, having passed through infantile and adolescent stages of development, really matured.

By the year 1750, the system of capitalism had become so well developed that it had reached its take-off point, the point beyond which it would never again stop growing. The maturity of the system was institutional, that is, it had by the early eighteenth century created economic institutions through which both money and goods could be moved easily and quickly. The most vital of all these institutions were the central banks, which concentrated capital as never before and dispensed it elastically in the form of credit. All over Europe, great central banks were founded between the time of Louis XIV and Napoleon I. The Bank of Sweden was established in 1656, the more prestigious Bank of England was created, by legislation, in 1694, and the Russian Credit Bank was set up in 1754. Napoleon was himself instrumental in the founding of the Bank of France.

Concentrating capital in certain key urban centers in Europe, about twelve or so, was just the first step in the process that stimulated trade. The second saw the great banks of Europe increase the amount of money available for use by means of new banking procedures. Starting with the Bank of Amsterdam, bankers stretched the value of their actual deposits by introducing bank notes. Prior to this time, trade had been limited by a heavy dependence upon specie—gold and silver. Now, banks issued bank notes at a rate of 5 to 1. The more reputable banks, like the Bank of Amsterdam, would issue these notes to a total of five times their actual deposits, thus literally increasing through this first form of paper money the amount of currency in existence by a good 500 percent. Thus, by purely artificial means they multiplied the amount of money, which Adam Smith called bank money, available to finance a growing commerce. All of this contributed so immediately to the flow of money in Europe that the English East India Company could readily borrow in Amsterdam and the Rothschilds could move from one money market to another, from Vienna to Frankfurt to Amsterdam to Paris, raising huge amounts of capital. The European money market had become integrated as well as concentrated.

The tendency to concentrate capital in certain banking centers was matched by the growing concentration of capital in the century's favorite type of business organization, the joint-stock company. Joint-stock com- panies meant an end to the family firms that had characterized commercial capitalism at a more youthful stage of development. Because merchants pooled their resources, they allowed for unparalleled concentrations of wealth. When the English East India Company was first organized in 1600, it had 200 investors, but by 1800 it was tapping the resources of more than 3,000 merchants, bankers, and aristocrats. The Dutch East India Company had no difficulty attracting investors; it paid an average of 18 percent in dividends per year for more than two hundred years.

By the eighteenth century, joint-stock companies were blossoming everywhere in Europe, either spontaneously or with government encouragement. By the early 1700s, France had, in addition to the French West and East India Companies, such major trading firms as the Guinea Company, the Company of Santo Domingo, the Chinese Company, and the African Company. The results were obvious. Through the course of the eighteenth century, French trade increased threefold, with imports and exports averaging more than a billion livres a year by the 1780s.[6] Even in lesser states like Sweden and Denmark, merchants, hoping to tap the colonial area, pooled their capital to form the Swedish East India Company and the Danish General Commercial Company, respectively. Meanwhile, the governments of Austria, Prussia, and Portugal were themselves encouraging the growth of joint-stock companies to participate in both the colonial markets and the carrying trade.

While the major European banks and stock companies were reaching ever higher levels of commercial sophistication in the 1700s, subsidiary institutions were also growing up, facilitating even more the expansion of trade. The most important of these subsidiary organizations was the national stock exchange. Initially, these exchanges served a variety of purposes. Futures were prominent, for wholesalers tended to buy and sell at the major exchanges—either commercial exchanges like those in London, Paris, Amsterdam, and Frankfurt, or industrial exchanges like that in Lyons—on the basis of samples. For a while, they

---

[6] About 2 billion current American dollars.

served as money markets not only for the exchange of currency but for loans as well, functions that were increasingly taken up, as time went on, by the great banking houses. Their final function became their most important one. They became security exchanges where the upper middle class could meet and invest in either government bonds or company stocks, although, if the German traveler J. W. Archenholz can be believed, more business was done in the coffee shops surrounding the London Exchange than on the actual floor of that institution. Underwriters, especially those dealing in marine insurance, were also to be found close to the exchanges. Marine insurance was necessary because of the risks of overseas commerce. So eager were overseas trading companies to protect themselves that two London companies, including Lloyd's, the world's greatest marine insurer, had by 1810 written premiums to a total of £140 million.[7]

Most of the goods moving into the European market from abroad were luxury items. This was especially true at the beginning of the eighteenth century, for the vast majority of workers in the cities and the peasants in the countryside lacked purchasing power. The great overseas adventure of the 1700s was accomplished primarily in the name of the great purchasers, the higher reaches of the aristocracy and the upper middle class. One could also list as consumers the gentry, master artisans, and peasant proprietors, but always to a lesser degree. Trade therefore was concentrated on commodities for the wealthy. Spices, such as peppers, nutmegs, cloves, and cinnamon were in great demand, as were furs, rugs, silks, tobacco, sugar, coffee and tea, the last two quickly becoming upper class drinks. Slaves were treated as a staple, but rarely appeared on the European continent. Many of the great fortunes of London, Amsterdam, and Lisbon were initially made in the slave trade, the Dutch introducing the first slaves to the colony of Virginia in 1619. They were the first of some of 450,000 to be transported to the United States up to 1808.

Toward the end of the century, the movement of staple items, especially indigo and cotton from overseas, indicated that commerce would eventually serve the interests of industry. Within Europe, the transfer of grain, coal, and iron ore was also a sign that the domestic carrying trade was rising just as quickly as overseas trade. The shift in the direction of staples by the 1770s, however, was not evidence of an emerging consumer market; members of the aristocracy and upper middle class were investing in some of the newer agricultural and industrial commodities in their private search for even greater profit.

The city, the center for profit, boomed, while the countryside

---

[7] This included customers both in England and on the Continent.

lagged. In 1750, even at a time when 85 percent of the population was on the land, the rural sector of Europe's economy accounted for only 40 percent of her gross international product. Commerce was simply more lucrative. It was here that money grew. And money begot other money, first through banking and then through newer areas of investment—shipbuilding, mining, the financing of the putting-out or domestic systems—and finally through agriculture itself. As merchant capital expanded, it began to search out other areas of investment. Among them were shipping and mining. The mammoth growth of trade during the eighteenth century required many more cargo-carrying ships. The result was a flurry of shipbuilding in the great ports of London and Amsterdam and even in more modest centers such as Bordeaux, Venice, and St. Petersburg. The premium was on sailing ships, and England was far ahead of the rest of Europe in 1800 with a huge fleet of 20,000 ships, about equal to the combined merchant marine of all the other Continental powers. Mining began to emerge as still another profitable area of investment for capital, especially that owned by the great magnates. Since mining was a rural enterprise, coal and iron tended to be discovered on the great estates. English, German, and Dutch capital was particularly active in this area, with, for example, the Austrian aristocracy financing almost exclusively the exploitation of mineral resources within the old Austrian Empire.

Merchant capital also made its way into the domestic system of production, formerly the monopoly of the guilds. The luxury and construction trades escaped the jurisdiction of merchant capital, but the textile trades fell to its influence in the eighteenth century and the metallurgical trades in the nineteenth. In the German town of Aachen, the textile guilds had fallen to the merchants by the 1780s. The merchant was the employer, the middleman his hired foreman, and the weavers, drapers, fullers, dyers, and shearers, even though they continued to work in their own shops, nothing but hired labor. This scene was repeated thousands of times no matter where one went, whether it was Rouen, Prague, or Florence. The increase in merchant capital in manufacturing was matched on occasion by spreading investment in agriculture. By 1800, 40 percent of the arable land in France was in the hands of the upper middle class, thanks to the seizure of church land during the French Revolution. Meanwhile, aristocratic capital, mostly from magnates but also at times from the gentry, was moving into the staple production of wool in England, sugar in Austria, and grain in Prussia and Russia.

Capital pools concentrating at the top of European society, either in the forms of rent or profit, were now beginning to stimulate the whole economy from above. In the cities of Europe's preindustrial society, the overconcentration of capital and wealth had its influence on the urban classes living below the level of the aristocracy and the upper middle class. Largely this meant the guilds, the small-scale manufacturers of the time. They now found themselves participating in this new wealth. Benefiting the most were the master artisans, who dominated the guilds and who formed the lower middle class element within the city. They could not come close to the wealth of the magnates or merchants in the cities but they did, because they owned and employed on a limited scale, derive sufficient income to enjoy a standard of living that was at least a modest reflection of that of the upper middle class. The same could not be said for the urban lower classes, the journeymen, the casual laborers, and the beggars. For it was at this level that the poverty of Europe's preindustrial society first revealed itself on a massive scale.

3

The Town Workers

Europe in the eighteenth century was still an overwhelmingly agricultural society; only 15 percent of her nearly 200 million people lived in cities and towns. The urban population was itself divided into three easily recognizable social groups. First of all, there were the upper class elements, magnates, merchants, and bankers, who together may have constituted between 10 and 12 percent of a city's population. They, of course, gave life to the city, pouring their money into the urban economy, making it dynamic, and denying the countryside an equal opportunity for growth. Sixty percent of the wealth of Europe was concentrated in the cities. Below the upper class were the guildsmen, the artisans of the time. Masters, journeymen, and apprentices, they were the majority. On the eve of the French Revolution, they constituted 60 percent of the Parisian population. There were some 75,000 artisans, of whom 20,000 were masters enjoying a lower middle class status, while the rest, because of income, were distinctly lower class. Manufacturing was inevitably the monopoly of the guilds, of which there were 100 or more in Paris, Europe's second biggest city, in 1789. But not all labor was to be found here. Far below the upper classes and the artisans was a large floating population. Primarily destitute peasants who had wandered into the cities, this submerged portion of the city's population, which Marx would later call the lumpenproletariat, barely survived. It was composed of a highly diversified group of day laborers, haulers, beggars, vagabonds, and criminals. When these people worked, they did much of the back-breaking and debilitating casual labor.

By the 1700s, the positions of master, journeyman and even apprentice was becoming hereditary within the guilds. Gone were the days when an individual might hope to move through the system by serving an apprenticeship of from two to eight years, then becoming a journeyman, someone who worked by the day, and finally a master artisan, owning his own shop. The nearly 100 guilds of London, the world's greatest city, were themselves divided into four categories by specialization. In the main, artisans were organized into the textile trades, comprising those who worked in cloth, sail, or lace; the metallurgical trades, comprising the smiths, forgers, and grinders; the construction trades, masons and carpenters; and the luxury trades, which included goldsmiths and jewelers. In each division, a handful of master artisans limited enrollment, set wages, prices, and standards, and made sure that their incomes were not threatened by too much competition.

Most journeymen were by the last century of the Old Regime little more than wage workers, living on weekly incomes that rarely included enough for savings or for social advance to the status of master. Even as most journeymen were being stuck in place, so were some apprentices, who by the 1790s, likewise became mere wage workers, forever fixed at the lower levels of the guild. The major exceptions were the sons of masters, who served their apprenticeships but regained their fathers' positions within the guild hierarchy by quickly becoming masters themselves.

The urban poor constituted a mass of people living below the level of respectability. Untrained, they had no share at all in the wealth of the city, which at least to some degree percolated down to the artisan level. These people did make a living on occasion. The more fortunate worked as haulers, carriers, street hucksters, wharfworkers, and casual day laborers. Outside the system of day laborers were the beggars, vagabonds, and criminals. They lived in the slums of London, Paris, and Amsterdam, usually diseased, quite often alcoholic, and subject to a very high death rate. The preindustrial city often had an excess of deaths over births, but it was the urban poor who did the dying.

The Lower Middle Class
Shopkeepers

Every European city and town had its shopkeeper class. For the most part, except for individuals such as grocers and butchers, the shop-keeping class was composed of master artisans who owned their own small outlets and tools. On average, they worked with two hired journey-men and took on one or two apprentices. The small shop was the outward symbol of master status. In one of the more typical towns of the time, the French city of Orleans, with almost 40,000 inhabitants, there were about 4,000 of these retail outlets, mostly combining produc-tion and sale, clustered by specialty. In Weissenburg, a southern German market town, shopkeepers were numerous. The town consisted of only 500 households yet it included 69 master butchers, 55 weavers, 34 shoe-makers, and 28 bakers along with a dozen tanners and another dozen brewers. The prevalence of trades concerned with the processing of agricultural products, indicates that Weissenburg was a market town, with master artisans serving the needs of the surrounding rural area.

Specialization, of course, depended upon traditional or local need. Venice was famous for its glassware, Lyons for its silk, Dresden for its porcelain. But usually the trades were more diversified and numerous than those particular cases would suggest. London had dozens upon dozens of trades, as did Paris. In London, with its highly elitist con-sumer market, the luxury trades were especially prominent, with a large group of skilled master artisans who made clocks, watches, cutlery, optical equipment, plate, jewelry, saddles, and furniture. Paris, nearly as affluent as London, had its corps of tailors, shoemakers, dressmakers, hatters, masons, carpenters, wheelwrights, and carriage-makers, all with business largely provided by the upper levels of urban society.

Within the guild system, there was a natural hierarchy based upon skill, income, and training. The luxury trades, with their greater incomes for master artisans like silversmiths and printers, were always considered on top. Below them in esteem were the metallurgical and construction trades, where training was vital. At the bottom were the less well trained textile artisans, grocers, and butchers. Social snobbery at the various levels was common. For example, among the poorest of the trades were the stocking-weavers, especially after the turn of the nineteenth century. When a group of London stocking-weavers approached the ruling coun-cil of master carpenters, who had a reputed treasury of £20,000, for a loan, the carpenters refused. They turned the stocking-weavers down, one observer recalled: "When they understood our trade had no regular fund to support itself, instead of lending us money, their noses underwent a mechanical turn upwards, and each [member of the carpenters' council] saluted the other with a significant stare." [1]

The social distinctions that separated one guild from another and masters from journeymen and apprentices were also reflected among the masters themselves. Within the various Parisian guilds, most masters were divided into one of three categories, *jeunes, modernes,* and *anciens.* Each category was separated from the other by about a decade of experience, with authority gravitating into the hands of the *anciens.* A small inner circle of three to six *anciens,* known in Paris as *jurés* and in Germany as *obermeister,* effectively controlled the individual guilds. In Paris, the power of these men was unchallengeable. Their prestige and influence rested upon their ability to supervise the various shops under their jurisdiction. They could condemn work of poor quality, chastise masters who paid journeymen above the rates set by the guild council, examine the efforts of journeymen, regulate apprentices, and if necessary, take a fellow master to the guild court for violations of guild practice. Their ultimate weapon was the ability to suspend the license of an unrepentant master artisan. Guild courts, under the senior members of the guild, also imposed moral standards and sought to regulate marriage and to condemn acts of theft and adultery that threatened the reputation of the guild.

The highly intrusive character of the guilds is nowhere better illustrated than in the regulation of business practices. Within the German guilds, the historian Mack Walker has discovered a powerful tendency toward both jealousy and rancor. Masters were condemned if they tried to attract customers from one another, cut prices, or sold door-to-door, instead of over the counter. They could be suspended if they hired too many journeymen or otherwise tried to introduce too much competition. The masters of the guilds disliked competition because it threatened their monopoly of what was at best a limited market. The result was inequities like those outlined by the nineteenth-century German economist Albert Schaeffle:

> Property rights in a trade and its territorial monopoly; subjection of the countryside to the town market; marriage obligations in the interest of masters' daughters and widows; fixing and limiting the number of masters, and of the apprentices and journeymen allowed them; brutality against real and imagined intruders [competitors]; overburdening of new masters with extravagant masterworks and all kinds of fees; silly journeymen and masterwork rites; price fixing and the elaborate regulation of work. [2]

[1] E. P. Thompson, *The Making of the English Working Class* (New York: Random House, 1966), p. 238.

[2] Mack Walker, *German Home Towns, Community, State and General Estate* (Ithaca, N.Y.: Cornell University Press, 1971), p. 89.

The guilds engaged in these practices largely because lower middle class shopkeepers lived in a precarious position. The few in the luxury trades had high incomes, often the English equivalent of £200 a year, enough to buy a house and enjoy a comfortable standard of living. But most master artisans were not that fortunate; masons in Paris could count on only seasonal employment and incomes of not much more than 180 livres a year, an income just above the level of subsistence. The same was true of the metallurgical trades. Since the guilds were often involved in the production of luxury goods, economic downturns could wipe out markets and income. Textile artisans were in even worse shape; masters in these trades often had incomes that barely allowed them to keep up with food, clothing, and shelter. So precarious was the position of most master weavers in places like Prague, Vienna, Nottingham, and Rouen that they often gladly gave up their rather uncertain independent existence in order to work for wages for some merchant. Given the fact that markets could collapse so readily, it was little wonder that masters tried to protect themselves by means of rather elaborate practices and legal devices.

It was in this atmosphere that the masters sought to keep their numbers limited, so as to guarantee income. In the north German town of Gruenberg, over the course of decades, the local bakers' guild admitted a total of 283 apprentices, of whom 213 were already the sons of master bakers. In London, new apprentices were kept out by means of astronomical apprenticeship fees. The master saddlers excluded others by charging apprenticeship fees of between £30 and £100. In certain small French towns like Tulle, where apprenticeships within given trades were limited, the hereditary character of the shopkeeping class was perpetuated by simply apprenticing the sons from one trade to another. So sensitive were the masters about penetration from below that they even resisted the attempts of government to apprentice orphans and street children on the ground that they were bastards and therefore socially unacceptable. Illegitimacy in the preindustrial city usually meant that the boy came from the urban poor. Governments wanted to train them, the guilds to exclude them. When the German Diet in 1731 declared bastards honorable and therefore trainable, one guildsman Justus Moeser replied sarcastically:

> Furthermore, it is certain that the trades and guilds suffered greatly from the recent ruling of the Diet requiring them to accept all bastards legitimatized by any palatinate count and, for that matter, almost any creature with two legs and no feathers.[3]

[3] Forster and Forster, *European Society*, p. 213.

In addition to internal practices, the guilds turned to the legal system to protect their individual monopolies and markets. The carpenters of Flensburg, in northwestern Germany, did no more than any guild when in 1711 they sought and won the legal right to monopolize all carpentry in the city and its environs. Exclusive control over a defined geographic area was imperative for many guilds; they could not have survived without it.

In the early part of the eighteenth century, guilds all over Central Europe, were successful in declaring illegal the work of free masters who operated outside the normal framework of the guilds. In Silesia in the 1750s the textile guilds demanded that free labor be brought under the legal jurisdiction of the appropriate guilds. In Aachen, the city government for a while protected the urban market for certain textile guilds, while in Barmen and Krefeld, in western Germany, the textile guilds were legalized and their markets defined. But legal protection did not really provide long-term safeguards, especially when the domestic system under merchant-manufacturers spread to the countryside, creating a new form of competition in the person of the rural artisan. Again, Silesia was a case in point. By the turn of the nineteenth century there were only 6,000 looms in the towns, but 29,000 in the countryside. The monopoly of the urban-based Silesian textile guilds on production was obviously gone forever.

The standard of living within the lower middle class was not uniform. Generally speaking, the greater the skill, the higher the income, a rule that gave an immediate advantage to masters in the luxury, metallurgical, and construction trades. For the more advanced tradesmen of the time profits ranged from £75 to £200 a year over all of Europe.[4] By contrast, masters in the textile trades probably flirted with the level of subsistence most of the time, although this was less true for tailors and more true for weavers. For a fair number of master artisans, profits were substantial enough to guarantee moderate comfort. Master artisans often owned their own shops, lived in houses or apartments that were practically furnished, and wore clothing that was respectable. Most important, they could afford the better food that was available in the cities.

By the late eighteenth century, the cities of Europe were not only draining capital from the countryside, they were also drawing increasing amounts of food from the rural areas. Market towns like Gagney and St. Denis around Paris, Floridsdorf outside Vienna, and Fulda east of Frankfurt and Hamburg saw a growing concentration of both meat and

---

[4] Again, the figure needed for subsistence for a master and four dependents would be around £50 a year in England, perhaps somewhat less on the Continent.

grain. From these centers, food was sold by wholesalers to grocers and butchers who distributed it in the major urban areas. In times of prosperity, master artisans could well afford to supplement the basic diet of the artisan class, bread, with additional items such as meat and vegetables. During this period, when the consumption of meat was more often than not a sign of social status, there is strong evidence that master artisans had meat available to them several days a week.

Master artisans were literate, since elementary education was imperative for those who had to run the guilds and to deal with upper class customers. Family ties were strong at this particular level of guild society. Women and children were expected to work, and women who did not have to work were considered to have attained a higher social standing. Sons, of course, given the intense conservatism of the lower middle class, were expected to enter their father's profession. Religion played a part, although much of the social life of this class seems to have revolved around the family and the guilds. For some 2 million European master artisans, life in the cities could never approximate the level of the great magnates and the upper middle class. Still, in the midst of a larger society suffering all kinds of deprivation, their way of life and standard of living stood out, especially when it was compared to that of those below them, the journeymen and the urban poor. Journeymen were too often borderline cases, individuals who had to struggle to keep from dipping below the level of subsistence. In the course of time, their rather uncertain existence was to be shared by certain apprentices who were acquiring a hereditary status at the very bottom of the guild social order.

The Wage-Earning Journeymen and the Apprentices

The guild system of Europe dated back to the Middle Ages and to the era when towns were first founded. In line with ancient custom and ancient expectations, the ceremonial book of the tailors of Leipzig listed, in 1708, the guild ladder—apprentices, journeymen, and masters. But actual movement up that ladder had long since been slowed in many parts of Europe. If and when a journeyman advanced, it was by means of his masterpiece. Most guilds spelled out their requirements specifically: For the potters guild of Alsace, they were

> Those who wish to be received Master Potters in the Brotherhood shall be required to work for a masterpiece three pots, each of three-quaters of an aune in height, a Colmar measure round and of proportionate width,

and each of these three pots shall be seen and examined by six master examiners . . . who shall carry out this task under oath.[5]

Very often, the requirements for a masterpiece would be set ridiculously high, or else the candidate gave up because he lacked the capital necessary to set up his own shop. Either way, journeymen were being increasingly frozen into place, their opportunities limited by unsatisfactory wage rates set first by masters and then later by merchant-manufacturers. The journeymen's response was to organize into unions. These journeymen associations often won legal recognition, but by the late eighteenth century they were becoming steadily more disturbing to the middle class because of riots and strikes. Probably the best-known uprising and strike by journeymen took place in Lyons in 1831 when, after a wage dispute, journeymen from the silk trades actually took control of the city.

Whether journeymen were employed by masters within the guild system or merchant-manufacturers within the expanding domestic system, the question of wages was vital to their survival. No overall pattern is discernible. For example, journeymen jewelers in Amsterdam often made more than most masters in other trades, but this was hardly the rule. In the London trades as a whole, real wages evidently declined for journeymen between the 1720s and 1810s. But the movement of wages was uneven, for the tendency was for the wages of those in the luxury, metallurgical, and construction trades to go up, while wages in the textile trades unquestionably sank as part of the general decline of the position of textile artisans. In the city of London, Dorothy George reports that journeymen's wages were on the rise in many trades, especially the more highly skilled ones. These advancing wages were pushed up even further by intense strike activity after 1793. Stocking-weavers and frameworkknitters were, on the other hand, always poorly paid. Whether good or bad, most wages paid to journeymen went for food; up to 1815, journeyman families in the English metropolis spent an average of 75 percent of their wages for food.

The same trend toward a rise in wages for the more favored trades revealed itself among construction workers in the city of Paris during this period. Wages for journeyman masons rose steadily through the century, doubling between 1727 and 1786. But even with better wages, the most fortunate journeymen could not save, they could only survive. At the beginning of the eighteenth century, the diet of the average journeyman in Paris consisted largely of bread and wine. It seems to have

<hr/>

[5] Sidney Pollard and Colin Holmes, eds., *Documents in European Economic History*, 3 Vols. (New York: St. Martin's Press, 1968–73), I, 52. Permission to quote from St. Martin's Press.

hardly changed by the end of the century, for 75 percent of the diet for some 55,000 families was, just as before, bread. Progressively increasing numbers of talented artisans, living in the great commercial centers, where business was livelier, knew some of the new luxury foods such as meat, butter, peas, tea, sugar, oatmeal, and cheese. Journeyman saddlers in London certainly had this kind of diet, but the majority did not, especially in the provincial cities of Europe.

In the German guilds, the custom of tramping developed. Upon becoming journeymen, apprentices would travel from one town to another, working for masters in different locales. Employment was possible only for those journeymen whose reputations were certified by their original hometown guilds. Prior to 1800, the tradition of the wandering artisan was a respectable one, but as the guild system eroded, all Europe came to know the tramping artisans. No longer the respected adolescent in search of new experiences, the tramping artisan was, after 1800, quickly becoming identified with the vagabond or criminal. Wandering journeymen were now involved in a desperate search for work of any kind. As the textile guilds crumbled, unemployment, especially among those who worked in the older cloths such as wool and flax, set journeymen wandering to such a degree that tramping took on a negative connotation. The idea of the tramp was born when the textile guilds began to go under. In northern England, where mechanization was taking place and the textile artisan was being displaced, the journeyman was often in trouble. Describing the plight of some of these textile artisans, one observer noted: "It is quite common [even] when trade was not bad to see weavers and spinners going from place to place seeking work, or to get a piece of cloth to work." [6]

The destitution that was beginning to eat away at the textile guilds demonstrates the fact that poverty was a constant companion at the lower levels of the guild system. In the eighteenth century 85 percent of the population lived below the level of subsistence, literally without enough food, clothing, or shelter. Below the aristocracy and the middle class, poverty was overwhelming. The lower classes of the city, of whom the journeymen are the first example, too often lived lives devoid of energy, health, and a sense of physical well-being. For journeymen, like some apprentices and the poor in the city, were undernourished. It is little wonder that the journeymen's riots of mid-century London, Paris during the French Revolution, and Zittau in Silesia in the summer of 1830 were either wage or food riots. Overly dependent on bread, journeymen lacked the vitamins to defend themselves from disease. They also lacked the protein and blood sugar that would have provided them with the

---

[6] W. B. Crump, "The Leeds Woolen Industry, 1780–1820," *Thoresby Society Publications*, No. 32 (1931), 28.

kind of day-long energy they needed. Even though food was more plentiful and existed in greater variety in the cities, that food was beyond the power of most journeymen to purchase.

For the lower classes of Europe, the difference in diet was often the difference between accomplishment and lethargy. If the lower classes of the city and countryside did not work as well or as consistently as aristocratic and middle class elements, it may have been the result of malnutrition. Quite often, the dividing line between the few who lived above the level of subsistence and the many who lived below it was access to certain foods, to meat, vegetables, and fruits. This is the reason why early death, disease, and malnutrition were more common the lower one went down the European social order of the eighteenth century. Many journeymen, especially the poorly trained in the less advanced trades, knew the edges of poverty and malnutrition. Their continued distress contrasted, of course, with the position of better-trained journeymen.

Apprenticeship for boys in Europe was not evidence of a youngster's social status, for apprenticeship could be either an avenue to lower middle class status, as a master, or to a fixed position within the lower class, as a mere wage worker. Apprenticeships varied. For the sons of masters, they were a guarantee that they would be able to follow their fathers' trade. But the poor were also being apprenticed, with governing authorities paying for their education. Whether they were trained formally by the guilds or in workhouses, it was likely that the only security they had gained was a chance for relatively steady employment as a low-paid worker. In the nineteenth century, apprentices were to show up again, this time in the domestic and factory systems. They were like the 10,000 journeymen and apprentices in the Austrian silk trade, whose apprenticeships were in name only, since they were unskilled laborers and distinctly lower class in income.

The formal contracts that were a part of every apprenticeship spelled out the responsibility of both parties. Typically, apprentices in the French gunsmith trade were bound, could not break their contracts, and had to pay the ubiquitous apprenticeship fee, either in full or in instalments. Sometimes the fees prohibited the entrance of any but the sons of other masters. Young boys were not bound to the more advanced and specialized skills until they were somewhat older. In Sheffield, a noted artisan center in northern England, boys might work in the shops when they were seven or eight, but glazers preferred youngsters who were ten and eleven, and some of the more intricate metallurgical trades, like the platers, kept the lowest possible age of entrance at thirteen and fourteen.

Among those destined for the upper reaches of the guild system, apprenticeship was not necessarily all that formal. During the latter part of Louis XIV's reign, authorities in Paris complained about apprentices being used to clean the silverware and for babysitting. Often apprentices in the Parisian guilds learned more from the journeymen than they did from the master who subscribed them to begin with. In London and Munich, apprentices were often found in the pubs or kellers buying ale or beer for journeymen and masters, who had a propensity for sipping the whole day. Depending on the skills required, apprenticeships could last from two to eight years.

The inconsistencies of the formal guild system of training were nothing compared with the abuses in the practice of apprenticing orphans, street urchins, and the poor. Throughout Europe, governments were interested in apprenticing the poor so that they might at least have a moderately self-sustaining occupation. But the guilds resisted; parish children, as they were called, did not make good workers. The more skilled trades avoided them. Only the poorer textile trades took them, often because the master needed the apprenticeship fee the local municipality would pay. Bad treatment was common. Apprentices were very often not trained, but kept on as simple laborers. The response of these children was often indolence. Adam Smith, ever perceptive, commented: "The boys who are put out apprentices from public charities are usually bound for more than the usual number of years, and they generally turn out very idle and worthless." [7]

Workhouses, if they were not like the Hôpital-Général in Paris, which did little more than enroll the poor, almost always had their own training programs. The workhouses in the Papal States, especially those in Rome, were a model of the benefits that public charity could provide. In fact, workhouses have a reputation that they do not necessarily deserve. An examination of the weekly menus of the Liverpool workhouses reveals a diet for apprentices that would have been the envy of most journeymen. Those in the workhouse got milk, bread, potatoes, and meat —sometimes described as paupers' beef, which might indicate its quality— on a daily basis. The reason why the diet of the workhouse was so good was because these institutions were run by middle class administrators, who tended to feed those being trained according to their own expectations.

The Urban Poor

At one point or another, usually at the lower levels of the guilds, urban society shaded off into the poor. Often transient, their numbers

---

[7] M. Dorothy George, *London Life in the Eighteenth Century* (New York: Capricorn, 1964), p. 230.

have been variously estimated. In London, they were referred to as "the sunken sixth"; in Paris on the eye of the French Revolution, they were thought to constitute about 20 percent of the population. In Cologne at one time they were judged to be a third of the population. Often unregistered and sometimes undetected, they had been identified in some cases only because they came into contact with such recordkeeping agencies as the police and charitable institutions.

The poor of the city ranged from respected, hard-working handloom weavers to haulers and carriers, to the indigent, the diseased, and the criminal. What distinguished them from other lower class elements in the city, journeymen and poorer apprentices, was the unrelieved poverty of their days and the absolute hopelessness of their existence. Preindustrial society had a positive penchant for classifying these people. A Spanish report of 1762 places the poor into three broad categories: the old and infirm who were actually unable to work; idlers and vagabonds, who constitute the majority of the poor; and those who suffered from misery because their jobs could not support their burdens. These last were known in Paris as the legitimate poor, those who seemed worthy of aid, as distinguished from the irresponsible and indigent who had little interest in work. Bourgeois administrators in the Berlin poorhouse made the same vital distinction, declaring that "the genuinely needy and the poor deserving sympathy shall be cared for better than hitherto, but the deliberate beggars shall more resolutely be made to work." [8]

Among the resolute poor in the cities were many who made their way as day laborers. Essentially unskilled, they did much of the heavy labor, carrying and digging. They were most often found working seasonally on construction or on the docks, depending upon the arival of cargoes. Day laborers were prominent in the construction trades, where they were hired by masters, always on a day-to-day basis. The actual skilled work was done by masons, carpenters, and turners, with the menial tasks left to the laboring poor. In the Parisian trades, material handlers were paid a wage below subsistence. In the 1780s, for example, they were receiving wages in the neighborhood of 25 sous a day, so that a family of five would have had to depend on the marginal income of the wife and some of the children in order to survive. An examination of wages paid to laborers in the English construction trades shows the same trend for the entire eighteenth century—substandard wages that left a man poor and undernourished. The fate of one Parisian family from among the laboring poor illustrates the point: In this instance, a husband tried to support a wife and six children on wages of 252 livres a year, when the level of subsistence for a family of five was estimated to require an annual income

[8] Pollard and Holmes, *Documents*, I, 166.

of 435 livres. There was no way this family could escape poverty, disease, and malnutrition.

There were plenty of pathetic scenes at this level of urban society, among them the sweatshops. These were tiny establishments employing a dozen women and children, usually in spinning and weaving. As society became more conscious of poverty and its ramifications in the early part of the nineteenth century, these poor were known to be suffering from a variety of conditions stemming from malnutrition and long hours of work, such as headaches, constipation, indigestion, colds, rheumatism, and the killer of the lower classes, tuberculosis. The struggle for daily bread on the docks produced its own sights. Every day on the wharves, representatives from the laboring poor would assemble in hopes of a day's employment. In the words of one observer, struck by the obvious debasement that he witnessed,

> Indeed, it is a sight to sadden the most callous to see thousands of men struggling there for only one day's hire, the scuffle being made the fiercer by the knowledge that hundreds of the assembled throng must be left to idle the day out in want. To look in the faces of that hungry crowd is to see a sight that is to be ever remembered.[9]

The chimney sweeps were among the classic poor in London. Sometimes sold by their parents, sometimes kidnapped or picked off the street, some 500 apprentices in the 1810s did some of the most dangerous and unhealthy work the metropolis had to offer. Medical reports showed most of them to be stunted, bleary-eyed, and undernourished. In the course of time, chimney sweeps became the symbols of urban poverty for an age just awakening to a condition that had been there not for decades, but for centuries.

The mistreatment of children so apparent in the case of chimney sweeps was noticeable elsewhere among the poor. Like their desperate parents, they lived in slums that were probably just as dank and just as forbidding as those of Liverpool in the earlier part of the nineteenth century. In the view of one Victorian, they were nothing more than unhealthy holes. Describing the situation in Liverpool, he commented:

> Those who have occasion to penetrate their dark and filthy recesses are generally thankful when they find themselves safe out again. In the winter these streets and courts are kept comparatively clean by the heavy rains; but in the summer the air fairly reeks with the stench of decayed fish, rotting vegetables, and every conceivable kind of filth. . . . The children, that seem to fairly swarm in this neighborhood, are nearly all of a pale,

[9] Francis Sheppard, *London, 1808–1870: The Infernal Wen* (London: Secker and Warburg, 1971), p. 365.

sallow complexion, and of stunted growth. Shoes and stockings and underclothing are luxuries they never know; and one good meal a day is almost more than they dare hope for. Cuffs and kicks they reckon upon every day of their lives.[10]

Children who were too much of a burden to their parents were commonly exposed. At the very bottom of urban society, the poor often engaged in infanticide, letting their children die in the streets because they could not care for them. How many infants died this way is not clear. During what appears to have been a representative year in the seventeenth century, a Paris physician estimated the number at about 600. By the eighteenth century, children who would have been exposed were becoming the wards of charitable institutions. During the terrible winter of 1708–1709, a total of 2,525 infants were deposited at the Hôtel-Dieu, the charitable hospital in Paris. Still, in 1739, if Thomas Coram, the English sea captain turned humanitarian, is to be believed, the practice had hardly subsided in London: "No expedient has yet been found out for preventing the murder of poor miserable infants at their birth, or suppressing the inhuman custom of exposing newly-born infants to perish in the streets." [11] Although London did come up with an expedient, the Foundling Hospital, some of these infants did not survive even when they became parish children. From 1768 to 1778, a number of London parishes received children under the age of six. St. Giles-in-the-Fields received 1,479, of whom 215 died. Since the overall death rate in the eighteenth century for the urban poor was better than 50 percent before the age of six, the record of the parishes was, relatively speaking, a good one.

As the cities of Europe grew more affluent, they also grew more charitable. All over Europe, public institutions were founded in the eighteenth century, mostly in the urban areas, for the training and care of the poor. Among them were workhouses, poorhouses, clinics, and the century's most frequent expression of aid, the charitable hospital. In Lyons, the Hôtel-Dieu was a model of neatness and order, caring for the poor who were ill as well as for foundlings, the wounded, the insane, and women about to give birth. The same institution in Paris, overcrowded in the time of Louis XIV and understaffed, came close to being a madhouse. Thousands died within its walls and were carted off for burial. In the 1780s its reputation was still bad, with one English observer noting the practice of lumping five or six to a bed. In Graz, Austria, the local lying-in hospital did try to improve the conditions surrounding birth for many women. Women were admitted whether they could pay

[10] J. E. Vaughan, "Nasty, Brutish and Short," *Local Historian,* No. 8 (1968), 102.
[11] George, *London Life,* p. 43.

or not, provided they were unmarried. Those who could not pay had only to prove their poverty and the fact that they became pregnant within the city limits. Just how they proved this last point to the middle class administrators of the hospital was not made clear.

Beggars and vagabonds were a conspicuous part of city life. Hardly given to the census, their numbers have never been adequately determined. Destitute, alcoholic, and diseased, they were the street people of preindustrial society. Local authorities were sometimes more interested in sweeping them from the streets than in anything else. One grand swoop by the Parisian police netted thousands of them. In Berlin, the municipal corporation was eager to establish a workhouse in order to get the city's numerous derelicts out of sight. The French police under Napoleon I were especially vigilant in enforcing a strict legal code designed to punish the so-called "sturdy beggar." In the period from 1806 to 1812, the association of two or more vagrants not of the same family was treated as a crime, punishable by deportation. The number of vagrants might rise suddenly, as in the disastrous winter of 1811 in France, when the authorities in Amiens estimated the number of vagrants in the district, both rural and urban, at some 60,000. The lower levels of the city also housed all types of petty criminals, pickpockets, thieves, and fences, to say nothing of pimps and prostitutes. London was supposed to have 6,000 to 7,000 ladies of the night, and day, during the early part of the Victorian era.

One of the leading social historians of France, Louis Chevalier, has demonstrated the unequal chances of the poor through the cholera epidemic of 1832. By the 1830s, recordkeeping had advanced, and the deaths recorded during this epidemic can be classified socially. The disease claimed capitalists, small employers, shop workers, day laborers and ragpickers. It touched the upper reaches of the city, but it ravaged the urban poor. To the municipal recordkeeper the rates of death for the various social groups revealed "the inequality before death" existing in French society. That inequality was in preindustrial society largely defined by a lack of food. The bottom 50 percent of the urban population was overly dependent upon grain for subsistence. Without meat and vegetables, they did not grow sturdy, nor were they filled with energy. Their lack of strength for all but a few years, their inability to initiate and to make a go of things, their propensity to disease were matched by the rural poor, for poverty was even more endemic to the countryside than it was to the city. It was among the peasants that malnutrition was most widespread. A few, the peasant proprietors, lived above the level of subsistence, but the vast majority did not. In many ways, rural poverty was more prevalent, but unlike urban poverty it was less concentrated and somehow less conspicuous.

many urban contacts with the village.

4

The Peasantry

The overwhelming majority of Europeans in the eighteenth century were peasants isolated from the more advanced intellectual and cultural centers of the time. Like other social classes, the peasantry showed a marked tendency toward division. Ever since the late Middle Ages, when serfdom began to decline in the West, the peasantry had divided into three conspicuous groups. First, there were the peasant proprietors, the rural counterpart of the lower middle class urban shopkeeper. Peasant proprietors owned up to 30 acres of land, a large amount by peasant standards, and represented the most productive element within the class, because they were capable of producing for the urban market. Often talented agriculturalists, they never formed more than 10 percent of the entire peasant population. Still, with their cereal and root crops and later with their highly specialized market agriculture, they helped to contribute, along with the great estates, to the expanding food supply flowing into the cities.

The 3.5 million peasant proprietors who functioned at the top of the European peasant order in the eighteenth and early nineteenth centuries were the beneficiaries of a long-standing agricultural development. For as serfdom dissolved, so did the practice of equalizing allotments. As the rough and ready type of democracy that characterized serfdom disappeared, deep economic divisions began to appear among the peasants, with peasant proprietors emerging as the most economically talented and advanced group.

The vast majority fell into the categories of middle or landless peasants. Middle peasants occupied exceedingly small plots of land ranging from 2.5 acres in Italy to 7.5 acres in France and western Germany. In the main they were subsistence agriculturalists, never participating in the market and living from year to year at the mercy of the soil and a single crop. They were numerous in some villages, amounting to 75 percent of the population in such areas as Haspengau, Julich, and Sudlimburg in the Netherlands. Some 60 million Europeans belonged to this group, which, while still owning, was nevertheless impoverished. By the year 1800, the majority of peasants in western Europe owned no land at all. They spent their time eking out a living as sharecroppers, tenant farmers, or farm laborers. By 1789, France, the classic land of the peasantry, had produced a tripartite peasant social order, with a bare 10 percent producing directly for the market and the remainder either middle or landless peasants. In fact, by the eve of the French Revolution, landless peasants numbered as much as 52 percent of the total.

In eastern Europe, the system of serfdom kept the idea of equal peasant holdings alive, in some areas, deep into the eighteenth and nineteenth centuries. This was particularly true in Russia, where a system of redistribution permitted the decennial equalization of landholdings among the peasants in at least half of the country. But even within the institution of serfdom, the tradition of equality and of equalizing peasant holdings was steadily being eroded. In Hungary the land had long since been allocated on the basis of the number of labor days a serf owed to his landlord. In Bohemia, unequal peasant holdings were common before 1750, while in areas like Moravia and in parts of Austria proper, a system of agricultural labor had grown up among peasants who had no land whatsoever. In sum, the deep-seated social divisions that characterized the peasantry in western Europe were now spreading to eastern Europe and separating the serfs in the east along the tripartite lines of the peasantry in the west. And once the peasantry was legally emancipated in Prussia, Austria, and Russia between 1848 and 1861, those divisions were to intensify.

The Peasant Proprietor

The social divisions that were part and parcel of peasant life were most blatantly reflected in the village, where the various levels of the peasantry lived side by side. The average population of 250,000 villages that dotted the rural European landscape was about 650 residents or about 175 households, since peasants did not have large families. Politically, socially, and economically, the village of the eighteenth century tended to be dominated by the relatively well-to-do and articulate group of peasant proprietors. The leadership provided by the richer peasants was sometimes complemented by men from the nonagricultural portion of the population, individuals such as ministers, schoolteachers, and rural artisans.

The basic institution through which the more well-to-do peasant proprietors and their social allies dominated local affairs was the village commune. The commune faded in the nineteenth century, but while it was alive it was a powerful institution. It decided what crops should be planted and just when the harvest should begin, on its own in western Europe and in cooperation with the landholder in eastern Europe. It also decided who would get the right to glean, exactly how the common lands would be used, and when and at what times pasturing could occur. It even regulated the folding of sheep, the hiring of the village shepherd, and the areas where the cattle could graze. If the village was mixed socially, if it included peasant proprietors along with middle and landless peasants, these vital decisions affecting the economic well-being of all were made by a few. On the other hand, in places like Brittany in western France and Galicia in southern Poland, where every village was poor, leadership by lower middle class peasant elements was, of course, lacking. The highly elitist character of most village communes was obvious since the deliberations of these bodies were supervised by village officials who were most likely either peasant proprietors or local artisans. In some areas of Provence, village government was already the monopoly of certain petit-bourgeois families, while in the villages of Switzerland, Austria, Germany, and Lithuania, the communes even had their own courts, which were usually dominated by a few village officials.

The leadership provided by lower middle class peasants at the village level, whether economically through the commune, politically through the village assembly, or legally through the courts, was the natural outgrowth of their own advanced economic and educational level. That position was gained by a very adroit combination of skill and energy, all of which made the peasant proprietor the most energetic and the most dynamic element in peasant society. Not necessarily as talented as farmers, they were nonetheless highly productive. Their agriculture was unique and their prosperity, gauged against the standards of the age, obvious in comparison with the poverty that existed all around them.

Although the majority of villages included all three levels of peasant society, here and there in Europe there were villages almost totally composed of peasant proprietors. The English traveler of the 1780s in France, Arthur Young, was duly impressed by such a village in the Midi, describing it as

> A succession of well-built, tight and comfortable farming cottages, built of stone and covered with tiles, each having its little garden, enclosed by thorn hedges, with plenty of peach and other trees. To every house belongs [fields], perfectly well inclosed, with grass borders mown and neatly kept. It is all in the hands of little proprietors, without the farms being so small as to occasion a vicious and miserable population. An air of neatness, warmth and comfort breathes over the whole.[1]

Villages just like the one that Young found in the Midi could be observed elsewhere in Europe, if one looked closely.

Such a village, unusual for eastern Europe, was Orašac in Serbia, located several miles from the capital city of Belgrade. The presence of an urban market, as it always did, stimulated Orašac's agriculture, but this was not the only reason for its success. For in the first half of the nineteenth century, Orašac was truly a self-sufficient village in a way that the vast majority were not. It could feed itself from its own produce. The village of Orašac was composed of 35 households, each with an average of five people. Each of these 35 peasant proprietors owned rather extensive plots, necessary because they raised both animals and crops. What was extraordinary about Orašac and what set its peasant proprietors apart from the great mass of the peasantry was the amazing diversity of its agriculture. The villagers of Orašac raised corn, somewhat unusual for Europe, beans, potatoes, onions, cabbages, and peppers, which they consumed along with cheese, eggs, bacon, and on important occasions other types of meat. The massive cultivation of vegetables along with plums, their basic fruit, meant an intensive type of agriculture, of which only a few within the European peasantry were capable. In addition to root crops, the village also raised pigs, thirty to two hundred per household, primarily as a cash crop, along with sheep for wool and goats for cheese. Cereal crops in the form of oats and barley were also grown, but

[1] Arthur Young, *Travels in France,* 2nd ed., 2 Vols. (London: G. Bell, 1906), I, 17.

again only as a cash crop, only for the urban market. In spite of the intelligence that was needed to engage in this type of agriculture, the villagers of Orašac were illiterate, unusual for peasant proprietors, who were often the only literate element within the peasantry.

Agricultural diversification along with the higher income levels that overproduction could bring naturally separated the peasant proprietor from the middle and landless peasants, who usually cultivated only a single crop and that just for subsistence. Still, diversification could be stimulated in the eighteenth century, as in the peasant villages of Saxony, where some of the newer industrial crops such as flax, hemp, hops, and cattle were increasingly being grown and sold. Agricultural diversification, the key to higher income levels, often took some peasants right into the category of farmers. Two villages, Wigston in the English Midlands and Osterstillinge on the Danish isle of Sjaelland, amply demonstrate this particular point.

Over the course of time, peasant proprietors in both villages had accumulated enough property that they could truly be called farmers. By the middle of the eighteenth century, some Wigston households had absorbed between 90 and 100 acres and in some instances as much as 195 and 215 acres, and were producing on all of it. The same trend toward accumulation of land was obvious in Osterstillinge, where certain prosperous farmers owned in separate instances 85, 95, 112, and 133 acres, respectively. Holdings of this kind meant not only a mixed arable and pastoral economy, but the existence of an extraordinary amount of agricultural knowledge. Needless to say, both villages were self-sufficient, with Wigston producing such commodities as meat, bacon, eggs, cheese, butter, milk, honey, apples, and herbs, food which the rest of the peasantry rarely saw, much less ate. So great was the agricultural potential at this level of peasant society that in a single year one French village, Azereix, located in the Pyrenees, was able to produce no less than thirty-nine different kinds of crops.

Not all peasant proprietors could match the obvious prosperity of those who lived in Orašac, Wigston, or Osterstillinge; some had to struggle just to maintain their lower middle class status and standard of living. And sometimes not even the prosperous could make it, for nature could be cruel, even to the more fortunate. In England, for example, major crop failures occurred in 1727, 1728, 1739, 1740, 1757, and 1758, to say nothing of intermittent downturns in production in other years. When either flood or drought struck, none escaped. In good times, however, peasant proprietors always survived with at least a modicum of comfort.

The peasant proprietors of Lourmarin, a French village in Provence, were typical of peasants who, in spite of their obvious talents, still had difficulty making a go of things. The men of Lourmarin diligently raised wheat, rye, fruits, vegetables, and nuts. But, unfortunately, the land was not fertile enough, their crop yields were relatively low, and grain was always in short supply. The resourceful peasant proprietors of the village made up the difference by producing a relatively unique cash crop, olive oil, the proceeds from which they used to buy the additional grain they needed. Their lives were somewhat marginal, and the slightest adversity found them easy victims. If either the grain or the olive crop failed, as happened in 1789, they were ruined. Beyond this, one of the great symbols of agricultural prosperity, meat, was often missing from Lourmarin diets.

The varied diet of the well-to-do peasant, which more often than not provided him with a reasonable balance of vitamins, proteins, minerals, and calories, along with the fact that he was partially literate, differentiated him from the other levels of the peasantry. His talent and skill were so well developed that they permitted him to live on right into modern times. In the eighteenth century, his life was often enough pleasant. Education came to the villages of England in the seventeenth century, to the rural areas of France after 1696, and to Prussia and Austria after the 1760s. Because of the costs involved, usually only the sons of the more prosperous peasants could afford to go to school. In a day when only 12 percent of the population was literate, education in the countryside was the rather exclusive monopoly of the aristocracy and the peasant proprietor. And because food was plentiful enough, people had the kind of sturdy bodies and alert minds needed for both farming and learning. A life, the son of one French peasant proprietor wrote in his memoirs, of hard work and quiet contentment.

The average peasant proprietor of the eighteenth and early nineteenth centuries was resourceful. It was from this level that the image of the sturdy and self-reliant peasant came. In 1820, the English traveler Thomas Hodgskin said of the peasant proprietors of northern Germany, "They think of what is to be done, and they themselves are the persons who do it." [2] Men built their own homes out of stone, wattle, or wood; women knew spinning and weaving. Since this peasant agriculture was so diversified, the presence of cattle meant that both butter and cheese had to be made. And since grain was consumed almost universally in one form or another, it had to be either baked or brewed.

Market agriculture required a certain amount of business acumen. Peasant proprietors often leased additional land from the aristocracy, paying rent. Since they produced for the market, they were normally required to travel to one or more of the market towns that surrounded the great urban areas. And since peasant proprietors were involved, in

[2] Pollard and Holmes, *Documents*, I, 35.

the market and the money economy, a limited amount of education was obviously needed, the real reason why peasant proprietors were willing to bear the cost of elementary education at the village level.

Proper nutrition was at its best somewhat accidental in the eighteenth century, yet given the variety of food available to the peasant proprietor, it was inevitable that he would emerge as the real leader of peasant society. The remainder of the peasantry could not come close to the type of foodstuffs available to the so-called small farmer. They were sentenced to a life of disease and malnutrition that must have contrasted starkly with that of the peasant proprietor. With limited acreage and a single crop, the poor peasant of the eighteenth and early nineteenth centuries presents us with a very different picture indeed of what rural life could be like before the coming of the Industrial Revolution.

The Middle and Landless Peasant

The majority of Europeans in the eighteenth century were middle and landless peasants condemned to perpetual poverty and early death by a backward and unproductive agriculture. These two lower levels of the peasantry were huge; they included perhaps 140 million of Europe's nearly 190 million people. They ranged from poor Irish tenants who averaged 2.5 acres apiece to the downtrodden serfs of Russia, the dark and illiterate *moujiks*. The middle peasant was not necessarily better off, for he was chained both by custom and by his own fierce possessiveness to a tiny plot of land that would not feed his family and that, because of circumstances, he had to leave one-third fallow. In the eighteenth century, the middle peasant inevitably lived out his life producing a single grain and clinging to his small plot, which in France and the western part of Germany extended to only 7.5 acres and in Italy to a mere 2.5 acres for each household.

The landless peasantry were even more numerous than the middle peasants. In places like Ireland and Wales, they were in the majority and survived only by cultivating the land owned by others as tenants. Tenantry was common elsewhere in western Europe, in the Low Countries, France, Germany, and Italy. In eastern Europe, where serfdom persisted, only a relatively few peasants could match the resources of the peasant proprietors of the west, and only in areas like Hungary and Bohemia. The vast majority of the serfs in eastern Europe prior to emancipation would have to be regarded as both tenants and middle peasants, simultaneously tilling their own soil and the soil of others, not as in western Europe for "half fruits," as the eighteenth century expression had it, but simply out of custom. Although the landless peasants, first in the west and later in the east, were often as equally undernourished as the middle peasants, at least they could find alternate sources of work as share-croppers, tenant farmers, or farm laborers.

The middle peasant was in a real sense a western European phenomenon to begin with. Almost everywhere he had trouble surviving, for the tendency was for the lower strata to expand at the expense of the middle. The middle peasant found himself in trouble because of his low level of agricultural knowledge and because he was a marginal producer. Living on the periphery, devoted to a single crop, usually grain before 1800 or a root crop after, he could be destroyed readily by bankruptcy or natural calamity or both. Central Germany was a case in point. In 1750 in Saxony, 50 percent of the peasant households had at least enough land to support a family; by 1843 it was only 14 percent, an indication that the middle peasant was being squeezed out. In northern France, in the Beauvaisis, the vast majority of villages had five or six well-to-do peasants, a huge number of landless peasants, and a constantly shrinking class of middle peasants, while the process had gone so far in the nearby area of the Nord that the middle peasant, with his tiny plot, had already disappeared by the end of the eighteenth century.

The appearance and disappearance of the middle peasant was again illustrated by events in the German states after 1807. In Prussia, land reforms went a long way toward establishing property rights for at least some of the peasants. All together, some 200,000, both peasant proprietors and middle peasants, got outright title to their land. But almost as soon as he began to emerge from serfdom, the middle peasant found himself in difficulty, especially if he was tempted simultaneously into the capitalistic market. For the marginal producer in Prussia, the cost of new seed, fertilizer, and tools often exhausted him financially, and bankruptcy was his fate, just as it was to be the fate of millions of other peasants in the nineteenth century.

In the last half of the eighteenth and early nineteenth centuries, the middle peasant survived not only as an agriculturalist, but also as an artisan. For the spread of the domestic system of production, particularly spinning and weaving, to the villages of Europe went a long way toward saving the middle peasant from outright extinction. He found an alternative source of income in the wages the domestic system was able to provide him. Between 1770 and 1830, rural spinning and weaving spread through the villages, and by the eve of the French Revolution, almost 2 million peasants in France, most of them middle peasants, were a part of the putting-out system. Very often the villages tapped were in marginal agricultural areas, as in the case of the semimountainous villages of the Lower Rhine, the Vosges, and northern Switzerland, but even in more prosperous areas, like Normandy and western Bohemia, the middle peasant still sought to guarantee his survival through his connection with the domestic system.

Although he shared the same economic fate as the middle peasant, the landless peasant often had more options open to him. He owned no land, but he could still work as a tenant farmer, sharecropper, or agricultural laborer. Tenantry and sharecropping were common because they were an important source of revenue for the aristocracy, which did not exploit its own land, but allowed the peasantry to do it in exchange for rent. Agricultural labor was also common not only on the great estates, but also at planting and harvesting time on the land of the peasant proprietors, who also hired. By the year 1800, landless peasants were the numerical majority in western Europe. In eastern Europe, they existed under the guise of serfdom, working full-time as agricultural laborers, as in Prussia and on the state-owned lands of the Russian czars, or simply as field hands for the local aristocrat a couple of days a week, as custom dictated, without pay.

In the British Isles, tenantry was a way of life in an area marked by landless peasants and absentee landlords. This was especially so in Ireland and Wales. There were relatively few landowning peasants in Ireland, where the vast majority were simple cotters, renting land and trying to win a living from plots that averaged 2.5 acres per household. Those who could not afford to rent worked as agricultural laborers. The standard of living of the Irish peasantry was just a cut above that of the serfs of eastern Europe, as the estimated annual income of £13 a year in 1814 [3] for an Irish cotter would seem to prove. If Irish tenants, dependent on a single crop, potatoes, lived below the level of subsistence in the first half of the nineteenth century, so did their counterparts in Wales. A few decades before, the English traveler Arthur Young, making a note on living conditions among Welsh tenants, declared, "The [Welsh] cottages [were] many of them not a wit better than Irish cabins." [4] He might also have added that like Irish tenants, the Welsh were also dependent upon potatoes and often lived below the subsistence level.

England, with its relatively advanced food supply for the age, always seemed to provide a better standard even for its poor tenants. The English agronomist Richard Baxter was taken aback because poor tenants did not have much meat to eat, yet elsewhere in Europe they often had none. Describing the class in England, Baxter added:

> The poor tenants are glad of a piece of hanged bacon once a week and some few that can kill a Bull eate now and then a bit of hangd beefe enough to trie the Stomack of an ostrige. He is a rich man who can afford

[3] The level of subsistence at the time would have required at the very least £40.

[4] David Williams, *The Rebecca Riots* (Cardiff: University of Wales, 1971), p. 99.

to eat a joint of fresh meat (bief, mutton or veale) once in a month or fortnight. If their sowe pigge or their hens breed chickens, they cannot afford to eate them but must sell them to make their rent. They cannot afford to eate the eggs that their hens lay, nor the apples or pears that grow on their trees (save some that are not vendible) but must make money of all. All the best of their butter and cheese they must sell, and feed themselves and children . . . with skimd cheese and skimd milke and whey curds.[5]

Here was the basic problem at the bottom levels of peasant society; too often the very foodstuffs that would have provided nutrition had to be sold for cash. This was the case even for the best agriculturalists. Some of the peasants who worked the land of the aristocracy were capable of a diversified type of agriculture, but they were, in fact, subject to penury because of the costs involved in paying rent. Too many farm products had to be sold for cash.

In western France, in the Vendée, peasants were in the habit of raising cattle, but always for market. After 1750, in western and southern Germany, in France, in Belgium, and in England, wheat was increasingly grown by tenants, but it was too valuable and so, just like meat, it became a luxury item, suited only for the rich. Sharecropping provided little better opportunity for economic advance. Traditionally, the landlord who provided the land and the tools took "half fruits," 50 percent of the crop, but the need to retain seed for the following year's planting often reduced the peasant's portion. An examination of sharecropping contracts in both France and Italy during the eighteenth century shows the sum actually retained for consumption to be closer to 30 percent. This was the case, again, even for men who proved to be talented agriculturalists. The great difficulty for both the tenant and the sharecropper was that he could not retain a significant enough portion of what he himself produced.

As at every level below that of the peasant proprietor, food and income were the perennial preoccupations of the peasant, who in numerous cases made his way as an agricultural laborer. The lot of agricultural laborers was often the most conspicuous because they worked the great estates. In Brittany, in the middle of the eighteenth century, this element was described in the following way by Arthur Young. He said, referring to the poor peasant, "the country has a savage aspect, husbandry not much further advanced, at least in skills, than among the Hurons . . . the people [appear] almost as wild as their country." [6] But the landless laborer was a vital part of the agricultural scene, for he did work no one else wanted to do. In places like Kent, Dorset, Wiltshire, Somerset, Devon, and Cornwall, he worked the great estates in return for a

[5] G. E. Fussell, *The English Rural Labourer* (London: Batchworth, 1949), p. 28.
[6] Young, *Travels,* I, 97.

meager wage that allowed him little more than bread, milk, cheese, and potatoes. And even that fare was better than most middle peasants could provide for themselves or what the landless on the Continent might hope for.

The money economy, so prominent in the cities, was not all that prevalent in the countryside. As a result, agricultural laborers were sometimes paid in produce, more often in both cash and kind. This was the situation in Brittany, where 100,000 peasants were totally dependent on day labor for survival. Their wages were low and their diet a combination of oatmeal, buckwheat, peas, and wine. Such poverty was matched elsewhere in Europe. As soon as the system of serfdom broke down in eastern Europe, agricultural laborers began to appear. Their numbers grew, replenished by middle peasants unable to hold on to their small holdings. Over the course of three decades, according to the German analyst Gustav Schmoller, 100,000 of them disappeared in Prussia, Brandenburg, Pomerania, and Silesia. Those surviving swelled the ranks of rural wage workers. Landless peasants who worked on the great estates as a permanent labor force were fortunate, for they were kept the year round. Those who were not permanently attached to an estate or a farm were less fortunate. For these people were dependent upon seasonal employment, particularly at planting and harvesting time, for a high proportion of their yearly income.

As early as the first part of the nineteenth century, migration became a permanent way of life for these people. The European climate allowed for the planting of both winter and summer crops, and therefore multiple plantings and multiple harvests. Migratory workers could move from one area to another seeking new wages during most of the year except, of course, in the winter months. By the beginning of the nineteenth century, the first signs of this emerging pattern were clearly visible in the Austrian Empire and elsewhere. Tens of thousands of agricultural laborers were pouring out of the villages of Moravia, Hungary, and Styria as the dispossessed, the young, and even some destitute middle peasants all joined in the seasonal migration.

Rural impoverishment, symbolized in the west by poor diet, was also characteristic of a fading form of serfdom in the east. In eastern Europe, serfdom was in various stages of disintegration long before legislative acts in 1807, 1848, and 1861 abolished its legal foundations throughout the area. Money payments, by way of illustration, were already replacing labor service in both Prussia and Poland by the 1810s. In Austria labor service still existed, but in many areas, the amount depended on one's holdings. Communal ownership, one of the oldest features of serfdom, still existed in Russia as did labor service, but even here, where serfdom was most recognizable, money payments were increasingly being accepted.

Whatever the actual state of the institution of serfdom may have been, the peasant was still heavily obligated to the nobility. The fruits of his labor were not his own, for he still had to work for the aristocracy, one way or the other. In Poland during the eighteenth century the large estates did move to commute labor service. Instead of depending on free labor a few days a week, the aristocracy showed a steady willingness to give up labor service and instead to lease its land to the peasantry. But this only forced the peasantry to sell off a portion of its grain to meet rental costs, since the lease was nothing more than a type of quitrent, an annual fee the peasant had to pay before the start of each growing season. Polish peasants really became nothing more than rent-paying tenants, just like their colleagues in the west.

Labor service remained a vital part of the local agricultural scene in the Austrian Empire. Peasants worked as agricultural laborers on the estates of the aristocracy, rendering free labor service in accordance with the size of their holdings. In Hungary, those with the largest holdings, 40 acres, were obligated up to 104 days a year, while those who held only 10 acres were obligated for only 25 days. In Lower Austria the obligation ranged from slightly above 100 days to 26 and in Carinthia from 156 to 39 days, again depending on how much land the individual peasant household cultivated. In most instances, this was less than 10 acres. Labor service was most extensive in Russia, where until the middle of the nineteenth century 70 percent of the peasants in European Russia were totally on labor service. Whether he gave service or paid rent, the serf of eastern Europe lost either a portion of his time or his income, or both, to the aristocrat.

It is at the level of the middle and the landless peasant that the vital statistics concerning the eighteenth century have the most meaning. For it was at this level that average life expectancy never went beyond twenty-seven or twenty-eight years. It was particularly the case among the peasants that 55 percent of the children were dead by the age of six. It was here that one of the scourges of the time, female mortality, was especially prevalent, for the average peasant woman of the eighteenth century only lived to be twenty-three. The high rate of infant and female mortality along with the lack of longevity were not exclusively a peasant monopoly; other social groups suffered as well. Only here the facts were especially gruesome because the poverty of the peasant masses was so continuously unrelieved. The average peasant of the eighteenth century drank no milk, consumed 8 ounces of meat a year, did not eat fruit, and saw only two vegetables a year beyond his basic diet of bread. What all of this spelled, of course, was really a state of permanent malnutrition for the peasant masses.

Unaware of bacteria, the average peasant, his home a one-room cottage or hut, lived in his own excrement and that of his animals,

without any idea that this own waste might actually do him harm. *living conditions*
Animals, far from being a source of meat, were regarded as agricultural
implements. Cows were vital first and foremost as a source of manure,
and sheep were kept primarily as a source of wool. Living conditions
were primitive. The peasant proprietor might have a house of stone,
furniture, and pewter to go along with his varied diet. But most huts
were made of wattle, mud, and straw; they were hot during the summer,
cold during the winter. There were no windows. At best, they served
as a crude form of shelter for the peasant and, if the family was lucky,
the peasant's animals. Far from being hard working, it is doubtful that
the lower levels of the peasantry worked, on a general average, more than
one hour a day. They probably did not have the energy to do much
more than that. In the atmosphere in which he lived, without sufficient
food, adequate knowledge, or shelter, one of the great consolations for
the peasant was his religion, still another of his traditions. For the
poorest peasants were also the most conservative.

The major cause of the poverty at the bottom levels of the peasantry
was a backward agriculture. Scientific agricultural knowledge may have
existed among the peasant proprietors, but it was not very pronounced
among the middle and landless peasants, who knew nothing of drainage,
seeding, irrigation, fertilizer, and animal husbandry. Instead, the middle
and landless peasant relied on custom and precedent, which meant that
he would continue to grow cereal crops virtually out of force of habit.
Barley, rye, and later wheat were the easiest crops to plant and grow,
for they required the least amount of attention. The problem, in the
absence of diversification that might have provided a more balanced diet,
was that grain was a liability. Not particularly nutritious itself, grain
exhausted the soil more than any other crop.

The results were simply disastrous, for at a time when the average
European peasant did not have enough to eat, one third of the land
had to lie fallow, unproductive. The peasant was condemned to a low
level of life by his own commitment to single-crop agriculture. Only
when he began to diversify, only when he escaped the past and turned
from the production of cereal crops, as he did increasingly by 1800
and thereafter, to the production of root crops, would he finally be able
to break out of the cycle of poverty that had bound him for centuries.

The Development
of Capitalistic Agriculture

The extreme poverty that characterized rural Europe deep into
the eighteenth century began to break down between 1775 and 1825
with the coming of agricultural innovations. Diversification became a

change

fashion both on the great estates of Europe and on the expanded holdings of the peasant proprietors. The result was a gain in the food supply
and the appearance of ever-greater quantities of vegetables, meats, and
finally fruits. At the lower levels of agricultural society, the bulk of the
peasantry also improved itself by finally turning away from the production of cereal crops to the higher-yield vegetable crops. The major consequence was that Europe was not only increasingly able to feed itself,
but the population now had levels of physical energy that had been
enjoyed only by those in the upper echelons of society before this. Perhaps the most conspicuous result of Europe's revolutionary increase in
food supply was that the population doubled after 1800.

Agricultural innovation on a large scale was, of course, only possible on the large landed estates. As at least a portion of the aristocracy
turned from rents to profits as a major source of income, the production
of staples for the market became vital. By the second half of the eighteenth century, some of the English aristocracy was producing both wool
and wheat for sale. By the 1780s, Arthur Young was reporting that the
large estates around Paris were experimenting seriously with the selective breeding of both cattle and sheep with an eye to the building of
herds. By the first half of the nineteenth century, agricultural societies
were springing up among aristocrats in the Austrian Empire just as they
had previously in the west. One after another, wool, sugar beets, and
potatoes all began to be cultivated on large estates throughout the
empire.

Aristocrats in Prussia and Russia soon followed suit with the large-
scale production of wheat and other grains. Staple production on the
large estates was directly linked, of course, to the growth of a class of
agricultural laborers, since their labor was needed by an agriculture
still characterized by sod-busting and hand-threshing. Estate production
could not match the highly diversified type of agriculture carried on
by Europe's peasant proprietors, the most talented agriculturalists of the
time, but it could and did increase the amount of certain foods available,
including grains and meats for man and certain root crops (turnips and
beets) for animals.

before 1800

The massive conversion from cereal crops, primarily barley and
rye and in some cases wheat, to root crops, in the first instance the
potato, spelled the beginning of the end of long centuries of malnutrition for the middle and landless peasant. Not only were barley, rye, and
wheat relatively low in nutrition, they exhausted the soil so badly that
they only added to the poverty of the bulk of the peasantry. At a time
when the average middle peasant, tenant, or sharecropper was cultivating
a meager patch of about 5 acres, he still had to leave a third of it and
in some instances half of it fallow. This was the inevitable result of

planting cereals, which robbed the soil of its nitrogen faster than almost any other crop imaginable. Poor peasants often traded the future for the present. In areas of Serbia, peasants planted the fallow yearly even though it exhausted the soil, saying they just could not afford to forego the greater yield.

Grain production also required heavy manuring, an expensive proposition. Manuring with either liquid manure (urine), regular manure (dung), or ash was necessary if crop yields were to be kept relatively high. In prime farm areas like Flanders and the rural areas adjacent to Lille, up to 60 percent of the cash outlay that a peasant might make during a year would be for fertilizer. Manure was an absolute necessity in places like northern Germany, where it could double the yield of a single crop during the growing season. The obvious tendency of grain to exhaust the soil is the real reason why cattle were kept as a source of fertilizer. Some areas of Europe, like Silesia, never had a domestic market in cattle until deep into the nineteenth century because cattle, the principal source of fertilizer, were never, ever, slaughtered. The widespread use of grain was, then, from a certain perspective, the real reason why a meat industry failed to develop before the nineteenth century.

The peasant proprietor could and did break with the past and diversify. The middle and landless peasant could not. Because he was a subsistence agriculturist, he could not afford to experiment; the failure of one crop could jeopardize his existence. As it was, grain crops, given the type of agriculture practiced, fluctuated sometimes up to 400 percent in yield from one year to another. Life was unstable enough without experimentation. The average peasant, then, hesitated to try something new, and only a major crisis could prompt him to break with tradition. The foundations of the new agriculture for the peasantry lay in disaster, in the failure of the grain crops, for example, in 1739 and 1740 in England; in 1770, 1771, and 1772 in the German-speaking areas; and in 1788 and 1789 in France. Crop failures often forced the peasantry to convert to root crops, in particular the potato. The peasantry resisted the potato for a number of reasons. It was ridiculed because of its taste and because it could not be stored, to say nothing of the common superstitions that it was either tubercular or poisonous.

The conversion of the European peasantry to potato cultivation began after 1750 in the Netherlands and in England. According to the French aristocrat Count Chaptal, peasants of the Sablons, in southeastern France, and the Grenelle, south of Paris, were delighted to find that the potato could sometimes be cultivated without using manure and even in years of only marginal rainfall, meaning that it was a more dependable crop than grain. The potato's reputation spread quickly. The Irish peasantry had gone over to the potato on a massive scale and by 1800 potato cultivation in Ireland matched the growing of grains. The potato also gained a reputation for improving health and stamina. The English traveler William Jacob in 1820 perceived that the potato spelled the difference between survival and disaster, noting that in Westphalia in western Germany, after the Napoleonic Wars, "peace has returned numbers to their homes in this country, who cannot find occupation, and would be an unsupportable burden on their families, if the general introduction of potatoes for a subsistence did not keep them from the extreme of want." [7] By the first half of the nineteenth century, potato cultivation had spread to Poland, Austria, and Russia. In Poland, its rise was symptomatic of soaring production elsewhere. In 1822, the landed estates and peasant plots in Poland produced 3 million bushels of potatoes; and by 1839, the figure was 23.5; by 1843, 41 million bushels.

The conversion of the peasantry to the potato gave them levels of energy and immunity never before known, in addition to greatly multiplying the food supply. Potatoes in places like Ireland and Poland yielded on the same plot four times the quantity of food previously produced by grain. Beyond this, the potato could be used as a fertilizer and also as fodder, freeing cattle for the production of food items such as cheese, butter, and meat. In addition to everything else, the potato was relatively high in calories and an important source of vitamins A and C. It gave the peasantry the ability to produce antibodies so that normal resistance to bacterial diseases was now possible. It is little wonder, then, that throughout Ireland and in other areas of Europe, like the Scottish Highlands, Alsace, and the Vaud in Switzerland, the population began to double within two decades of the turn to potato cultivation.

As William Jacob was to note on the European continent, the conversion to potato cultivation was the only form of agricultural innovation that could be seen in some areas. Still, the idea of innovation did attract some peasants, just as it proved a lure for some aristocrats. New industrial crops could now be grown, crops that could command ever higher prices after 1750. The general inflation that touched all commodities in Europe after 1750 tended to send the prices of agricultural goods upward. That price rise, on the average 2 percent a year, proved a temptation for all agriculturalists from the estate owner right on down to the sharecropper. As the prices of grain, vegetables, industrial crops, fodder crops, meat, and poultry rose, many tried to take advantage of the rise to gain extra income. The period from 1770 to 1800 was especially tempting in northern Europe because prices rose sharply in areas like England, the Low Countries, and Scandinavia.

The new agriculture required new knowledge. It was generally intensive, requiring a great deal of care and specific skills, rather than

---

[7] Pollard and Holmes, *Documents*, I, 36.

the old extensive type that had required only minimum effort. The older type had been dependent on sod-busting, broadcast seeding, pasturing, and hand-threshing. Now more scientific knowledge was required of the agriculturalist. Even potato cultivation required a greater preparation of the soil than grain at planting time, plus intensive weeding. The first major change, as might be expected, was a variation on old methods that took several forms. One of them was to mix cereals. By the late eighteenth century this was common in England and France, where wheat and barley were planted together. In Alsace, spelt and rye were often combined; in the Netherlands, rye and barley. In terms of improved yields, however, the most significant break came with the introduction of buckwheat. This cereal, which evidently originated in the Netherlands, had several advantages: It could be grown on marginal soil, its yields were high, and it grew quickly. The great disadvantage of the crop was that it could not be made into a flour and had to be consumed as a porridge.

The new root crops were, in addition to the potato, turnips and sugar beets. Turnips were especially favored. They replenished the soil with nitrogen, thus effectively eliminating the waste in letting fields lie fallow, they could be used as fertilizer, and they made excellent feed, especially for England's growing sheep industry and later on for cattle. The sugar beet was an equally viable crop in eastern Europe. Just as turnip production spread through the British Isles after 1750, sugar beet cultivation spread in central and eastern Europe after 1800. As with turnips, sugar beets were first grown on the Continent on the large estates and then adopted by the peasantry. Cultivation began in areas like Bohemia and Lower Austria around the early 1800s and then spread quickly to the rest of the Austrian Empire. Sugar beets not only provided standard fare for the peasantry; like turnips, they were good for the soil, could be used as a fodder crop and, once more, had cash potential. Since West Indian sugar did not reach central and eastern Europe, the sugar beet soon became a cash crop for Austria's growing sugar industry.

The sugar beet was an industrial crop, like so many other crops that could now be sold for cash. Flax production for the growing linen industry, for example, was encouraged throughout Germany. By the late eighteenth century, all levels of the peasantry in both Saxony and Silesia were increasingly producing for the market. By 1800, flax was known throughout Flanders and, after 1800, it proved a vital cash crop for the Irish peasantry. Flax was rightly regarded as the peasant's crop, since it could be grown profitably on as little as 2 acres of land. Its great disadvantage lay in the fact that it had to be carefully seeded and needed rather extensive fertilization. As the brewing industry grew and developed in Europe, beginning in the eighteenth century, grain, hops, and potatoes suddenly became good cash crops for those peasants who could either grow hops or overproduce grain and potatoes. The production of hops developed first in the Netherlands and then spread to England and Germany, to be thereafter largely confined to those three areas. For the peasantry, hops could be a boom-or-bust crop, since its price tended to fluctuate violently. In the Netherlands, it varied from 10 to 130 guilders for a hundred-pound unit.

As the sheep and cattle industry began to grow, fodder crops could now be regarded as a cash crop. And as the fallow began to disappear in the eighteenth century along with the commons, which was being sold off by the commune or subdivided, pasture lands took on a new significance. Hay and clover production were expanded. The peasantry, in general, was now able to supply fodder crops as well, since turnips in England and France, potatoes in Germany and Russia, and sugar beets in Bohemia and Hungary could all be used as feed for livestock. Fodder crops not only helped to improve the size of livestock herds, they guaranteed their growth. The size of animals improved noticeably. In Holland, the average weight of cows probably increased by more than 125 pounds to 700 pounds during the eighteenth century, while sheep in England seemed to advance in some cases from a scrawny 25 to 30 pounds to 70 or 75 pounds.

What all this means is that the food supply was being measurably increased all over Europe. Although those who benefitted the most were those at the top, still it is fair to say that the population as a whole probably did experience a nutritional advance after 1750 and most particularly after 1800. Not all the peasants, however, were better off as a result of the expansion of the market. The peasant proprietor experienced an ever-rising standard of living primarily because he was a good agriculturist. But many below his level, and in particular the middle peasants, found themselves in trouble even if they did enter the market. The new agriculture required not only new capital outlays but an exact knowledge of soil preparation, planting techniques, proper drainage and moisture levels, the precise use of fertilizers, and more intense labor. For many peasants with marginal resources any expenditure for new seed or fertilizer was a burden, especially in areas like France, where the peasantry prior to 1789 was still forced to pay up to 7 percent of its annual income to the aristocracy in the form of feudal dues, money that might have gone for agricultural improvements. In the east, serfdom was a threat to the new labor-intense type of agriculture, for it took the peasant away from his own land for too many days a year. The new agriculture separated the good agriculturist from the bad, and many in the aristocracy—and many more in the peasantry, during the nineteenth century— would not succeed in capitalistic agriculture precisely because they lacked the necessary knowledge.

5

Stresses and Strains
in the
Old Regime

Although the Old Regime seemed stable through the eighteenth century, it was subject to certain stresses and strains. Those tensions were among the first indications that society was about to enter upon a bold, new era characterized by industrialization, urbanization, and a rising standard of living. The pressures within the old order in Europe did not guarantee the coming of the new society—that would be the work of the machine— but they did indicate areas of dissatisfaction with society as it was. They predicted that a new elite was about to take over in European society and that something would have to be done to alleviate the widespread economic distress that was still characteristic of most areas even after 1800.

European society had been essentially aristocratic ever since its founding. Around 1500 the upper middle class had emerged dramatically as a second elite, but the merchants and bankers, for all their vitality, had never been able to accumulate through profit the wealth that the higher reaches of the nobility could command through rent. The result, in the eighteenth century, was social tension as merchants, bankers, and industrialists showed a greater and greater unwillingness to accept an inferior social and political position, especially when their wealth began to rise in absolute terms during the commercial revival. More often than not, the challenge of the upper middle class—the new elite in nineteenth-century society—to the aristocracy was peaceful. But on three occasions, 1789, 1832, and 1848, it threatened to inspire violence. And that threat was in itself a rather spectacular sign that the upper middle class was about to take over after centuries of aristocratic rule.

In accordance with their growing political consciousness, the upper middle class may have been more and more interested in governing, but the masses were still economically oriented, seeking food and trying to guarantee their own survival. This fact is borne out by an examination of any of the rural or urban riots that periodically plagued the countryside and the cities of Europe until the middle of the nineteenth century. Whether peasants or artisans, the cry was always the same—lower food prices, better wages, or some other basic economic improvement.

Even as these riots were taking place, European society was changing in a way too subtle for the mass of men to perceive. The change was happening on the estates and peasant plots of Europe and slowly and inevitably increasing the food supply. More food, better food, meant rising levels of energy. Indeed, it is doubtful that the Industrial Revolution could ever have taken place if the energy level of the peasant had not increased by the time he entered the factory system. Only a rise in his standard of living, defined here in terms of nutrition, could have made increased production possible. Not only did men improve biologically, but more survived. Infant mortality declined, as did female mortality. Communicable diseases were, at last, undermined. The consequent increase in population could have swelled the rural population to unbearable limits and created even more pressure on the land. Fortunately, Europe in the nineteenth century had an alternative, the growing cities with their factory jobs. Economic growth in the urban areas spelled one thing, of course, sociologically—the end of aristocratic rule and the triumph of the upper middle class, the group that was directing and would control the process of industrial change.

The Upper Middle Class Challenge
to the Aristocracy

The presence of two elites in European society, the great magnates and the upper middle class, whose wealth by the early 1800s was about to be equivalent, created irreversible social tensions in Europe between 1789 and 1848. The result was that the upper middle class was on three separate occasions to challenge the governing authority of the higher nobility: in France in 1789, in England in 1832, and in most of Europe in 1848. These episodes have been referred to as revolutions or near-revolutions. From a sociological point of view, a revolution is a situation in which two events are occurring simultaneously. First, there is the political challenge of one elite to another. These challenges are always, in the words of the great French historian Georges Lefebvre, juridical, bloodless, representing an attempt at a legal transferral of power. They were always accompanied by a good deal of rioting by artisan and peasant elements whose concerns were not political, but rather the satisfaction of immediate economic wants. When these two events occur simultaneously, there has been a tendency to describe the situation as revolutionary.

This is exactly what happened in France in 1789, in England in 1832, and in the various German states in 1848. In each case, the political challenge was accompanied by popular disturbances that had a way of amplifying and exaggerating the somewhat peaceful political demands of the upper middle class. The rich and powerful banking families of Europe, the Barclays, the Pereires, and the Rothschilds, just to mention a few, were not tempted to go into the streets to accomplish their aims any more than the well-to-do merchants or industrialists running the domestic system were tempted to commit acts of violence. The rich did not man the barricades; they had neither the numbers nor the inclination to do so. Instead, they permitted either their own representatives or the somewhat less successful members of the professional bourgeoisie to speak for them against the old order, using a parliamentary platform to get their ideas across.

The French Revolution is the story of an attempt on the part of one elite to replace another. It began as an organized effort on the part of the aristocracy to compromise the power of monarchy. The aristocracy, however, was forced to close ranks with Louis XVI in the wake of a determined bid by the upper middle class to kidnap the revolution and turn the Estates-General into a legal device for dismantling the Old Regime. The upper middle class in this instance was led by renegade aristocrats like Lafayette and Mirabeau, but this should not hide the obvious bourgeois character of the political challenge laid down in 1789.

The world of merchants, manufacturers, and bankers was, in a sense, only partially represented in the Third Estate, soon to become the heart of the Constituent Assembly. They totaled 85 out of the 648 middle class delegates elected to the Estates-General. Still, their interests and the interests of those outside the legislature were served not only by themselves but by the professions, especially by the more than 400 lawyers who made up the greatest bloc in the Constituent Assembly. About half were practicing lawyers; the rest were probably notaries, judges, municipal officials, and bailiffs—public servants, many of whom were originally from the upper middle class. Though overcrowded, the legal profession was prestigious enough to attract many sons from wealthy business families. The stranglehold that the professions, especially the legal profession, had on the events of this crucial period of the French Revolution continued, only punctuating the highly selective and elitist character of the Constitution of 1791, France's basic constitution during the 1790s. That constitution really assigned responsibility for government in France not to the people, but to some 50,000 rich and well-to-do men, the so-called electors, the only ones who were allowed to vote directly and the only ones legally permitted to hold office. This total obviously included some great magnates, but mostly it meant bankers, merchants, and industrialists.

Once the business and professional elements were in power, the interests of the upper middle class in France were well served by a spate of legislation that legally undermined the Old Regime and guaranteed the political, economic, and social advance of the wealthier members of French society. As the national legislature replaced the monarchy, the upper middle class could feel safe in its increasing acquisition of office after 1789 at both the national and municipal levels. The door was now open to political penetration of the existing system of administrative control. The upper middle class also benefitted economically, because it was the great beneficiary of the seizure and sale of the lands of the Catholic Church, which totaled nearly 20 percent of the land in the country.

If the French Revolution did not signal the absolute triumph of the upper middle class in French society, it did propel that elite in the direction of ultimate control, for now it could progressively match its newly acquired political power with its own ever-growing economic prowess. The great magnates would have to move over, for the second elite within society was on its way to the top. Not even Napoleon could afford to ignore the power and influence of the upper middle class, for the 10,000 notables, guaranteed public office by the so-called Napoleonic Constitution of 1799, were the real pillars of his regime. And again as in the Constitution of 1791, they turned out to be, for the most part, the rich and well-to-do members of bourgeois society.

The Reform Bill of 1832, passed under nearly revolutionary conditions in England decades later became law in an atmosphere similar to that of France in 1789. For here, too, there was a confrontation between the aristocracy and the upper middle class over who would rule. Perhaps the reason England was only brought to the brink of violence was because its aristocracy was divided in sentiment about the upper reaches of the middle class. The Tories, surely representing the principle of aristocratic resistance, were much less willing to accommodate the political aspirations of the wealthy bourgeoisie than were the Whigs, who were actually seeking some kind of accommodation with middle class interests. The more liberal aristocracy was led by Lord Grey, who was not a liberal in the classic sense; rather, he thought of himself as an aristocrat by both nature and position, with a definite preference for older institutions. He was a man who was trying to stop innovation by means of innovation and that meant, at the very least, taking into account the political desires of the highly influential upper middle class. It was good strategy to enfranchise the members of that class in order to prevent a repetition of the events in France, where the haute bourgeoisie had taken over the government and enfranchised itself to the detriment of the aristocracy.

In England it was not a matter of creating a national legislature; it was basically a matter of the franchise. Pressure for an extension of the franchise came from within and without Parliament. The upper middle class did have its spokesmen in the House of Commons, for by 1831 merchants, bankers, and industrialists made up 25 percent of the lower house. Though they did not have numerical superiority in comparison with the aristocratic Tories and Whigs, they obviously spoke for a clientele of growing importance. The pressure that they could exert was equaled on the outside by public opinion mostly created by the wealthy and their articulate allies in journalism.

The Reform Bill passed in 1832. It did not disturb the still characteristically aristocratic leadership of English politics, but Great Britain was not any less bourgeois. For even the aristocracy realized that with first some 200,000, then 300,000, and then 400,000 new middle class voters, they would now have to respond to upper middle class legislative initiatives. And an examination of the legislation, passed after 1832, especially business legislation, reveals the existence of a political system more and more responsive to the will of that class. Whether aristocrats or bankers passed that legislation is less important than the fact that it was passed, guaranteeing the triumph of the financiers, the merchants, and the industrialists. The upper middle class had won. The battle in the final analysis was only superficially for political leadership, for the real conflict in both England and France had been for a certain type of legislation conducive to upper middle class interests. Indeed, the haute bourgeoisie might have supported aristocratic leadership in France too, at least for a while, if it had taken their interests into account. It did in England, which is why it survived for a few decades after 1832, although progressively at the will of the upper middle class.

The pressures that led to 1789 and 1832 reemerged in 1848 to send out yet another revolutionary shock wave, this time through the whole of Europe. Once again, the sociological proportions were the same. Bourgeois elements from the upper reaches of middle class society threatened the governing authority of the aristocracy, for so long Europe's only political leaders. The bid by upper middle class elements for political power in 1848 was accompanied all over Europe by rioting, but not the sustained kind that had occurred in France after 1789 and in England during 1830 and 1831. Rioting in 1848 was more short-lived, which is probably why the old aristocratic order did not give in either totally as it did in France in 1789 or partially as it did in England in 1832. The old order in Europe in 1848 was not sufficiently intimidated by rioting from below to surrender either all or part of its political monopoly.

Nothing demonstrates this last theme better than events in the Germanies in 1848 and 1849. Once again, the upper levels of the bourgeoisie reached for political power. As in 1789 and 1832, that bid was, by and large, legal. Representatives of the upper middle class sought to gain their way juridically through the creation of a national assembly or legislature, in this case the ill-fated Frankfurt Assembly. Even though elections to that assembly were widely based, they produced a pattern of representation similar to the French Constituent Assembly. As in both France and England, prominent business elements were represented, but they were not numerous, only 75 out of a total of 799 delegates. And the professions were well represented, setting a tone for all of modern political life. For the modern tendency is for the professions to seek political prestige while the upper reaches of the middle class run the economy. Besides, in places like France in 1789, England in 1832, and Germany in 1848, the professions were usually staffed from the upper reaches of the middle class, so it is proper to speak of the business and professional elements in society in a single sociological breath, as sharing a community of interests.

In the Frankfurt Assembly, the professions were represented out of all proportion to their numbers in society. Of a total of 799 delegates, 157 were civil servants, 130 lawyers, 123 university professors, 119 judges, 45 clergymen, 36 writers and journalists, and 25 doctors. Once again, the balance was with the civil servants, judges, and lawyers, just as it had been with the Constituent Assembly in 1789, which was also elected by a system of near universal manhood suffrage. The same thing was to happen in England after 1867. Political leadership would start to fall to the professional element within the middle class once the franchise was actually opened up; it had not opened up enough after 1832 to produce that particular result.

The Frankfurt Assembly in 1848 and 1849 progressed the way the

political forces more diverse than the author maintains

French Constituent Assembly and the English Parliament did, by trying to advance its own interests legislatively. It failed, as indeed the whole political movement by the business and professional elements within European society failed in 1848, not because of what it did but because of what did not happen in 1848. The German bourgeoisie did not win the day because the rioting that was such a key factor in determining the outcome of events in 1789 and 1832 did not occur in 1848. In France and England it lasted for years; in Germany, only two months. The failure of the rioting from below to sustain itself reduced the fear of the ruling elements in 1848, allowed them to recoup and fend off the demands of German liberalism, and to make at best only grudging concessions. If the rioting had sustained itself, German liberalism—a code word for the political thrust of the upper middle class—might have won totally as French liberalism did in 1789 or partially as English liberalism did in 1832. The future did belong to the upper middle class both in terms of political representation and vital political interests, but the upper middle class in Germany in 1848 would have to wait until it was stronger to achieve the same results, and they would come not by revolution but by a chain of evolutionary events.

The Sources of Urban and Rural Rioting

These attempts on the part of the upper middle class to seize power from the aristocracy make a rather spectacular chapter in what was otherwise to be an evolutionary process. Since the political triumph of the upper middle class was almost inevitable, given its ever-increasing domination of the economy in the nineteenth century, the actual change, as will be seen later, was to come legislatively rather than violently. Rioting motivated by economic want was not unusual, for it had been commonplace in both rural and urban areas long before 1789, 1832, and 1848. But it was only when these riots were joined with the political activity of the upper middle class that a truly revolutionary climate actually existed.

The upper middle class may have been motivated by politics, but the lower orders of society, especially the artisans and peasants, were driven on not by ideology, but by some kind of actual economic threat to their existence. Artisans and peasants interpreted life in more immediate terms than did the middle class. Their vital concerns were much more with the price of bread than with political ideology. In fact, it may be said that bread, or better, the price of either grain or bread, was by far the major cause of the numerous food riots in Europe between

1700 and 1850. Rural rioting, while it was economically motivated, really had a tamer character than riots in the cities. In the case of major rural riots like those in France in 1709, 1725, 1740, 1749, 1768, 1775, 1785, and of course, 1789, they usually took place in a market town and revolved around the price of grain. The same was true of the riots in England in 1710, 1727, 1735, 1758, 1766, 1771, 1772, and 1791, where underlying economic motives were again quite conspicuous.

Two riots, one English and one French, may be said to be characteristic of the larger pattern of rural rioting in the eighteenth century. The English food riots of 1766, which swept through Devon and the Midlands during the summer, were provoked by a precipitous rise in the price of grain. Shortages of wheat, along with spiraling prices for other commodities such as butter, cheese, and meat, set off a series of riots that convulsed one market town after another. The rioting began in the market town of Honiton in Devonshire, but it did not get out of hand. The poor did force sellers to reduce the price of a bushel of wheat, but once what they considered to be a just price was reestablished, calm returned. The episode was typical of the rural riot: its focus was limited, its goals immediate, and its temper short-lived. Some of the English rioters in the summer of 1766 did participate in the damaging of flour mills in places like Tipton and Sidbury, and later on thefts were reported in Wiltshire. But considering that the riots spread over a fair proportion of England, the amount of damage actually done was minimal. Far more conspicuous than the violence was the forced reduction of prices.

If the English country riots of 1766 demonstrate the less ferocious and somewhat limited character of country rioting, an examination of the French rural riots of 1775 gives evidence of their highly spontaneous character. According to local officials, rioting broke out at Beaumont-sur-Oise, a market town twenty miles north of Paris, when bakers refused to bake more bread and when grain merchants refused to lower their prices. Starting on April 27, the riots, fed by similar causes, spread quickly. By May 3, most of the major villages north of Paris had experienced disturbances; by May 9, Corbeil, Melun, Milly, and other centers south of Paris felt the sting of peasant revolt. Here, as in the case of the English rioting, the military, helped by the fact that the rioting had spent itself, easily restored order.

The rural rioting that periodically disturbed the countryside in most areas of Europe was, then, a more or less continuous phenomenon that was eventually to underscore and exaggerate some of the major political events of the time, the most obvious being 1789. The hunger riots of 1789, more popularly known in the rural areas of France as the Great Fear, were a direct result of the crop failures of 1788 and 1789. This time, the economic threat was not simply a temporary rise in prices; famine actually stalked the countryside. The revolt started in March and

April and spread quickly, as before, through areas like Provence. Given the dire need of the peasants, the riots took on a more sinister nature, especially for the aristocracy. For the rural revolts of 1789 were not aimed at middlemen, but often directly at the aristocracy: Peasants were demanding an end to the tithe and to feudal dues. When peasants in the Dauphine refused to pay feudal dues they were not, however, doing it for political reasons but out of sheer economic want. The 7 percent loss of income represented by the dues was simply too much for peasants already faced with two years of declining crop yields and increasingly dependent on the purchase of grain for mere survival. If the rural revolts did have political significance, it was because the upper middle class used their violence to intimidate the aristocracy.

The "bread riots" that periodically shattered the king's peace in the eighteenth century, sometimes during periods of political turbulence and sometimes not, gave way in the nineteenth century to a different kind of riot. After 1815, rural rioting was still economically focused, only this time the threat was a long-term one, for now the peasantry was predisposed toward rioting by threats to its very existence as a class. This was true in 1830 and 1831 during the rural risings that predated the English Reform Bill of 1832 and also on the Continent throughout 1848. In England, the threat was mostly to agricultural laborers whose very existence as a stratum of the peasantry was being challenged by, among other things, the introduction of threshing machines. The wave of wage riots that followed in the summer of 1830 in Kent and Sussex spread and continued through 1831, with arrest records showing that agricultural laborers made up the overwhelming majority of the crowds.

Fear of loss or fear of displacement were motives behind the peasant upheavals of 1848, which were on occasion made more serious by crop failures. Here, the protests were primarily directed against the order of serfdom. When German, Czech, and Hungarian peasants resisted the old order in 1848 and in some instances engaged in arson, their protest was against forced labor, which deprived them of a real opportunity to work their own land, and the tithe, which took away from their marginal income or capital for improvements or both. Both the peasant riots of the early 1830s and those of 1848 might have occurred on their own; it happened that they were obviously coupled with overriding political developments.

The same was true of riots by artisans. In certain instances they took place in conjunction with vital political events, but in other cases they were purely isolated outbursts, although like all the conflicts from below, their origin lay in the threat of economic distress. Artisan rioting in the cities followed a pattern similar to that of peasant disturbances. Often, these were not much more than bread riots, especially in the French Revolution. Food shortages in Paris occasioned by crop failures prior to 1789 set off artisan elements whose daily diet was mainly composed of bread. That rioting, which continued off and on right into 1795, has sometimes been covered over or explained in ideological terms. Too often, these disorders have been seen as support for bourgeois elements challenging the old order, when in fact what they were actually seeking was a guaranteed food supply or increased wages.

Two case studies prove the point. The march to Versailles in October 1789, immediately after the crops had failed for a second year in a row, may have intimidated the king politically, but the real catalyst that sparked this protest by artisan wives was the threat of a bread shortage. The same was true years later, when artisan elements rioted at the demise of the Jacobin regime not for political reasons, but because inflation had become a serious threat. Artisan riots were just as spontaneous as peasant riots had been. But in the cities, these rebellions sometimes took on a more vicious character; they could and did on occasion lead to bloodshed. The cause of this may well have been ideology, in particular political ideology, which seems to have added a more intense note to urban riots. For once political factors were added to economic distress, the results could be and were precipitous. Again, because propaganda seems to have stirred them to an even higher pitch, antagonism was added to the fears motivating the crowd to begin with.

Artisan uprisings inspired by economic distress, as well as peasant rebellions, punctuated the closing decades of the Old Regime. Most of them were not bloody; they were more like strikes that got out of hand and turned into riots. In Germany a number of these revolts flared up only to be put down, as so often was the case, by the military. One such riot occurred in Monschau in 1774, when weavers attacked representatives of merchants who were trying to export wool to the surrounding countryside for spinning and weaving. The weavers rightly saw the move as a clear threat not only to their guild monopoly of production but to their livelihoods, since work was already in short supply. Similar motives were behind the revolt by master and journeymen weavers in Elberfeld in 1783. Here the textile guilds were protesting higher standards of workmanship that were being demanded by merchant-manufacturers supplying them with raw materials and markets. As more and more guildsmen slipped into the putting-out system and became dependent on wages, wage rates became a subject of dispute. In Krefeld in 1828 there was a mass uprising by silk weavers on the announcement of an immediate reduction in wage rates. Perhaps the largest single case of artisan discontent over wages took place in 1831 in the French silk center of Lyons. Here, journeymen weavers, their fear of economic disaster amplified by falling wages, actually seized control of the city for a short period of time.

In some ways, artisans were a declining class long before some other groups in Europe's preindustrial society underwent the same experience. The most vulnerable of them, the textile artisans, especially feared the introduction of labor-saving machines that seemed to threaten their whole way of life. This anxiety apparently lay behind the so-called Luddite rebellions by artisan elements in England in 1811 and 1812, which featured the highly symbolic destruction of textile machinery. Steam looms were attacked and destroyed at Stockton, Middleton, and Westhoughton in the belief that their destruction would save the jobs of certain weavers. After this, machine breaking became more common, a kind of symbolic protest by artisans against the coming of the machine age. A striking illustration of this type of impulsiveness took place in Annaberg in the state of Saxony in 1846. During November of that year ribbon and lace makers rioted when the rumor spread that mechanical lace-twisting machinery was about to be introduced by one of the companies. In fact the rumor was not true, but the artisans summed up their plight in a declaration which stated that the introduction of machinery would make them redundant and cause pauperism among them.

Artisan uprisings, like peasant disorders, accompanied the major political upheavals in England in 1832 and on the Continent in 1848. The revolutionary potential of popular disorders in England between 1830 and 1832 was measurably increased by major artisan participation. More articulate than the peasantry, rural and town artisans were in the forefront of the disturbances. Indeed, in certain cases, they constituted up to one-third of the rioters who were deported to Australia.

The presence of artisan elements in the events of 1848 was even more pronounced. They supplied the overwhelming bulk of the fighters killed or wounded in the street fighting of June in Paris. They formed the crowds of demonstrators in Saxony and the Rhineland appealing to the Frankfurt Assembly for redress of their economic ills. And it was artisans who stormed factories in places like Bohemia in a desperate attempt to get across to the larger society the fact that they were losing out economically. The cotton printers of Prague may be said to have represented the whole group when they attacked new cotton printing machinery in the heady days of 1848. In their declaration they explained, "we are not rebels," but "unfortunately our patience is at an end, for we cannot adequately describe to you the woes that pursue us." [1] They may have summed up well the cause of much of the artisan and peasant rioting during the eighteenth and early nineteenth centuries.

[1] Stanley Pech, "The June Uprising in Prague in 1848," *East European Quarterly*, I (1968), 344.

The Standard of Living

Estimating the standard of living of eighteenth- and early nine-teenth-century Europe is not something that can yet be done with precise accuracy. Still, the main outlines of an essentially impoverished society can be seen even if our information is not yet total or complete. In the eighteenth century, Europe's capacity to grow in any direction was lim-ited by low agricultural production. It limited the size of cities, since they could be fed only from surpluses. It kept population growth to a minimum, largely because of undernourishment and lack of immunity, especially to bacterial diseases. Population did not increase from the Middle Ages down to the time of the Old Regime, on average, at a rate of more than 20 percent each century. This may be compared to the period from 1800 to 1900 in Europe when the population doubled and then nearly doubled again in the fifty years after 1900. The marginal gains that were made before the industrial age were the result of a pains-taking process of increased crop yields in many areas. The fact that the Continent could not meet its agricultural needs left food in relatively short supply, particularly as one went down the social scale, and made nutrition accidental rather than deliberate. Because food was in short supply and because the average European was a grain eater, he lacked the energy needed to be truly productive. This was especially true of the agricultural population. One of the reasons, besides tradition, why grains were so extensively cultivated was because they represented an extensive type of agriculture which minimized the amount of labor needed to grow them. The cultivation of grains required much less attention and much less energy than almost any other type of agricultural commodity, in fact, much less than the more intensive types of agriculture-truck farm-ing, dairying and viticulture—which came into vogue in the nineteenth century. If the peasants had only limited energy, the result of poor nutri-tion, grain was the ideal crop to grow, since, like all grasses, it in a sense grew by itself.

Below the level of the aristocracy and the upper middle class, life in Europe was overly dependent upon the level of nutrition. The mass of Parisian guildsmen in the eighteenth century was just as dependent on grain for survival as the peasants in the countryside. In the upper reaches of society, meat, fruits, cheese, and other foods that often fell into the category of luxury items were readily available. With food supple-ments like these, the well-to-do could have better nutrition. The masses, overly dependent on breadstuffs, got along on the relatively high propor-tion of calories in grain, but lacked the vitamins, protein, and minerals that might have raised resistance to bacterial diseases like tuberculosis, typhus, and cholera, lowered the high rate of infant and childbirth mortality, and lengthened the rather short life expectancy for Europe as a whole of only twenty-eight years.

Tuberculosis was probably the steadiest killer in Europe's preindustrial society, largely because the respiratory system was the weakest system in the human body, given the conditions existing in the eighteenth and early nineteenth centuries. The almost universal lack of vitamin A in this period not only led to the characteristic skin disorders and poor eyesight of the time, it robbed the respiratory system of its ability to counteract the entrance of bacteria. Death might come in a more spectacular way through epidemics of two other bacterial diseases, typhus and cholera, which attacked the intestinal tract. This age also knew influenza, but the greatest cause of death was from bacterial diseases and not from viral disorders.

Infant mortality was one of the great scourges of the age. A study of family bibles in Slovakia reveals a steady rate of infant mortality among the peasant classes of about 50 percent. The peasants were not the only ones to suffer. The composer Johann Sebastian Bach, a self-reliant member of the middle class, was likewise to see half of his children die in infancy or childhood. Some educated estimates place the number of conceptions failing to achieve adulthood at perhaps two-thirds, pregnancy being terminated by natural abortion, quite common in this age, stillbirth, or in the case of an actual live birth, infant mortality. This very high rate of termination can also be traced to the lack of certain nutrients in the European diet. The major cause of death in these cases was apparently organic failure, organs that never developed because the fetus was starved for vitamins A, C, and E and because of the absence of both protein and calcium in the general diet.

The high rate of female mortality during this age may also be explained nutritionally. On the average, women in Europe's preindustrial society lived five years less than men. One of the factors that shortened their life spans was the danger inherent in childbirth. At one stage during the eighteenth century, the London lying-in hospital reported that 10 out of every 100 women died in childbirth. In some areas of Europe, up to 15 percent of women of childbearing years died in childbirth. Here, the principal cause of death seems to have been hemorrhaging which midwives were often unable to stop. The cause of this excessive bleeding would seem to have been a direct result of lack of calcium in the diet, for without proper levels of calcium in the system, the blood was unable to clot.

If there was a conspicuous absence of key vitamins and minerals from the diet of those living below the level of the middle class, the lack of protein was just as obvious. It is true that grain can provide protein, but the amount of protein the average European got was limited because he ate somewhere around two and a half pounds of food a day, not enough to produce adequate levels. As a result, bones were not well developed, and most people were small and relatively short.

The lack of protein and of proper levels of sugar in the blood caused by the absence of fruits and vegetables in the diet left the average European far more lethargic than energetic. Our vision of this society comes largely from an appraisal of those who were better off and more energetic—the aristocracy, the business community, the peasant proprietor, and the artisan. Even the widespread alcoholism of the lower classes in the cities and in the countryside during these decades may have been less a matter of moral decay and more a physical desire for the residual carbohydrates left after the brewing process had been completed. Alcohol simply meant quick energy for groups that normally did not have high blood sugar levels.

The impact of poor nutrition on family life must also be mentioned. As the American historian Gideon Sjoberg has pointed out, the extended family was, by and large, the product of the city, not the countryside, and to add to his point, more a consequence of a certain level of economic attainment than of poverty. The frequency of death in the form of infant and young adult mortality suggests that the family was constantly being reconstituted, under the pressure of rural poverty, in the form of step-mothers and step-fathers, half-brothers and half-sisters. It would appear that blood relationships may actually have been reduced and that the natural family was more of aristocratic and middle class than peasant origin historically. Peasant proprietors were surely able to maintain their families more readily due to their higher standard of living. The real pressure was on the middle and landless peasants, the two largest groups in European society.

The Growth of Population

The population of Europe doubled between 1800 and 1900, from less than 200 million to slightly more than 400 million, and this figure does not include the 30 million who emigrated abroad. This gigantic increase was due after 1850 to major improvements in sanitation and medical facilities. But the population was already shooting up before this date due to the increase in food production and improvements in nutrition. Underlying the great gains of the nineteenth century was the Industrial Revolution, which not only increased the standard of living in Europe but provided Europeans with something that had never characterized them up to this time—longevity. There were signs all over Europe, even before 1800, that population was on the rise. It was obvious in areas of northern Europe, where agricultural improvements were more advanced, but even in countries like France, where the food supply was increasing less rapidly, there were gains. Between 1700 and 1800, Great Britain's population grew from 8 million to nearly 15 million; the population of the Netherlands, from 1.1 to 1.7 million; and Sweden's population, from 1.6 to 2.3 million. The population of France, growing more slowly, went from 23 to 28 million by the time of Napoleon.

The increase in population during the period before and after 1800 was not due to an increase in the number of live births. Peasants, who formed the bulk of the population and contributed most to the statistics, did not have large families. Peasant women normally delayed marriage until their mid-twenties and then strung out their pregnancies until their late thirties. In Bourgogne, Dauphine, Provence, and other representative areas in the 1750s, French women averaged 4.5 live births. But the mortality rate was so high that more than half the children did not survive to adulthood. The increase in the population of France during the second half of the eighteenth century was not the result of any noticeable increase in the number of births. For example, the number of children born in 1770 was 950,500; in 1784, it was 965,000. Yet the population increased by 1.5 million during this period, obviously because infant mortality was being reduced, at least slightly. More children were, in fact, living, and living longer than before. For when the death rate was first cut, it declined most obviously in the case of infant mortality.

There were, of course, other factors that limited population growth in the eighteenth century. One was the rate of childbirth mortality, and another the fairly high rate of voluntary celibacy. Although statistics in this area are not what they should be, it would appear that an important minority of women never married and never conceived, or else never remarried. Celibacy in the form of unmarried elements in the population was common, for example, in Ireland. A specific study of women in Boulay, in the Moselle area of France, between 1720 and 1800 showed that between 15 and 30 percent of the female population at certain times was unmarried even though of childbearing age. The percentage may have been just as high elsewhere, since some women were evidently unwilling to take on the burdens of marriage and childbearing. Another cause of celibacy was a relatively high rate of young adult mortality that sometimes left an important segment of the female population without spouses.

The extremely low life expectancy in Europe in 1800 meant that its population was young. Contemporary French demographers estimate that 52 percent of the population in 1775 was under the age of twenty and that two-thirds of the population in that year had not yet reached their thirtieth birthday. The number of people in French society over the age of sixty-five, an extraordinary age in the eighteenth century, was most likely less than 2 percent of the entire population. Statistics for the Scandinavian countries show a similar pattern. There was a slightly higher life expectancy in Sweden in 1750 than there was in France, but the generalizations still hold. In Sweden in the middle of the eighteenth century, 55 percent of the population was under twenty-four years of age, and 62 percent was under the age of twenty-nine. The number of those over sixty-five was only slightly higher than it was in France, a little less than 4 percent. The same statistics would seem to hold for the rest of Scandinavia during this period, because of its somewhat higher standard of living.

As Europe industrialized during the nineteenth century, the birth rate per 1,000 inhabitants remained the same in some instances and in others actually declined. The major difference, again, was the number of children living. Great Britain may be taken as a kind of yardstick. In 1700, the rate of infant mortality was about 50 percent; by 1800 it had dropped to 25 percent; and by 1900, to a low of 10 percent. Other evidence points to a decline in the death rate. During the second half of the nineteenth century, the Netherlands continually gained in population in spite of the fact that the birth rate per 1,000 dropped from 33.7 in 1851 to a 1905 figure of 31.5. And Soviet statistics show the same trend. Between 1887 and 1914 in Russia the birth rate fell from 49.9 per 1,000 to 46.9. During this period, Russia nonetheless increased her population by some 30 million people. When the death rate did decline, the areas affected first were infant and childbirth mortality, followed by declines in adolescent mortality and finally in mortality among the older segments of the population.

In order for life expectancy in Europe to rise from twenty-eight to fifty years during the nineteenth century, changes would have had to take place. Before the age of medicine and sanitation, those changes had to be of a nutritional character. Medicine was a thing of the future and sanitation still not considered vitally important, either in the cities or in the countryside. The population of Europe was simply growing stronger, more capable biologically of warding off disease. Epidemics such as the influenza that hit Marseille in 1720 were fearsome in their impact. The attack of that year claimed 40,000 lives at a time when the total population of Marseilles was only 90,000. A similar tragedy struck Messina in 1743, when an epidemic carried away half of that city's population. After this, however, epidemics declined somewhat in their ferocity, especially after 1831, when a major cholera epidemic struck Europe. From mid-century on, Europe was not to be visited by another epidemic until 1918.

The population explosion of the eighteenth and nineteenth centuries was a rural phenomenon to begin with but quickly became more of an urban experience. As the population grew, so did the cities, absorbing, by the second half of the nineteenth century, the bulk of the excess. In 1801, England had a population of almost 9 million citizens, of whom 1.5 million were town dwellers. By 1851, her population had doubled to 18 million, of whom 6.5 million lived in the major urban areas. All of this means that about half the expanding population of England had been absorbed by the cities; by 1891, the major urban areas were taking in 75 percent of the growth. Once the Industrial Revolution began in Germany, the rural population remained stagnant at 26 million from 1871 on; every bit of population increase after that went to the cities of the new German Empire. A somewhat similar story can be told for France after 1851. In the following four decades, France's rural population actually declined by some 2 million, while her urban population increased by 5 million.

The traffic from the countryside into the city was especially heavy in the nineteenth century. Out of every 1,000 new inhabitants that Rome added in the 1880s, 893 were immigrants. For some other representative cities, it was 881 for Turin, 717 for Manchester, 654 for Belfast, and 558 for Dresden. Fortunately for Europe, urbanization and industrialization, along with emigration abroad, provided new opportunities for a population the land could never have absorbed.

Part Two

The Social Impact of the Industrial Revolution 1789-1914

The Industrial Revolution was Europe's greatest revolution. It steadily transformed Europe in the nineteenth century, bringing down most of its older classes and ushering into existence an entirely new social order. This process of social transformation came within two generations. By the end of the century, average life expectancy had jumped from twenty-eight to fifty years. The standard of living had risen as never before; a smaller percentage of the population was suffering from poverty than at any time in the past. Food, clothing, shelter, and commodities were being mass produced on an unprecedented scale. The result of economic change was industrialization, urbanization, and the growth of new social classes. If Europeans were much better off in 1900 than they had been in 1800, it was because the Industrial Revolution was the cure for poverty, not its cause.

The process of industrial expansion tended to follow a set pattern. Mass production first won out in textiles, then metallurgy, then chemicals, and finally electronics. Different stages struck different countries, from England to Russia, at varying times. Amplifying the process of industrialization was the growth of transportation. Whether it was cotton or wool, iron or tin, salt or soda, industry had to be fed and improvements made shipping and mining as vital and lucrative as industry itself.

Most of the old classes in society were to find themselves without the talents required by the new industrial age. Some great magnates made it during the nineteenth century, but most did not. Those who survived did so not on their own terms, but rather by compromising and then becoming bourgeois. The artisan element was hard hit by industry. The class conflict of the new century was largely between the upper middle class and the artisans, between the new forms of mass production and the old craftsmen. Once their markets were destroyed, one after another of the guilds collapsed, as first the textile and then the metallurgical and construction trades were eliminated by the coming of industrialization. The luxury trades survived, but only as anomalies. The peasantry was also to be challenged and scattered; the middle and landless peasant failed to survive on the land, and became in time the factory worker of both Europe and America.

The growth of industry, of mass production within the factory system, was bound to have an economic impact. Its most immediate consequence was to expand measurably the wealth already concentrated in the upper reaches of the middle class. As capital gravitated there, the upper middle class emerged triumphantly as the new elite, in control politically and economically as a consequence of its own managerial talents. After this, it was the values of the upper middle class that percolated down through the levels of society.

The size of the middle class expanded as industrialization continued. The middle class never became a majority, but it did produce a new level in the form of the middle middle class, and its lower levels were extended. The newest stratum, born of the needs created by industrialization, was the middle middle class, the professions. To the list of doctors and lawyers was now added new categories—scientists, engineers, journalists, and architects. As a result of continued economic expansion, the size and proportions of the lower middle class also increased. In the city, the master artisan tended to disappear in favor of the retailer, the clerk, the foreman, the schoolteacher, and other new petty bourgeois types.

The largest class resulting from industrialization was the working class, chiefly factory workers, but including as well transport, dock, and municipal workers. Largely drawn from the peasantry, with a steadily rising standard of living, the working class was ultimately to constitute better than 50 percent of the population once Europe achieved a truly mature state of industrial development. The greatest metamorphosis during the industrial age was the reversal of proportion of the peasantry, which declined from fully 85 percent of the population to a mere 15 percent by middle of the twentieth century. The peasant proprietor endured, but the other levels of the old peasantry were literally to vanish.

Nineteenth-century Europe was a society in flux, and it is little wonder that most observers thought change would never end. It was everywhere. The urban areas of Europe, with their opportunities for employment, were proving a boon to emigration. During the course of the century some 80 million peasants would leave the countryside for the cities. Social mobility was becoming commonplace; not only were many now gaining economically, they were changing social position. Most of the movement was in an upward direction, although substantial numbers were experiencing downward mobility as well. Even though Europe, especially her cities, offered historically unparalleled chances for advancement, millions of Europeans, maybe up to 40 million before it was over, left for foreign lands. Those who left were principally middle and landless peasants. Underscoring all the advances of the nineteenth century were the gains most people were making in their standard of living. Toward the end of the century, alcoholism, illiteracy, poverty, infant mortality, childbirth mortality, hunger, and bacterial disease were all being conquered to one degree or another, proving that this era of social transformation was also an era of accomplishment.

6

The Process
of Industrial Expansion

If one identifies the growth of industry with the introduction of machine production, then it may be argued that the Industrial Revolution spread from England in the 1820s eastward to Russia in the 1890s. Through the course of the nineteenth century, almost every country industrialized, at least to some degree, each passing through the various stages of mass production of textiles, metals, chemicals, and electronic equipment. Although different areas of Europe experienced these stages in different ways, still they were there in every case. As one stage grew into another, profit built up, which is the reason why capital tended to flow from west, where industrialization began earlier, to the east. Indeed, the wealth of commercial capitalism, more concentrated in the west than in the east prior to industralization, was now being magnified once more, this time as a result of investment in industry and its associated enterprises—shipping, mining, and transportation.

The first area to be stimulated was textiles. Not only were cotton goods being produced, but the older cloths, wool and linen, were also being subjected to the machine. The key invention was, of course, the steam engine, which really made the factory system viable. The spread of cheap, durable clothing, accompanied by an increase in the food supply, made life more comfortable. Thereafter, the construction of warehouses, factories, and trains was, by itself, a direct consequence of the emerging metallurgical industry. Until 1865, the new construction material was pig iron; then came steel. Industry was again indebted to steam, because the steam engine made possible both the deep mining of coal and iron ore and the railroad. The major breakthroughs industrially thus came in the form of the mass production of clothing and new construction materials. In the 1890s, a chemical industry would develop that would fashion even newer products like fertilizers and medicines. Finally, prior to the turn of the twentieth century, electronics would begin to come into its own, aiding communication by means of telephones and telegraphs, and improving the quality of life by means of electrical appliances.

The rise of industry meant urban growth. Even though mass production, the domestic system, and mining began in rural areas, industrialization after 1820 was increasingly an urban phenomenon. At first, industrial towns like Birmingham, Mulhouse, Barmen, and Kiev became prominent, but eventually industry attached itself to the older commercial centers as well. By 1900, industry was ubiquitous. Whether in one of the old commercial centers or one of the new industrial towns, the spread of the factory system meant millions upon millions of industrial jobs. Attracted from the countryside, tens of millions of peasants would, before 1914, come streaming off the land to become the new factory working class.

The Four Stages
of Industrial Growth

As one country after another entered upon the various stages of industrial growth, the transition from an agricultural to an industrial society obviously began to take hold. Sometime or another, probably deep into the second stage of growth, these differing industrial states began to reach a take-off point. That point was the critical juncture beyond which industrial growth could literally not be stopped. The only question after this was a question of pace. But, the take-off point was achieved only after capital had been sufficiently mobilized, raw materials had been secured, managerial and organizational ability had appeared and a trained, talented work force had come into existence. England was probably at this stage by the 1840s, Germany by the 1870s and Russia by the 1910s.

The beginning of take-off occurred in textiles, and here England was far ahead of the rest of the Continent. By 1850, her textile industry was highly mechanized and employed 500,000 men, women, and children. Because of the superior quality of her textiles, especially cotton cloth, which had great appeal because it was both durable and easy to clean, England dominated the European market to the point of stunting the growth of the textile industry elsewhere. Belgium was forced to concentrate on woolens; France emphasized silk products far into the nineteenth century; Germany was noted for linen. Italy, once it industrialized, moved rapidly into cotton production. Up to this point, she had been famous for her silks, but by 1914, primarily in the northern cities, she was successfully establishing a major cotton industry. By 1914, Italy, with almost 120,000 looms, was ready to challenge the British. Austria had one of the most diversified textile industries in Europe. By 1900, she had more than 400,000 individuals employed in this industry, some as artisans, and a higher proportion in the factory system. Russia, which had the fastest rate of industrial growth of any country in Europe in the 1890s, again made one of her breakthroughs in textile production. To some extent she was building upon the past, for as early as 1850, Russia was already the world's fifth greatest producer of cotton cloth.

Among the industrial countries of Europe, Britain and Belgium moved the fastest into the second stage of industrial growth, metallurgy. The fact that Britain and Belgium had quantities of coal for coking and iron ore for processing into plate accounts for the initial rapid rise in their pig iron production. Pig iron was the most dependable building product that Europe had ever had; it made possible bridges, ships, rails, and railroads. By the 1890s, Britain was producing nearly 3 million tons of pig iron a year, some of it for export. Pig iron was produced to a lesser extent elsewhere, of course, but when Germany industrialized after mid-century, she emphasized the production of iron and later steel.

When Germany emerged around 1900 as the second greatest industrial power in the world (after the United States), one of the most visible signs of her growing preponderance was the fact that she now outproduced England in steel. Britain's production of steel in 1900 was 6 million tons a year; Germany's, 7.5 million. And steel, with even greater tensile strength, was fast becoming the premium building material of the late nineteenth century. The great metallurgical centers, Birmingham and Essen, were now the symbols of a more advanced industrial age. Other countries moved into this area as well. Kharkov, in the Russian Ukraine, Graz in southern Austria, the Thionville industrial complex in

France, and Cornigliano in northern Italy were all well-known metal-lurgical centers by the early part of the twentieth century. Still, production in Russia, Austria, France, and Italy lagged in comparison; these four powers in 1900 were able to produce, in combination, only as much iron and steel as Germany produced alone.

As the nineteenth century wore on, two entirely new industries appeared, chemicals and electronics. The chemical industry was the logical outgrowth of improvements in mining techniques that by the 1850s allowed the recovery of sulfur, rock salt, potassium, and phosphate. The movement and use of minerals was facilitated by the continuous expansion of rail traffic. Now, for example, fertilizers could save soil that for centuries had been subject to steady depletion. At first Britain, Belgium, and France led in this area, but by 1900, Germany was catching up and destined to surpass all others. Chemistry had become a versatile and magic tool—it meant fertilizers, rubber products, cleaning agents, explosives, medicines, and chemicals for industrial use, especially bleaching. Other countries in Europe established chemical industries because of their contribution to the growth of armaments, but none could match Germany's growing dominance. By 1913, Germany, her production based on places such as Barmen and Leipzig, led Europe in the processing of sulphuric acid, nitrates, phosphates, and potassium. Great Britain maintained its former lead only in the production of common salt.

The electronics industry grew quickly, especially after the 1890s. As was so often the case, Britain and Germany were in the forefront of development, while Belgium, France, Italy, Austria, and Russia followed. The great era of growth came in the quarter-century before World War I. The electronics industry in Britain employed only 12,000 men in 1891, but by 1900 employment had jumped to more than 100,000, an eight-fold increase in less than a decade. Germany kept pace. By 1907, she was employing more than 100,000 workers in her industry as well. The electronics industries in the two countries produced a variety of products—lights, cables, generators, transformers, and appliances. Once again, the Germans emerged in first place. Through concerns like Siemens in Berlin, they even surpassed the United States, producing in 1913 no less than 34 percent of the world's output of electrical goods. Except for France, the rest of Europe, without a significant electronics industry of its own prior to 1914, bought first from Germany and then Britain.

With industry increasingly concentrating in towns and cities, urbanization was spurred. The great lure of the city became the new opportunities for employment and gain in both industry and commerce. New industrial centers grew up, but along with the factory towns, the older commercial centers also grew. In these cities, the number of artisans, especially those in the luxury and construction trades, actually increased, largely because of the demand being generated for their services by the upper reaches of middle class society. As the number of artisans multiplied, so did the number of factory workers. Old and new cities were becoming crowded.

The new factory towns that were being founded all over Europe were usually isolated from the old commercial centers. Representative of these new industrial centers were Lille in northern France, Barmen in western Germany, Wels in Upper Austria, and Lodz in southern Poland. Lille was the classic industrial city, growing from a population of 59,000 in 1804 to 131,800 in 1861, its mechanized industry eventually producing cottons, woolens, and linens. Lodz in southern Poland was another typical city, dominated again by the textile industry, its population jumping from 31,500 in 1860 to 314,000 in 1897. Barmen's growth was spurred by both the textile and chemical industries, its population increasing from 36,000 in 1850 to 170,000 in 1910. Even some of the smaller industrial towns like Wels in Upper Austria turned out to be dynamic. Wels, originally a village, grew into an industrial town of 37,000 people. Even though it was small, its economy was surprisingly diversified; it produced textiles, machine tools, paper, agricultural machinery, and hats. At first the factory system was confined to these industrial towns and cities, but by the turn of the twentieth century, industry attached itself to the great metropolitan centers. London acquired an automotive industry, as did Paris, while Vienna was to see the growth, in time, of a chemical industry.

Employment opportunities in the cities were now unparalleled not only for artisans willing to move into the factory system, but for unskilled peasants penetrating the urban areas. By 1847 Lille alone offered more than 6,000 jobs in the cotton industry and 5,000 in the woolen mills, and employed an additional 3,600 men, women, and children in the production of linen cloth. By the middle of the nineteenth century, Birmingham, England's great iron center, offered more than 50,000 jobs in metallurgical factories and shops. As Birmingham's industry diversified, thousands of new jobs were created in allied occupations. By 1891, more than 8,000 workers were engaged in the manufacture of bicycles, and by 1911, another 16,000 were working in the automotive industry. In the iron and steel center of Sheffield in northern England, employment opportunities increased by 71 percent between 1891 and 1911. The Bayer chemical works in Leverkusen in western Germany first employed a few thousand and then some 25,000. Decades later, the Soviet Union would follow the same pattern, establishing industrial centers in the Ukraine like Zhdanov and Kramatorsk where a full 55 percent of the jobs were for factory workers.

In addition, the industrial age opened up employment in areas such as mining and railroading. In 1851, Britain had 217,000 men mining coal and an added 28,000 men mining iron ore. Even in the less well developed countries, like Austria, mining employed more than 100,000 workers by 1900. Railroads required a large labor force. The Russian state railroads hired hundreds of thousands of workers in the early 1900s. In Austria-Hungary, at the same time, there were close to 40,000 railway workers. Opportunities for jobs in basic industry or in allied occupations were, of course, just part of the story. Shopkeeping grew as the retailing of food and goods became more and more prominent. At the same time, the number of clerical positions in banking, commerce, and industry expanded. The Industrial Revolution, starting with the factory system, was offering the average European the chance for steady employment within a more advanced urban economy. Those who came usually benefitted, for the Industrial Revolution meant for the majority a step upward. But some social classes could not or would not respond to the new age. Aristocrats, artisans, and peasants were, as a consequence, to go under, first to be disrupted and then progressively overwhelmed by economic and social forces most of them never saw or understood.

7

The Older Classes

The immense prosperity of the commercial revival of the eighteenth century and the Industrial Revolution of the nineteenth century temporarily kept afloat some of the older classes in European society. Excise taxes on trade were a source of revenue for the monarchs of the period. With tax money they were able to build up their bureaucracies and strengthen the financial position of the aristocracy through government service. The emphasis on consumption among the rich in the cities also sustained large numbers of artisans in the luxury and construction trades. Indeed, the growth of capital in the cities even led to the financing of the domestic system, which ultimately employed millions of poor peasants as weavers and spinners. But although the growth of urban wealth went a long way toward keeping alive a portion of the older social classes in European society, the uplifting character of this wealth did not last. Between 1750 and 1850, elements of the older society began to decline. The gentry, the textile artisan, and the middle peasant were all going under by 1800. The forces contributing to this decline were often subtle, inflation in particular having a very destructive but uneven and diffuse impact.

As the agrarian sector of the economy declined and land became less important, the aristocracy began to go into eclipse. The first group to fall was the gentry; less viable economically, it began to lose land and become déclassé. Some elements of the gentry in England, Prussia, and the Baltic states did fight the inflation that was sapping their incomes by turning to capitalistic agriculture. But this often brought debt and sometimes actually speeded the process of social disintegration. The great magnates, meanwhile, entered the nineteenth century as the wealthiest social group in society, but they were constitutionally unable to hold that position. They lost out because they failed to respond to the new investment opportunities offered by shipping, mining, and industry but relied instead on the traditional rents or, in some marginal instances, on capitalistic agriculture. Those who survived in this way did so only by coming to terms with the new age, only by becoming essentially bourgeois.

Some of the old bastions of aristocratic control over society likewise fell. The new political institutions that came into existence were progressively taken over by the upper middle class. Bureaucracies grew to the point that aristocrats were often swamped by middle class recruits. Even in the military, the number of bourgeois officers was by the end of the century outstripping the number of aristocrats. The individual national churches, often dominated by nobles, were also on the defensive in an age of increasing anticlericalism.

Meanwhile, the various levels of the artisan class gradually lost their independent status and disappeared. This trend was not apparent at first, for the number of artisans increased in England up to 1850 and on the Continent until 1870. But they would nearly all be gone by the beginning of the twentieth century. The first to suffer were the textile artisans, for the textile trades had begun to fall to merchant capital even before 1800. The metallurgical trades held out longer but they, too, were eventually absorbed, this time by the iron and steel industry. The luxury and construction trades survived the longest. In 1870, Paris had no less than 100,000 construction workers and another 110,000 men in the luxury trades. The size of her artisan class had expanded many times, but the momentary affluence of these trades was to end by 1900. Construction workers would in time become mere wage workers, a part of the much larger working class in industrial society. The luxury trades persisted, but they too finally knew the disintegrating effect of mass production. Although it took a hundred years longer, the luxury trades were also assimilated into the much larger factory system.

Along with the upper middle class, whose wealth financed the Industrial Revolution, peasant proprietors survived down to the present. Europe, which had never been able to feed itself before the nineteenth century, needed food even more desperately once urbanization began. The more talented members of the peasantry, primarily the peasant proprietors, took advantage of the situation to switch to the more profitable truck farming. In conformity with changing dietary patterns, they began to produce the fruits, vegetables, eggs, meat, and milk that were in the nineteenth century being consumed by the many, instead of just the few. Middle peasants were often tempted to profit from the market as well, but they could not seem to keep up with the demands of the new agriculture. Often in debt, some began to sell out, some to migrate to the city. Those who did not leave simply fell into the category of landless peasants. Prior to the introduction of machinery, agricultural labor was in great demand, especially on large tracts owned by great magnates or the upper middle class. But once these entrepreneurs turned to labor-saving machinery, the landless peasant too began to desert the land, like the middle peasant eventually moving to the city.

The Decline of the Aristocracy

European aristocrats did not respond to the new economic possibilities posed by industrialization. By and large, they did not invest. The one area they moved into, to any extent, was for them, the more familiar area of staple agricultural production. The reluctance of the gentry to invest is understandable, given their limited incomes. But the great magnates, the richest per capita group in European society in 1800, did not use their capital to profit from either commerce or industry—or, for that matter, agriculture. They too shunned the new economic opportunities.

In Spain during the eighteenth century, the Count of Aguilar established a factory for the manufacture of taffetas, and the Duke of Infantado started a tapestry works, but they were the exceptions. During the reign of Louis XIV, a number of prominent aristocrats made huge profits in business, but the practice of aristocratic investment in France did not survive into the following century. Later on, in the middle of the nineteenth century, a number of great magnates in Austria were tempted into the stock market, but the crash of 1873 scared them off. The lordly Schwarzenbergs did have sugar and paper mills, but the rest of the Austrian aristocracy resisted industry. Some aristocratic capital showed up in the domestic system in Silesia, supporting the production of linens, but again, characteristic of the class, the German aristocracy did not normally invest. And capital from aristocratic sources did finance some mining enterprises in England and Austria. One study of ship-owners in England showed that of a total of 338 owners, only 24 were aristocrats. Still committed to the idea of inherited wealth, aristocrats tended to downgrade acquired wealth, for after all, in the words of one apologist, "riches are an ornament, not the cause of nobility." [1]

The response of this class to the inroads of a steady inflation of about 2 percent a year brought on by the expansion of the European economy through the late eighteenth and early nineteenth centuries varied. A few tried and succeeded at market agriculture, at least for a while. Others sought to exact more dues and labor from their peasants. Still others went into debt and eventually lost their estates. Even when the aristocracy did not completely lose out, its relative position declined as agriculture contributed less and less to an expanding gross national product. Worse still, the price of food, after an initial upward surge, declined toward 1850 with the coming of mass production. All these factors made market agriculture actually less profitable.

While agricultural prices were relatively high (between 1750 and 1850), some aristocrats were tempted into the market and did convert to staple production. In Great Britain, numbers of magnates and gentry survived by means of good management, staple production, and high rents. But land taxes, the costs of enclosure, upkeep, and competition from foreign countries supplying grain to the British market inevitably took their toll of aristocratic incomes. The consequence in Great Britain was the relative decline of the aristocracy in relation to the upper middle class. After 1878 in Great Britain, aristocratic income fell precipitously as much as 50 percent, dooming the class to even further economic de-cline. Most did not sell out, but few survived at their former standard of living.

On the Continent, the situation was often far worse. Again, the problem was income. High standards of living coupled with declining income meant the loss of a great deal of land, the traditional prop for aristocratic society. The aristocracy tried to exact more rent and labor from the peasants, but peasants could afford to pay just so much. After serfdom was abolished in central and eastern Europe, the aristocracy discovered that in substituting rent for labor there was again a limit to what the peasantry could afford. Economically squeezed, the Conti-nental aristocracy too moved into market agriculture.

The Austrian aristocracy after 1815 saw opportunities for profit in the new root crops, sugar beets and potatoes, and in the production of

---

[1] Arthur J. May, *The Hapsburg Monarchy, 1867–1914* (Cambridge, Mass.: Harvard University Press, 1951), p. 159.

falling food prices

wool. Later in the century, the Hungarian aristocracy began producing meat, especially pork, for the protected market they had in Austria. Some of the Prussian Junkers specialized in rye, while their aristocratic counterparts in the Ukraine turned to the mass production of wheat. But those aristocrats who depended on grain were, of course, to be disappointed after the 1870s and 1880s, because the world price of grain fell sharply. Here and there, some aristocrats even tried to raise livestock, but many were ruined by plagues that periodically claimed a high proportion of their herds.

When financial disaster struck, either as a result of declining income or the exhaustion of capital resources, the aristocrat had no choice but to sell. In Prussia, a full third of the estates owned by the Junkers was bought up by middle class elements between 1815 and 1848. After the Napoleonic Wars, land in Austria was likewise being lost to middle class purchasers. As early as 1791, the French bourgeoisie had 40 percent of the arable land in the country in its possession; by comparison, the aristocracy's share was only 20 percent. The passage of land into the hands of the middle class sometimes occurred at a fairly rapid pace, especially in and around the cities. For example, in one forty-year period, a full 80 percent of the land surrounding the German city of Breslau fell to middle class control. In the twenty years that followed the emancipation of the Russian peasantry in 1861, the amount of land owned by the Russian nobility dropped almost immediately by 18 percent.

The aristocracy of the nineteenth century was also being stripped of its legal privileges and protection. The legal systems of the time turned toward the interests of the upper middle class. The most conspicuous attacks came in the guise of peasant emancipation. In France in 1789, and then more spectacularly in 1848 in Prussia and Austria and in 1861 in Russia, the remnants of feudalism were legally destroyed. Feudal dues, like quitrents and other annual payments, were swept away. All over Europe, the aristocracy lost the right to establish road and river tolls on their own land. Their exclusive right to hunt was ended, except, of course, on their own preserves. Monopolies that had guaranteed income in the past, such as the right to maintain grain mills and wine presses the peasants had to use, were also terminated. The traditional safeguards for aristocratic landholding, entail and primogeniture, became mere custom when and where they could be maintained against increasing economic pressures. The final blow came with written constitutions, beginning with France in 1791 and followed elsewhere, that established equality before the courts. Aristocrats were obviously no longer set apart.

As far as Crown Prince Rudolph of Austria was concerned, the economic and legal decline of the aristocracy was actually robbing that class of its "ambition to excel." In his opinion, the aristocracy was losing its élan, its willingness to lead society. Writing in 1878, Rudolph commented:

> The unprejudiced observer will be surprised at the extent to which the Austrian civil service is neglected by the members of the landed aristocracy. Especially it is astonishing to see the heirs of the old military nobility of Austria turning away more and more from a military career, whereas at all times the aristocracy has claimed for itself the right to be the favored bearer of the knightly way of life, and the military actually has been the gathering place for the youth of the nobility. The explanation of the regrettable present state of affairs lies in circumstances which are in no way a source of pride for our contemporary nobility.

Rudolph also noticed a trend toward vulgarity among aristocratic women. Condemning the situation, he added:

> The coarsening of manners has spread not only among the young men, but to no small degree it has won over some of the ladies too. In Vienna there are smoking rooms for aristocratic women whose conversations, carried on until into the night, recall in tone those of the low-class theatre and the art world, and indeed not in the best sense.[2]

Rudolph's words were a fair description of the declining political and social position of the European aristocracy. Slowly and irrevocably, they were losing their former positions in government, the bureaucracy, the military, and the church. Their loss of power largely took the form of a recession, beginning in western Europe and then spreading eastward as the nineteenth century ended. In France, the aristocracy managed to reassert itself after 1815, but then quickly lost political power. It controlled 60 percent of the seats in the Chamber of Deputies, France's new national legislature, in 1815; in 1821, the proportion fell to 58 percent; and in 1827, it tumbled to 40. After this, aristocrats were never again to be a majority in any of France's national legislatures. By the same token, under Napoleon III, the powerful Consultative Commission was little more than a political tool of the Parisian bourgeoisie. The army was supposed to be a bastion for the aristocracy, but even this was changing. Many senior officers were still of aristocratic birth, but one study of the Austrian general staff between 1867 and 1918 revealed that 89 percent of the officers permanently attached to the general staff actually came from various levels of the bourgeoisie.

[2] Eugene N. Anderson, et al., eds., *Europe in the Nineteenth Century*, 2 Vols. (Indianapolis: Bobbs-Merrill, 1961), II, 79, 87.

Aristocratic control over the expanding European bureaucracies also slipped. In 1888, aristocrats constituted 80 percent of the district administrative chiefs in Prussia, but by 1914, nonaristocrats had nearly 50 percent of those positions. Competitive examinations for civil service jobs in England and elsewhere did much to open up the bureaucracy to bourgeois penetration. The size of the Italian bureaucracy swelled from 63,000 in 1861 to 640,000 in 1901. Obviously, there were just not enough aristocrats to fill all those positions. The conservative churches of Europe were yet another institution through which the aristocracy had exercised control over society. But here too, they were on the defensive. The anticlericalism that led, for example, to the separation of church and state in France in 1905 was really an attempt by bourgeois politicians to limit the impact of the aristocracy. More than anything else, the growth of free secular education after 1870 deprived the aristocracy of one of its exclusive characteristics and the church of a great part of its influence. And once the religious monopoly on education was broken, the teaching profession was open to middle class penetration.

The erosion of aristocratic dominance in European society was to end, to a large extent, on the battlefields of World War I. So many aristocratic officers died in the war that in the west, the aristocracy was permanently eclipsed. In Russia, war and revolution quickly ended their role, while in central and eastern Europe, those who hung on met eclipse in World War II.

The Collapse of the Artisan Class

The gradual elimination of the aristocracy's role in European society was matched by the decline of the artisan class. The coming of industrialization initially increased the size of the artisan class. It grew until the middle of the nineteenth century, perhaps not at the same rate as the industrial working class, but still steadily. Up to 1850 in England and 1870 on the Continent, artisans comprised a full half of Europe's working class population; it was only after these dates that their numbers began to decline. What kept the artisan class afloat for so long was the new prosperity. The capital concentrated in the older urban centers—London, Paris, Hamburg, Vienna, and St. Petersburg, to mention just a few places—was now being compounded by industrial investment. With even more wealth available at the upper reaches of society, and in industrial society this meant the upper middle class and the new professional element, the luxury and construction trades had more business than ever. The number of artisans increased in response to demand.

What was true of some levels of the artisan class was not, however, true of others. Textile artisans were already being displaced or absorbed by the new mass production techniques, the domestic and factory systems. Although prior to 1850 metallurgical artisans were on the verge of being absorbed by the factory system, their skills were now needed by the iron and steel industry. In time, a similar fate would befall other artisans, so that by the end of the century, this class too would have disintegrated.

During the first half of the nineteenth century, artisans, both urban and rural, still seemed ubiquitous. France had more than 2 million peasants employed in the textile trades on the eve of the French Revolution. They were an integral part of the domestic system, which emphasized mass production carried out in the workers' own cottages and shops. After the Napoleonic Wars, one estimate placed the number of artisan shops in Prussia at about 325,000. In England, where mechanization and the factory system grew only after the 1820s, there were 240,000 hand looms in 1830 and only 60,000 steam-powered looms. Between 1836 and 1849, the number of textile artisans in Saxony doubled. The artisan population of Paris jumped between 1789 and 1871 from 100,000 to 500,000, with those in the luxury and building trades showing the greatest increase. The rapid advance in the size of the artisan class, which did not peak until the middle of the nineteenth century, only magnified the differences between the skilled and unskilled.

Incomes and wages rose at the higher levels of the guild system. In the London building trades, wages for journeymen rose a full 80 percent between 1800 and 1850. Even laborers benefitted, their wages improving by about 33 percent during the same time. In Paris, wages for journeymen painters, stone masons, plasterers, and carpenters increased somewhat more slowly, advancing by about 40 percent between 1825 and 1860. Meanwhile, in the provincial cities of France wages were rising at about the same rate. In Belgium, purchasing power for the artisan class as a whole was moving upward, especially after 1830, and a similar situation existed in Spain.

Rising wages were a necessity, because prices were also going up. Despite an inflation of about 2 percent a year, however, purchasing power did increase after 1850 because the price of food and clothing, now being mass produced, began to fall. But there were still poor journeymen, just barely making it. In the German port of Bremen in 1847, two-thirds of their wages went for bread and potatoes. Such poverty was even more evident among the declining class of textile artisans. Their numbers were too great, their incomes and wages too limited, and their futures bleak because of the spread of mechanization. The growth of the domestic system meant that more and more masters were losing their independent status and becoming wage workers, just like their journeymen. The system spread from linen, wool, and silk to the production of cotton, until millions of urban and rural artisans were working for upper middle class merchants. There were many like those described in 1783 by the Englishman Caleb Herring. In an obvious appeal for help, he described their plight:

> Behold the man worn out with age and infirmities; the man who by spending his youth in the finer branches of the trade, whose eyes are thereby become dim, . . . behold this man, and consider how exceeding small must be his earnings, and what poor pittance there is for himself and his family: add to this the high price of provisions; . . . [and] the prospect of a flat trade, with all its accumulating miseries; can any gentleman view these things in a proper light and not see the cruelty of reducing the price of labour? [3]

Herring had struck a vital point. For the domestic system, just like the later industrial system, was also subject to periodic depressions. When they hit, either wages were reduced or there was unemployment. Sometimes, the artisans' reaction was violence in the form of rioting. In fact, textile artisans were responsible for a major share of the rioting that took place in the cities of Europe between 1789 and 1848. It was almost as if most textile artisans were predisposed to riot by their declining economic position. The predisposition seemed, if anything, to spread, as artisans from other trades also suffering economic loss formed the core of groups rioting all over Europe in 1848. And even the Paris Commune of 1871, backed primarily by artisans, was to some degree an expression of the fact that incomes and wages had failed to keep pace with steeply rising prices.

Of course, most artisans did not riot. But artisan rioting, so characteristic of the period up to 1871, was undoubtedly a symptom that the class was in decline. Many textile artisans found themselves in factories not because they wanted to be there, but because they were forced by economic necessity to become a part of the new working class. No matter what their guild, artisans found the adjustment to the factory both difficult and degrading.

In the 1830s a German journeyman, Johann Dewald, a man of obvious perception, roamed through central Europe exploring the new factory system, taking a job first here and then there as he moved from Munich to Prague to Milan. While employed as a factory hand in Prague, he summed up the differences between the guilds and the factories in his diary:

[3] Stanley D. Chapman, "Memoires of Two Eighteenth-Century Framework Knitters," *Textile History,* I (1968), 107.

A factory like this is quite different from a master's house and there is no unity among the employees. Each goes his own way and pays little attention to the others. Guild-like conduct is lacking and there is no intercourse as among regular journeymen. Moreover I do not like the work; all day long one has to do the same thing, and so loses all sense of the whole. Of course it has to be in a factory, but I can't adjust to it and always feel as if I only half ply my trade.

In Milan he found another characteristic of the age, the all too apparent decline of the guilds. Commenting on the situation, he declared: "[In Milan], the old handwork customs are here completely disappearing. No feeling of comradeship and the worst behavior. The guild house was more like a pothouse than a respectable lodging." [4]

For many metallurgical artisans, there was nowhere to turn except to the factory system. In the 1830s and 1840s, the Krupp works in Essen, destined to become one of Europe's greatest iron and steel centers, was attracting its own unique labor force. Although many with rural backgrounds were employed, a good percentage of those who formed the original work force were of artisan origin. And within that special group, a majority had a background in metallurgy. Many were attracted by the wages, for factory wages were high for those who had skills. Among the artisans entering the Krupp works were blacksmiths like Heinrich Struenk, who rose to become a foreman of one of the steel works, and men like Ernst von Oerdingen, originally trained as a key maker, who worked as a grinder. Regarded as a fine worker, von Oerdingen's wages rose steadily from 433 marks a year in 1846 to 1,936 marks in 1884.

In the English iron and steel center of Sheffield, artisans were not drawn into the factory system quite so fast. Noted for its cutlery, Sheffield had been a metallurgical center long before industrialization, and for a long time the factory system existed side by side with trades still functioning on an independent basis and still perpetuating the guild tradition of small-scale production. The modern steel industry was born in Sheffield between 1850 and 1890. In 1851, heavy industry employed a quarter of the work force, and by 1891 it was up to two-thirds. For several decades, however, local artisans refused to enter the factory system, and the vast majority of new workers were drawn from the countryside. But after 1880, forgers, grinders, and filers from the guilds began to enter the factories as the prosperity of the guilds waned.

The factory system did not pose a threat to the construction trades, but their guild system did splinter and divide. In cities like London, master artisans progressively became contractors, and journeymen, apprentices, and laborers steadily slipped into the category of wage workers,

4 Anderson, et al., *Europe*, I, 116–17.

losing in the process their guild identities. The luxury trades were not challenged by the factory system until the twentieth century.

The decline of the artisan class during the course of the nineteenth century was matched by certain legal attacks on the guild structure. For long before economic forces began to eat away at their position, the guilds had been legally abolished. The Le Chapelier Law of 1791 eliminated them in France; the Anti-combination Act of 1799 produced the same result in England. Prior to 1815, through most of western Europe they had lost their legal right to exist.

The legal assault against the guilds was primarily the work of upper middle class interests. The old and new systems of production clashed during the eighteenth and nineteenth centuries. The upper middle class merchant or banker financing the domestic and factory systems saw the legal prerogatives of the guilds as an impediment. The guilds had a legal right to set wages, prices, and standards, and had often had monopolies on the production and marketing of goods within certain geographic areas. The new entrepreneurs wanted to be able to hire unskilled labor without that individual having to go through an apprenticeship. They did not like the guilds setting standards for the manufacture of certain textile and metal products. Large-scale employers wanted to vary their standards to produce quality goods for the luxury market and products of lesser quality for the mass market. The same was true for wages. Merchant-manufacturers and industrialists wanted to increase or lower wages depending on circumstances. They did not want a legal system that permitted master artisans to set wage rates for them. Finally, the upper middle class wanted to market goods freely, whereas guild monopolies denied them access to certain areas. There was class conflict in the nineteenth century, but it was not between the emerging system of industrial capitalism and the factory working class. Class conflict in this century was primarily between the upper middle class and the artisans. Their interests clashed, which is probably why artisans and not factory workers went into the streets or to the barricades over and over again during this era.

The Displacement of the Middle and Landless Peasant

For the first half of the nineteenth century, the various levels of the peasantry could be relatively hopeful about the future. The peasant proprietor, who had helped supply the preindustrial city, was in an even more favorable position after 1800. The urban market expanded gigantically as the cities and towns of Europe added one million new residents a year through the course of the century. Often a grain producer, the peasant proprietor could conquer the urban market because he also produced a diversified array of crops. The city had always been the center for the luxury foods that the majority of the urban population would soon demand as necessities. These were products the peasant proprietor could and did supply, and prices were everywhere on the rise. The middle peasant of western Europe, up to now a subsistence agriculturalist, did not do well in the new market, but his misfortunes were obscured by the advantages befalling other levels of the peasantry. For example, before mechanization the demand for agricultural labor increased tremendously as the estates, both aristocratic and bourgeois, took up staple production, which made farm labor more necessary and better paid.

Meanwhile, in the east, legislation brought about the end of serfdom. The first law designed to emancipate the serfs was announced by Prussia in 1807, but the real wave of change came later, in 1848 with the release of the Prussian and Austrian peasantry from bondage, and then in 1861 when legislation emancipated the Russian and Polish peasantry. But in spite of new hopes and the gains in the agricultural market up to 1850, the middle and landless peasant, west and east, began to disappear, another victim of the new economic forces.

The period from 1800 to 1870 was one of unprecedented opportunity for the sturdy peasant proprietor. Peasant proprietors were everywhere pushing up production. Already involved in the production of grain and the newer root crops, some peasants at this level were moving on to even newer areas, especially milk and meat. Milk was virtually unknown to most of Europe before 1800. After that date, peasant proprietors in the Maine in France, the Vaud in Switzerland, and throughout England were not only increasing the size of cows, but doubling milk production. No beef industry appeared, but a livestock industry based on pigs and calves developed. Pig farming turned out to be a profitable enterprise, because these animals required much less land than livestock of greater size.

While the peasant proprietor continued to make his way in an increasingly capitalistic and apparently profitable market, the middle peasant was lured in the same direction, but with different results. The social structure of peasant society in the west was already undergoing modification by 1800. The classic division into peasant proprietor, middle peasant, and landless peasant was being subjected to tremendous economic pressures. The peasant proprietor was holding his own; the middle peasant was not. And those who dropped out of this segment of the peasantry inevitably fell into the landless category. The so-called small farm was the characteristic plot of the middle peasant. In France in the early part of the nineteenth century, some 3 million peasants owned an average of 2.7 acres apiece, from which they tried to eke out a living. Most did not succeed. Costs overwhelmed them: the middle peasant had to pay for seed, fertilizer, livestock, and new tools, and if he tried to lease more land, he had the additional cost of rent.

When they did not succeed, which was often, middle peasants usually sold out to peasant proprietors who were constantly expanding their own holdings. In Belgian Flanders, small landowners were still prevalent during the first half of the nineteenth century. For example, in the middle of the century some 86,000 peasants still occupied land amounting to no more than 7.5 acres apiece. Most of them were middle peasants, hanging on to their meager plots decade after decade. But those who were potato farmers were wiped out by the blight that struck in 1845. The cause of the Irish famine of the 1840s, this blight also hit other parts of Europe, including the Low Countries. When it struck the Netherlands, it had the same economic consequences as in Belgium; many middle peasants who had converted from grain to the new root crop were driven from their holdings. In Saxony, the middle peasantry had developed slowly over the course of time, their small holdings dotting the countryside around Hohndorf, Ottendorf, Kleinmilkau, and Godelitz in the eighteenth century. A few generations later, they were impossible to find; they and their holdings had disappeared.

The gradual disappearance of the middle peasant in Saxony, so typical of developments all over western Europe, was the result of population pressure as much as natural disaster and indebtedness. As the population expanded, the small plots of the middle peasantry became less and less viable. The system of serfdom in Prussia, Bohemia, and Hungary prior to emancipation only hid the fact that a middle peasantry also existed in the east. For example, in the Austrian Empire, one can identify this class fairly easily. In Moravia in the 1840s there were about 38,000 such households, in Styria about 26,000. Their position was protected under serfdom because they held their land intact as long as they fulfilled their labor obligations. But once serfdom was legally abolished in 1848, they were like their counterparts in the west, largely unable to hold on to their small holdings. Those who lost their land often tried to maintain contact with the soil by becoming tenants. In the words of one English observer, William Mure, they now lived "with the dreaded rent day ever hanging over them," watching "their children grow up in complete ignorance," the whole family forced to "share in the daily routine of labour and anxiety." [5]

By the 1850s, Europe's once huge class of middle peasants was disappearing. Some middle peasants left for the cities of Europe and Amer-

[5] "Letter from William Mure," *Royal Statistical Society Journal,* No. 33 (1870), 150.

ica; others remained, swelling the size of the landless peasantry. As before, these peasants survived as tenants, sharecroppers, and agricultural laborers. Their numbers were legion in England, where they worked the great estates. In France as of 1800, the landless constituted more than half of the 5 million peasant households in the country. By the early part of the nineteenth century, more than 2 million peasants in Prussia and the Mecklenburgs made their living exclusively as farmhands. In the Austrian Empire, even before emancipation, a distinct class of landless peasants was emerging as migratory laborers. In this connection, the district president of Danzig admitted to an English visitor that low-paid agricultural labor had become an integral part of the German agricultural scene. He confessed that "this price of labour, or amount of 30 dollars . . . a-head annually, yielding no more than what a person wants for bread, salt, clothing, taxes and minor objects, cannot be diminished without lessening the power of labour and its usefulness." [6] In order to survive in the 1810s at the minimum rate of 348 marks a year in Germany, women and children in the family also had to work as farm laborers alongside the father.

The system of staple production on large estates between 1750 and 1850 required the existence of cheap, abundant farm labor, for agriculture at this level was still essentially a hoe-and-harvesting type of effort. The result was the appearance of an entirely new type of peasant community, like those of the Nivernais in the central part of France, entirely composed of agricultural laborers. There were no owners left. At least most of this new agricultural proletariat found work until 1850. The demand for farm labor even caused a rise in wages, especially during the harvest, in places like England, Germany, and Austria, although in fact the money was never enough for the laborer to lift himself above the level of subsistence. Soon a new dimension was added when payment in kind changed to money payments.

Beginning in the 1850s, a combination of factors began to destroy this class. Mechanization was the first threat. In the 1830s in Britain, one harvester could replace a hundred hands. The doubling of the European land population created a situation where there were just too many laborers willing to work, a consideration that kept wages low. Even worse, after the 1870s the importation of staples from abroad, primarily grain and meat, made production in Europe less lucrative and caused widespread unemployment among the landless. By the second half of the nineteenth century, the landless were also beginning to leave the countryside.

[6] Theodore S. Hamerow, *Restoration, Revolution, Reaction* (Princeton: University of Princeton Press, 1958), p. 52.

Underscoring the decline of the peasantry were the periodic outbursts that convulsed Europe in the late eighteenth and early nineteenth centuries. Peasant riots were not unusual. Most European countries had the same experience as Hungary, which had uprisings in 1735, 1751, 1753, 1755, 1764, 1766, 1784, and 1790. Most of these riots were limited in their impact and were contained by the military. Nineteenth-century peasant riots took on a somewhat greater significance, for they were increasingly directed against institutions. Peasant revolts during the French Revolution had as their aim the abolition of feudal obligations, dues, and fees that ate away at incomes already low. During the early 1830s in England, rural rioting very often had an immediate economic goal. In West Kent and Essex, the demand was for higher wages; in East Suffolk, laborers often called for an end to the tithe. In other instances, they wanted reduced rents.

The final wave of peasant rioting on a large scale came during the revolutions of 1848 in areas where serfdom was still prominent, primarily Germany and Austria. Peasants protested inequities of all kinds. In Baden, they marched on the castles of the nobility to burn records of indebtedness. Bismarck, the future Chancellor of Germany, viewed the peasant upheavals of 1848 with some apprehension. He wrote at the time, "Beneath the ashes of seeming tranquility all the glow of desire for a plot of land is still alive among the day laborers." [7] Undoubtedly, many among the older classes desired a return to the past. Magnates longed for the time of aristocratic dominance; guildsmen wanted to return to the older system of production; peasants yearned for the land they had lost. But a new society was coming into existence, one within which many of the classes of the past would be forever lost.

[7] Hamerow, *Restoration,* p. 110.

8

The Upper
Middle Class:
The New Elite

The Industrial Revolution brought into existence a new middle class society. Not only did it expand the size of the middle class from 15 to 25 percent of the population, it added entirely new strata and caused growth in those that already existed. Emerging on top, and on top of society as a whole, was the upper middle class. Just below the new elite was a developing class of professionals, of middle middle class origin. Unlike the tiny professional element of preindustrial society, the middle middle class was not drawn from the upper reaches of society, but was increasingly being recruited from below. In other words, it was mostly formed as a consequence of social mobility, especially by 1900. The lower reaches of the middle class, like the upper middle class, expanded in response to the new opportunities presented by the industrial age. It was the largest element in the middle class, and just like the petty bourgeoisie of old, the most insecure about its middle class status.

As wealth and achievement replaced titles and birth as the most distinguishing features of the elite, the upper middle class, carried along by expanding profits from investment, soon became dominant in nineteenth-century society. It replaced the aristocracy and, in the process, presented a whole constellation of names. The upper middle class was composed of many men whose family wealth had been gained in commerce and banking before the advent of factories. But as far as the nineteenth century was concerned, they did not so much personify the age as the dynamic class of new entrepreneurs and inventors who had made their way to the top. The rise of certain industrial giants like Werner Siemens and Friedrich Bayer in Germany and John Marshall and John Heathcoat in England seemed to characterize the growth of the factory system much more than the accumulated capital in the banks of Europe. In this great age of change, people needed to personify the development that was occurring so rapidly around them, and so industrialists, inventors, and scientists became symbols of "progress"—in fact, the new royalty.

These new entrepreneurs possessed one quality indispensable for the large-scale production and complex financing of industry: managerial ability. Almost as soon as shop production gave way to mass production in the factory, managers became vital. Production existed on a scale not previously known. More raw material than ever was needed. The various stages of production had to be integrated under a single factory roof. Labor had to be recruited and disciplined to work along with the machine. And the finished product had to be marketed. For those who had this kind of ability, whether it was in the Europe of the nineteenth century or the Soviet Union in the twentieth, the rewards could be high.

As more and more wealth concentrated in the hands of the upper middle class, the new leaders of the economy were able to parlay managerial ability into increasing control of the whole society. The reins of power were now corporate and political. As long as the upper middle class dominated the banking system of Europe and the emerging corporations of the time, they were economically secure. They had a solid base from which to influence not only the course of the economy, but political developments as well. Not even the aristocracy, still in control in some places politically, could really afford to challenge the economic system being fashioned by this group. They had to conform to it and they did, just as later bourgeois political leaders would, by adapting the legal system to the interests of the middle class. The challenge in France in 1789, England in 1832, and on much of the Continent in 1848 was not decisive; but it was a signal that the upper middle class would replace the aristocracy not violently, but juridically. The transfer of power was built decade after decade by subtle economic changes and by changes in the existing legal system, the two pillars upon which bourgeois political strength would ultimately rest.

The Entrepreneurs [1]

In order for the Industrial Revolution to proceed, men had to be willing to invest in the newer enterprises. The vast majority of projects, from the building of railway systems to the establishment of factories of any type, usually required a fairly large outlay of funds. Although the upper middle class was often conservative in these matters, there were still those who were willing to try—even to gamble—at certain moments. These individuals came to be known as entrepreneurs. In a social sense, they were the ones willing to finance large-scale industry and its associated activities, mining, shipping, and railroading. Sometimes the new industrial plants were relatively small. The city of Strasbourg in Alsace, for example, had by the late eighteenth and early nineteenth centuries begun building a system of light industry. Already by 1800, the Hannong family, of Dutch origin, had established a clay pipe factory. One of the city's wealthiest merchants, Pierre Mayne, built a tobacco works, and the factory of Jean-Joseph Lamiral produced tapestries. The jump from relatively small entrepreneurship to large-scale projects is demonstrated by the Pereire brothers, the French financiers Émile and Isaac, originally from Bordeaux. Together with the great French banking houses of Rothschild, Eichthal, Thurneyssen, and Davillier, these two financiers put up nearly 5 million francs in order to begin France's first great spate of railway building in the 1830s.[2]

The search for capital could sometimes be tedious. John Heathcoat, England's great pioneer in machine-made lace, was stymied until he got initial support from William Jockett in the neighborhood of £20,000. With that capital a partnership was formed that not only helped Jockett but became the foundation for Heathcoat's own considerable fortune. Mining, no less than manufacturing and railroading, required significant capital outlays. By way of illustration, the great German coal firm, the Society for Hard-coal Mining, based in Düsseldorf, needed an original capital expenditure of some 640,000 talers in mid-century to start excavating.[3] The willingness of banks and merchants in the west to invest was not always matched in central and eastern Europe, especially during the early part of the century. In Prussia, many investors were fearful of low returns. Some of the leading Prussian entrepreneurs argued that it was

---

[1] In this section of the book I am highly indebted to the small but significant study by W. O. Henderson, *The Industrialization of Europe, 1780–1914,* one of the few books that does not neglect business history.

[2] About 7.5 million current American dollars.

[3] Somewhat over a million 1974 American dollars.

up to the state to create the preconditions for safe investment by building roads, canals, and railways and by backing new banking endeavors. The less timid, like the leading Austrian economist Franz Riepl, pushed for investment and development no matter what the source of capital.

Some investments, especially when they were combined with technological advances, were particularly successful and propelled certain "new men," the term with which Saint-Simon, the French aristocrat and social critic described them, to national prominence. Three men, all of middle class origin, represent the type of fortune those with capital and a certain amount of ingenuity could accumulate from industry. These three were John Marshall, the English textile magnate; Alfred Krupp, the pioneer of the German iron and steel industry; and Werner Siemens, who foresaw the coming of the electronics industry. Each man saw the possibilities in new production techniques or in new products. Marshall turned from cotton to the mechanized production of wool. Alfred Krupp actually built on his father's confidence, for his father was absolutely convinced as early as 1819 that iron was the building material of the future. Siemens was without a doubt almost clairvoyant; he understood the significance of the telegraph and foresaw the electrical industry four decades before it actually developed.

John Marshall's father had already accumulated a modest fortune as a draper in the latter part of the eighteenth century. In combination with Samuel Fenton and Ralph Dearlove, the young Marshall leased a production site outside Leeds. From the first, he was interested in mechanization, but got nowhere until he linked up with Matthew Murray, a young mechanic of considerable engineering talent. Murray's invention of a flax-carding machine paved the way for mechanization in Marshall's mills. By 1803, he had more than a thousand workers in his woolen plants. He bought out his partners in 1815, and his fortune began to grow. Throughout his career, Marshall continued to look for new and better ways to improve the process of mechanization.

Marshall's awareness of the importance of technological innovation was a quality shared by the German Alfred Krupp. Krupp inherited a rather small steel works from his father. Convinced that cast steel would inevitably find a wide-ranging market, he first specialized in rolled plate, dies, tools, and small machine parts. In 1835, with the help of his cousin, Fritz von Müller, he invested some 10,000 talers [4] in a foundry, certain that he needed steam power to increase production. Krupp eventually settled in Essen, which became the center of his giant steel complex. With the railway building boom of the 1850s in central Europe, Krupp was on his way to becoming one of the greatest steel magnates of all

---

[4] Almost $17,000 in current American purchasing power.

time, his name synonymous with the whole mass production process. From ore deposits to coal mines to a manufacturing complex with 6,000 workers, Krupp proved that bigness could still mean quality and control.

Werner Siemens was yet another entrepreneur of the age who combined managerial skill with inventiveness. But, unlike Marshall and Krupp, it was he who did the actual inventing. It was Siemens who first solved the problem of conducting electrical signals over long distances by means of insulation and it was he who, at the age of fifty, invented the dynamo (1866). After a military education, he and the talented German mechanic J. G. Halske established a factory to build telegraph equipment in 1847. From the beginning, he grew with the industry. Using family funds, his factory literally supplied Russia with all her telegraph equipment for a long period. Then he went into the production of electrical cable when demand rose. His inventiveness never flagged. As late as 1880, he invented the first electric elevator, and a year later he helped to set up the first electric tramcar in Berlin.

Men of middle class background dominated the entrepreneur group, but not all those helping to shape the new industrial age were bourgeois. The wealthy Hungarian magnate Istvan Szechenyi was of an impeccable aristocratic background. Szechenyi had wide-ranging economic interests, most of them dictated by the opportunities offered by the new economic age. Like most members of the higher nobility, Szechenyi's wealth originated with the land. But, unlike most of the others in his class, Szechenyi did not hesitate to invest. With the vision of the banking bourgeoisie, he moved his wealth into one area after another. Originally an improving landlord, he imported cattle and pigs, engaged in the scientific breeding of sheep, and went over to the new root crops. From agriculture he moved into commercial banking, shipping, food processing, and finally metallurgy, all the while earnestly condemning those who fought against industry and the coming of steam power.

In the east, government often stepped in because the private sector of the economy was either too weak or too timid to do so. Key government officials acted as entrepreneurs, investing from the government's treasury instead of from private sources. Such a man in Russia was Count Sergei Witte, the minister of finance from 1892 to 1903. Witte was the man behind the development of railway links throughout European Russia and the real supporter of the Trans-Siberian Railway. Heavy government investment in this area, he reasoned, would stimulate the iron and steel industry and increase mining activity. At the same time, he promoted foreign investment inside Russia to stir industrial growth.

Men willing to promote and willing to invest either their own or government capital undoubtedly quickened the pace of industrial growth in the nineteenth century. Through propagandists like the Englishman Samuel Smiles, a new entrepreneurial creed began to develop. The idea grew that men who worked just as hard as the great entrepreneurs could not help but go a long way and become successful. The notion was fostered that wealth and prominence were within the reach of anyone who would adopt the upper middle class values of thrift, hard work, and self-discipline. Actually, few went all the way up the social ladder in the nineteenth century. Most men of prominence and public esteem already had technical backgrounds or money or both, but still the myth of social and economic gain was held out to the mass of men. Samuel Smiles, preaching the doctrine of work, implied that if a person only practiced the upper middle class virtues of "diligent self-culture, self-discipline and self-control," [5] he too could succeed. Few did, but the myth did encourage social mobility.

The Development of Managerial Skill

The rise of large-scale enterprise established basic economic units of hitherto unknown size. Because of the administrative problems that came with bigness, entrepreneurs placed a premium on managerial ability, the capacity to see the various stages of production both compartmentally and as a part of overall development. Managerial ability meant the capacity to draw in raw materials, integrate production, discipline labor, transport and market the product. To those who could do this went a commanding position in the managerial class, a social group that was to attach itself to the upper middle class by virtue of ability and financial success.

During the early stages of the Industrial Revolution, the idea of management was closely linked to ownership. This was overwhelmingly the case because so much of industry began as a family enterprise or as partnership. It was only when the smaller company gave way to large corporations that a separate and distinct class of industrial managers actually emerged. John Marshall and John Heathcoat, the two English textile barons, both managed, as did Alfred Krupp. When the textile industry was first established around 1810 in Austria, leading industrialists like Franz Radler, Samuel Vogel, and Lorenz Rhomberg all took part in the active management of their plants. In France and Italy, family enterprises continued to be the norm for decades. The de Wendel interests in France, involved in the production of iron and steel products,

[5] Reinhard Bendix, *Work and Authority in Industry* (London: Wiley, 1956), p. 110.

kept most of the company's management and financing in family hands right up to 1905. Later on, during the automotive age, Gottlieb Daimler administered his own plant at Canstatt in western Germany.

The eventual growth of industrial bureaucracies in the late 1800s can in part be told by the history of two of Europe's greatest corporations. The first involves Brunner, Mond, one of the forerunners of Imperial Chemical Industries of Great Britain; the other, the electrical firm of Siemens, which eventually became a part of the much larger German Allgemeine Elektrizitäts-Gesellschaft (A.E.G.). At Brunner, Mond, the day-to-day administration of the plants was primarily in the hands of John Brunner and Ludwig Mond during the industry's early years. Later on, Brunner and Mond assigned some functions, but only to a group of scientists and engineers. From the start, they seemed to distrust anyone without a technical background. The break in this pattern did not come until the 1890s, when new and different managerial recruits appeared. The most famous of them was J. H. Gold, a lawyer by training. He was followed by H. D. Butchart, an accountant. The addition of these types indicated that Brunner, Mond was now willing to rely on managerial ability, no matter what a person's background.

At Siemens, there likewise seemed to be prejudice in favor of men who had strong technical backgrounds; 55 percent of Siemens' top managerial personnel in 1910 were graduates of technical schools. But it would seem that Siemens ranged more widely in its search for talent, for 25 percent of its managers had little more than a general business background, while another 10 percent were distinctly of lower class backgrounds.

A postscript to the story of the growth of managerial talent was written inside the Soviet Union in the 1920s. Russia clearly had a class of factory managers prior to the revolution. After all, she was the fifth greatest industrial power in the world even in 1914. Like their counterparts in the west, these men managed corporations primarily concerned with the manufacture of textiles and metallurgical products. As in the west, they were originally drawn from the various levels of the middle class, showing a talent for direction either as a result of training or the acquisition of practical knowledge. This group was largely destroyed by the revolution of 1917.

Afterward there were no longer private corporations but public trusts, and these had to be administered. In 1922, even before the first Five-Year Plan, there were 430 trusts administering more than 4,000 production facilities. In this situation, the Party began to develop a whole new class of industrial managers. By 1928, the trusts were dominated by Communists, many of whom were of lower class backgrounds. For example, in 1928 about 80 percent of the trust managers were Communists, but less than a quarter of them had higher educations.

At the local level there was even less preparation, a full 95 percent of all Communist plant managers lacking higher education. Still, the Soviet Union brought into existence a managerial elite, not of the same social background as that in the west, but in the course of time about as successful.

No matter where the managerial class came from, socially it was still confronted by the same problems. For the difficulties inherent in management were essentially an outgrowth of industry, not of ideology. *Problems* The managerial element had to deal with a certain set of problems that hardly changed from the nineteenth to the twentieth century, or from industry to industry, or—for that matter—from economic system to economic system. For example, managers were overly dependent on mining, shipping, and railroading in order to get the resources they needed. Krupp sought to solve this problem by owning and operating his own coal and iron ore mines, but his solution was an unusual one. Probably the greatest problem was difficulty in recruiting and training labor. Not only did the worker have to be trained, but the former artisan or peasant had to synchronize his activity with that of the machine, something that most new workers were unable to do. Finally, there were cost accounting and marketing. Accounting problems were solved by means of double-entry bookkeeping, which allowed for a day-to-day assessment as well as an overall check on financing. This practice, which originated with the English estate system, was carried into industry by stewards once the Industrial Revolution began. For the most part, marketing was not considered management responsibility; it was left to the lower middle class, which through the nineteenth and early twentieth centuries marketed the goods of industry through small retail outlets.

No problem facing the new managerial elite was so pressing as that which surrounded the actual training of labor. Most artisans and peasants were unaccustomed to what Lenin would later call labor discipline. Their previous pattern of work had been highly disorganized. When they worked, they labored in spells, ranging from 10 minutes to a few hours, never consistently in the shops and never daily in the fields. In preindustrial society, labor was intense only during certain peak periods. The English inventor, entrepreneur, and factory administrator Richard Arkwright faced a continuous problem "in training human beings to renounce their desultory habits of work, and identify themselves with the unvarying regulatory of the complex automation." He "had to train his work-people to a precision and assiduity altogether unknown before, against which their listless and restive habits rose in continued rebellion." [6] The managerial class not only learned how to

---

[6] Sidney Pollard, *The Genesis of Modern Management* (Cambridge, Mass.: Harvard University Press, 1965), pp. 183–84.

educate workers to follow the machine, they also came to the realization that workers who ate better were more productive, and this is the real reason why industrial wages, particularly for the skilled, rose so continuously through the course of the nineteenth century.

The Foundations
of Corporate Power

From the beginning of the eighteenth century until the start of the twentieth, family enterprises and partnerships in banking and business steadily gave way to corporations. The growth in size of financial and commercial organizations was one of most conspicuous features of the age. From industry to mining, shipping, railroading, and agriculture, there was an uninterrupted trend in the direction of bigness, until finally the corporation emerged both dominant and strong. The growth in size made necessary both management and capital. An industrial bureaucracy was already coming into existence; the next step was for the corporation to coax as much capital as possible out of investors so that it could sustain growth. This was done legislatively; new laws were passed that safeguarded wealth and made investment easier. By 1914, giant corporations like the French bank of commerce Comptoir d'Escompte and the Italian metallurgical combine Consorzio ILVA were taking over. The trend in the direction of sustained growth went on unabated, until the banking and business corporations literally had control of the economy.

The basic tool of the upper middle class, the corporation, got needed capital from both banks and the public at large—primarily the various levels of the middle class. The great central banks formed during the previous century were still in existence. Only now the central banks, both the older ones like the Bank of Hamburg and the newer ones like the Bank of France and the Russian State Bank, were serving an expanded function. They were supervising, somewhat informally at times, a sprawling banking system, a system with ever greater variety. And newer types of banks came into existence to attract as much capital as possible by offering different inducements and different opportunities.

The growth of the French banking system in the nineteenth century illustrates this point. The older banks in France, dominated by the Rothschilds, Heines, Mallets, and Hottingers, actually slowed the growth of French commerce and industry by sticking to older types of investment, especially safe and sure government bonds. A new banking system was actually needed to push growth through the accumulation of capital and the issuing of short-term loans. The more adventurous Pereire brothers filled the gap by organizing the Crédit Mobilier in 1852. Using the extraordinary device of paying daily interest, the bank first aimed at the acquisition of 20 and then 60 million francs. The brothers hoped that the lower middle class, peasants, and even laborers would be tempted to invest so that all the capital in society would be mobilized for large-scale investment in industry.

The immediate success of Crédit Mobilier was matched by the Comptoir d'Escompte, like the Crédit Mobilier also dealing in commercial banking and short-term loans for industry. Founded in 1848, its original capital of 6.5 million francs shot up to 80 million by 1866. Attempts to fill gaps in the investment picture were aided by still other novel banking institutions in France, such as Crédit Agricole, Crédit Foncier, and Crédit Lyonnais. The proliferation of this type of banking, more directly involved in the newer investment areas, was an irreversible trend. Similar institutions popped up everywhere; in Belgium it was the Société Générale; in Germany, the Diskontogesellschaft; in Italy, the Banca Generale; and in Austria, the Credit-Anstaltverein.

The economic reserves of society were being concentrated more and more in the great central and commercial banks, giving a handful of upper middle class bankers unparalleled power over the economy. For example, in the nineteenth century, the Bank of France maneuvered itself into such a powerful position that it was said that a mere two hundred individuals could not only dominate the money market, but could dictate to the government and control the economy. Their power, often masked by the impersonal character of the corporation, was at times approximated by the directors of the great business corporations. Often, they were the same individuals. For instance, the powerful Dresdener Bank claimed in the period prior to World War I that its directors sat on the dominant boards of more than 200 separate German corporations. Meanwhile, the various business corporations were, like the banks, always in search of greater and greater funding. Toward the end of the nineteenth century, they found it in the form of the cartel.

The emergence of four or five leading producers in each industry seems to have been one of the characteristics of the time. In the English textile industry, the leading producers were the Ashton Brothers, Horrocks, Miller and Co., Dale and Owen, the Grant Brothers, and the Strutts. In the French iron and steel industry, Terrenoire, Audincourt, Alais, Dacazeville, and Schneider-Creusot were early leaders. In Italy, where corporate enterprise came somewhat later, the metallurgical industry was developed by ILVA, Ferreire Italiane, and the Alte Formi e Fonderie di Piombino. The competition these companies offered one another was often debilitating economically, and to solve this problem businessmen developed a new form of enterprise, the cartel. The cartels of Europe represented an overconcentration of economic wealth and power that could only be matched by the banks. For example, when in 1883 the firm of Werner Siemens and that of Emil Rathenau's German Edison Company merged to form the Allgemeine Elektrizitäts-Gesellschaft (A.E.G.), it meant a virtual monopoly of the German electrical industry for the firm.

The growth of cartels in the quarter-century before 1914 was spectacular. By 1906, there were nearly 400 of them in Germany. They grew up elsewhere; Norway had 418 cartels in 1921 when new legislation forced them to register. In France, the Comptoir Métallurgique de Longwy, founded in 1876, controlled the production of 400,000 tons of steel a year in 1893. A similar cartel, Comité Français de la Filature de Coton, regulated the manufacture of cotton goods. In England, unlike on the Continent, the cartels were not legal, but they grew up in the form of mergers. In the banking industry, the number of banks in Great Britain fell from 600 in 1824 to 55 in 1914, and later to 11 in 1937, under the aegis of the five big banks—Midland, Westminster, Lloyd's, Barclay's, and National Provincial.

The Rhenish-Westphalian Coal Syndicate in Germany established in 1893 was a typical cartel of the times. It controlled 50 percent of coal production in Germany, regulated levels of production, set prices, divided up the market, and determined the rate of reinvestment for each of the various corporations involved in the cartel. The inevitable consequence of the formation of these cartels was higher prices and profits. As was almost always the case with upper middle class institutions, the legal system worked to their benefit. English common law normally forbade such restraints on trade, but new legislation allowed for the creation of mergers that turned out to look suspiciously like the cartels on the Continent. French law forbade price fixing up to 1884, but this legal restraint was dropped after that date. In Germany, cartels were legalized on the grounds that they helped to rationalize production and marketing.

The change in legal attitudes that permitted virtual monopolies to grow and grow was indicative of the age. The whole legal structure of Europe had turned against the older classes in society and in favor of the upper middle class. The new elite came to power not in any sudden or spectacular way, but slowly, decade after decade, by legislative means. Never before had the legal system of Europe been so structured in favor of those who had money. The Napoleonic Code, adopted in so many other countries besides France, was outspokenly prejudiced in favor of property rights and the individual owner, the "one who has." The code virtually guaranteed the existence of wealth and protected its perpetuation through inheritance. To bypass the tendency of the aristocracy to squander inheritances, it even legally denied the right of owners to waste their acquired wealth. When wealth was perpetuated "dangerously," in the case of minors and women, the so-called threat to the bourgeois estate was limited by guardianship and trusteeship. Family wealth was thus continued in an uninterrupted way. Limited liability laws, passed in Great Britain, France, and Germany between 1855 and 1870, capped this process by allowing individuals with money to invest without their personal family fortunes being jeopardized. Thus were the capital pools accumulating in the upper middle class protected.

The Emergence of New Political Institutions [7]

Nowhere were the power shifts protecting the interests of both the older and newer elements in the upper middle class so obvious as in the field of politics. Older political institutions like monarchy and the aristocratically controlled French Estates-General and the Diets of Central Europe either atrophied or died. They were replaced by institutions that better served the interests of the upper reaches of the middle class. At the level of national government, this usually meant a parliament, with obvious middle class representation, and a bureaucracy increasingly passing out of the hands of the aristocracy and under the control of those who had strong business or professional backgrounds. At the local level, this quite commonly meant legislation that forced the countryside to submit more and more to the jurisdiction of the city, so that with the growth of urban government, a larger and larger portion of the population was living either directly or indirectly under the sway of the city.

The retreat of monarchy was a fact of life in nineteenth-century Europe. The process was completed in 1918, when the German, Austrian, and Russian monarchies all collapsed. Monarchy disappeared first in France in 1848. It was on the decline in both Great Britain and Italy, where it was constitutionally limited. In Austria, the monarchy was deliberately weakened by the Constitution of 1867. It was able to reassert itself only because the legislature bickered so much that it could not hold on to its original victory. In Russia, the czar's position was strong up to 1905, after which he had to share power with the Duma. In Germany, the emperor remained a vital force in the political life of the country after 1871, but the voice of the legislature was growing.

[7] The gradual process by which the upper reaches of the middle class took power by redesigning the political structure of Europe is best examined in a truly extraordinary book, Eugene and Pauline Anderson, *Political Institutions and Social Change in Continental Europe in the Nineteenth Century.*

As monarchy faded or was at least challenged, attention was increasingly focused on the role of national parliaments, especially the lower houses. In France, the Chamber of Deputies, originally under aristocratic control, fell to the bourgeoisie by the late 1820s. In England, the House of Commons remained aristocratic for a sustained period but was eventually overcome by middle-class interests. Centralized parliaments, generally mixed socially, emerged suddenly in central Europe in mid-century. The Italian Chamber of Deputies, the Austrian House of Representatives, and the German Reichstag were all formed between 1861 and 1871. The last major legislative body to be brought into existence was the Russian Duma, established in 1905.

The essentially middle class character of government at the top in the nineteenth century was preserved by means of a limited franchise. It was well into the century in Great Britain and France before the masses got the right to vote; in Great Britain it was 1867; in France, 1875. Germany had universal manhood suffrage from 1871 on, but it was blunted by a system of national representation so structured that it thwarted lower class representation. The lower classes did not receive the right to vote in Russia, Austria, and Italy until 1905, 1907, and 1912, respectively. In almost every instance prior to this, the right to vote was limited by a property qualification or an educational standard. In this way, the middle class character of the vote in England was maintained between 1832 and 1867, although more levels of the middle class did qualify. In France in 1830, the franchise expanded from 100,000 to 200,000 individuals, meaning that at best the business and professional elements could exercise it. Austria, which first established the right to vote in 1873, limited it to those with high property qualifications. It extended the franchise to the lower middle class in 1882, but then left it there for a quarter of a century. Italian legislation followed a somewhat similar path. The system, which had a highly elitist character to begin with, was enlarged in 1882 so that it reached down to the lower middle class, but here it was also stopped.

The system of political representation passed not from aristocratic elements to the upper middle class, but from the nobility to the middle middle class, the professions. The dominant banking and business elements were never more than marginally involved in the active pursuit of politics. They never constituted more than 10 percent of the representatives elected to the French Constituent Assembly in 1789, the English House of Commons after the Reform Bill of 1832, or the ill-fated Frankfurt Assembly of 1848–49. So actual political participation tended to fall to the professions, increasingly allied to the interests of the upper middle class after 1800 and more often than not representing their attitudes.

It was this element that helped pass the spate of legislation which built an essentially middle class conception of society in the nineteenth century. For example, after the 1860s, four out of every five British cabinet members of middle class origin came from the professions—the clergy, the law, the civil service, or medicine. Only 20 percent had backgrounds in banking or business. The tendency for political leadership to concentrate in the hands of the middle middle class was conspicuous in the case of the Frankfurt Assembly, where academicians and civil servants were represented out of all proportion, a trend that would continue in the Reichstag. Between 1893 and 1914, a full 54 percent of the members of the Reichstag were from the so-called free professions. The leader of the powerful Constitutional Democrats in Russia was Paul Milinkov, a historian. Even left-wing political parties saw the rise of men with distinct professional backgrounds. Karl Lueger, the head of the Christian Socialist party in Austria, was a trained lawyer. His chief rival, Victor Adler, the leader of the Socialist party, was a medical doctor.

The growth of national bureaucracies in the period after 1800 represented still another area of penetration by the upper reaches of the bourgeoisie. The size of the Prussian civil service tripled from 1821 to 1901. For Germany as a whole, the state bureaucracy consisted of some 1.2 million jobs, and most of the senior positions were occupied by the upper middle class. France showed a similar propensity toward the proliferation of bureaucratic positions, for it too had more than a million public officials by the end of the century. A French author has estimated that in 1910 there were for every 10,000 inhabitants in Belgium, 200 officials; in France, 179; in Germany, 113; and in England, 73. Pressure by middle class elements steadily reduced the grip of the various aristocratic groups on the bureaucracy. By the end of the century in the various ministries of the Prussian government, for example, the number of Junkers had slipped to a mere 16 percent, and they had virtually disappeared in the Ministry of Justice in favor of bourgeois types. In England after 1870, educated upper middle class elements progressively made it into the civil service, but only at the junior levels. It was several decades before they would emerge in senior positions of power.

The movement of well-to-do middle class elements, either business or professional, into positions of power on a national level was mirrored by their growing control of local government. The city was not only absorbing a larger percentage of the population but in many areas spread its jurisdiction to the countryside. After 1815 in France and 1861 in Italy, the commune became the center of local government. Either elected by a limited franchise or appointed, the commune under the control of the propertied bourgeoisie took over government functions at the local level in both countries. It kept up roads, provided schooling, recorded vital statistics, paid the police, and maintained poor relief for both the local urban center and the surrounding rural area, even when the district was largely composed of agricultural elements. In both Austria and Prussia, a weighted system of voting gave upper middle class taxpayers a much higher percentage of the vote, guaranteeing bourgeois control of the cities. In fact, in Austria, the lower classes did not get the right to participate in urban·elections until 1918. In Great Britain, essentially urban from 1850 on, the majority of the population was automatically under the control of the upper reaches of the middle class.

The tendency of rich bourgeoisie to prevail at the local urban level can be proved by looking at two fairly typical urban centers, the English town of Exeter at the start of the nineteenth century and the Austrian city of Graz half a century later. An examination of Exeter's records shows the franchise in 1831 limited to 1,125 voters out of a total population of 20,000. Of that total, 365 electors were artisans, the rest upper and middle middle class elements—bankers, businessmen, brewers, lawyers, clergymen, and other men of personal wealth and fortune. Those elected to public office came overwhelmingly from these groups even as the franchise expanded in time, with lawyers making up the largest group elected. Graz by 1910 was an industrial center of 150,000. The Municipal Corporation Act of 1869 in Austria reserved the suffrage for those in Graz and other Austrian cities to those who held the greatest amount of property. Businessmen actually dominated the city council up to 1918, but progressively they found themselves sitting next to civil servants, doctors, lawyers, and academicians, especially after 1890. In the case of Graz, the professions were a close second to businessmen among those holding public office.

The upper middle class moved into positions of power during the nineteenth century. Using old and new wealth, accumulated capital, and the boldness and talent of its entrepreneurs and managers, the upper middle class steadily took over society, enriching itself as it went. It replaced the aristocracy by taking over certain key institutions with which it maintained its hegemony. Upper middle class control of capital and its ability to funnel that money through the banks to the corporations for loans and investment gave it a commanding position. So did its ability to control the new legislative and local governing bodies of the century, which in combination with the bureaucracy gave a peculiar upper middle class stamp to nineteenth-century politics. In all of this, the upper middle class would find an ally in the new professional element within society, a social group that in time had an equally privileged position in the new society.

9

The Formation
of the
Middle Middle Class

Europe's preindustrial society had produced its own class of lawyers, doctors, writers, and notaries, but their numbers had been small. Moreover, they were so closely allied to the upper classes that they were barely distinguishable from them in either social origin or attitudes. The professional elements of the eighteenth century came sometimes from the aristocracy, sometimes from the upper middle class. Either way, they tended to reflect elitist concepts of society. The same was true, sociologically, of the new emerging middle middle class of the nineteenth century. Its members were distinctly upper class to begin with, but as time went on, the class received more and more recruits from below, from the lower middle class or the lower class itself. Especially after 1850, the middle middle class became the object of social mobility, in particular because the upper middle class was so hard to reach. For the socially ambitious, professional status in society was a major achievement. But once in, even these elements would quickly take on the upper class attitudes that had always characterized the professions in Europe.

As the size of the middle middle class expanded, the old professions grew along with some of the newer ones being created by industrial change. Among the older professions expanding in response to the new age were the clergy and the officer corps. In England, the clergy was still the largest profession, numbering 50,000 as late as 1881, twice as large as the legal profession, its nearest rival. As the military grew during the nineteenth century, so did the overall strength of the officer corps. By 1914, Germany was to have three officer corps, one drawn from the aristocracy, one from the upper reaches of the middle class, and another from the lower reaches of the middle class. In response to the great medical breakthroughs of the period after 1850, the number of doctors jumped considerably. The law, ever a haven for the aristocracy searching for a career, continued to train both nobles and nonnobles alike for careers in the civil service and the judiciary.

The growth and expansion of the old professions would never have been enough to produce a middle middle class nearly twice as big as the upper middle class. The most spectacular increases were achieved by the addition of entirely new professions. Engineers, architects, authors, scientists, chemists, electronics experts, and inventors all added to the dimensions of the new society.

What characterized the upper middle class was wealth, business acumen, and managerial ability. What distinguished the new middle middle class was advanced education, specialized training, and a certain inventiveness. Although the monetary rewards that went to the middle middle class were not as great as those accumulating at the top of society, they were amply rewarded, enough to classify them economically among the privileged. The professions, even when staffed from below, were part of the emerging Establishment of the nineteenth century. They designed the homes of the rich, educated the sons of the well-to-do, did the research that could be patented for profit and industrial gain, and legally guaranteed the position of the upper middle class. And in all of this they reflected the interests of Europe's new dominant elite, the upper middle class.

The Older Professions

During the nineteenth century the older professions were revitalized largely as a result of education. Medical schools, military academies, and universities became the centers from which the doctors, army officers, and civil servants of the time emerged better trained than ever before.

The most progressive and dynamic were the medical schools. At a number of leading medical facilities, notably Leyden and Paris, new courses were added to the curriculum as a result of growing medical knowledge. The advances in clinical knowledge that characterized the late eighteenth century were, in fact, the prelude to the breakthroughs of the nineteenth century. The leading preindustrial centers were the two Scottish universities, Glascow and Edinburgh, plus Leyden, Paris, and Vienna. From the work done at these universities came new discoveries in anatomy, dermatology, and pathology.

As the work of one generation contributed to the next, the human body became less and less of a mystery to the medical profession. In the field of physiology, the French doctor François Magendie produced, during the first part of the nineteenth century, findings on the significance of the spinal cord. His accomplishments were followed by those of Dr. Jean Cruveilheir, the first man to hold the chair of pathology at the University of Paris. Cruveilheir was convinced of the chemical basis of disease, an assumption that gave greater legitimacy to the emerging biochemical conception of life. This research soon had practical application, especially as the functioning of the body's neurological system was more fully understood. By the 1880s, for example, the anesthetic qualities of cocaine had already been recognized by two noted surgeons, Dr. Paul Reclus in France and Dr. August Bier in Germany. Louis Pasteur, still another of the great French pioneers in medicine, had by 1863 established a germ theory for most diseases. Pasteur's intellectual feat was matched by that of Joseph Lister, a Scotsman. Experimenting in 1865 with carbolic acid, Lister came up with a usable antiseptic. Lister, a surgeon and professor at the University of Glasgow, was deeply concerned about the high death rate among amputees (about 45 percent). Antiseptic, which brought that toll down, was first used extensively in 1870–71 by French army surgeons to lower the death rate among battlefield amputees during the Franco-Prussian war. In the 1880s, Dr. Emil von Behring of the Berlin Institute of Infectious Diseases discovered immunizations for both diphtheria and tetanus, and the Spanish physician Jaime Ferrán, for cholera and typhus.

The medical discoveries of the nineteenth century contributed enormously to improved public health. Combined with better diet, the advances in medicine brought relief from some of the diseases that had plagued Europeans for centuries. Perhaps the most obvious case in point was the work of the English country doctor Edward Jenner. Jenner's successful vaccination against smallpox helped to eliminate a disease that one medical historian estimates had taken a total of 60 million lives through the centuries. In 1807, a grateful British Parliament awarded Jenner a prize of £30,000 for his discovery but did little else despite pressure from the Royal Academy of Physicians and other national bodies for a national system of immunization. The mortality rate from smallpox remained high until the second half of the century, when large-scale vaccination programs in England and on the Continent finally brought the disease under control.

The dramatic accomplishments of the medical profession in the nineteenth century were accompanied by steady growth in the other professions, notably the military. Until the middle of the eighteenth century, military education was, generally speaking, largely unknown. The British continued to ignore it even after that date; training at one of the great public schools—Harrow, Eton, or Winchester—was considered sufficient for any gentleman bent on a military career. On the Continent, however, education played a much more dramatic role. The Austrians had the oldest tradition of military education in Europe, their Institute for War and Engineering dating back to the middle of the seventeenth century. By 1768, the Prussians had an Academy of Engineers at Potsdam, and by 1781, the French had a number of military academies with specializations in both artillery and engineering. The English, meanwhile, held out, the Royal Military Colleges at Sandhurst and Woolwich gaining fame only late in the nineteenth century.

The training of officers became more and more important, especially as armies became more unwieldy. The Prussians put 480,000 men into the field in 1870, a force so large that it required 42,000 junior and senior officers to command it. Warfare was also becoming more complex. Armies had to be supplied, troops had to be moved over terrain that engineers had to make passable, and artillery was becoming more deadly. The English, without a land tradition and accustomed to fighting in small, compact units, still had some 15,000 army officers in 1881. After this time, the size of the officer corps proliferated uncontrollably, especially with the introduction of universal conscription. By 1914, Germany alone could field an army of 1,540,000 troops, supervised by an officer corps of nearly 150,000 men. The French, drawing on lesser resources, nevertheless matched the Germans in numbers in both enlisted men and officers.

During the second half of the nineteenth century the military grew in political importance as well as in numbers. It found ways of protecting its interests: Former officers sat in the English Parliament, the French Chamber of Deputies, the German Reichstag, and later on, the Russian Duma. After 1871, for example the French Chamber of Deputies had a solid block of thirty former officers well disposed toward the military. Meanwhile, officers were becoming more and more prominent. Generals Kitchener and Gordon were household words in Great Britain. In France it was believed that General Boulanger had designs on the government, and the Dreyfus Affair certainly focused an unprecedented degree of public attention on the French officer corps. The Austrian commander in chief von Hötzendorf played a decisive role in determining Austria's attitude toward Serbia in the fateful summer of 1914.

The noticeable rise in the number of doctors and military officers in Europe during the nineteenth century paled, however, in comparison with the gigantic growth in the number of civil officials. The wealth governments were absorbing from an expanding economy in the form of taxation was being used to develop bureaucracies with hundreds of thousands of employees. Not all government employees were middle class, but the various ministries and offices needed tens of thousands of managers to run them. Once again, higher education available only to some, became the avenue by which the middle class entered another burgeoning profession. In open competition for civil service positions in Prussia, the aristocracy did poorly. And although aristocrats did try to improve their chances by attending the universities in greater numbers, by 1852 only 32 percent of those entering the upper reaches of the bureaucracy were aristocrats; nonnobles—that is, middle class elements— were already supplanting them. Civil service positions in Great Britain had long been filled from the graduates of Oxford and Cambridge. Now the emerging Indian Civil Service absorbed those from other schools with bureaucratic ambitions.

By the end of the nineteenth century, after nearly two centuries of evolutionary development, the mammoth civil service establishments in Europe were now middle class in character. Merit rather than birth was being rewarded, salaries were on a graduated scale, and both promotions and pensions had become part of the system. Recruitment by means of open competitive examinations had helped to end the aristocratic stranglehold.

When the century began, the social origin of most professionals was distinctly upper class. By the 1860s although still recruiting from above, the professions were more and more being filled from below. Even as these groups combined to form a distinctly professional class, they were absorbed into a single social layer in the middle class, more allied to those above them than to the masses. In other words, they were part of the elite in industrial society, their incomes and educations separating them from those lower down in the social scale.

New Professional Opportunities

While the Industrial Revolution was expanding some of the older professions, it was also spawning entirely new ones, especially in engineering and science. For the older professions, education had been vital; for the newer ones, it was mandatory. Initially, many of Europe's leading engineers were either artisans, like the Englishman James Watt, or mechanics, like the German August Borsig, men with a great deal of practical experience, but not necessarily any formal education. The French were the first to lead in the development of scientific and technological education, motivated perhaps by the words of the great French *philosophe* Condorcet in 1792, who said:

> The sciences offer a remedy for prejudice, for smallness of mind. . . . Those who follow their course see the coming of an epoch when the practical usefulness of their application will reach greater dimensions than were ever hoped for, when the progress of the physical sciences must produce a fortunate revolution in the arts. . . . Literature has its limits, the sciences of observation and calculation have none.[1]

In 1794, the École Polytechnique was established. Its original curriculum emphasized both mathematics and science as the real foundations of an engineering career. Among its early faculty members were scientists such as Gaspard Monge, J. L. Lagrange, and Pierre de Laplace, all renowned in their own right.

The impact of the École Polytechnique is actually somewhat difficult to assess. Not only did it turn out graduates who went into the military, government, industry, and engineering, it also produced a whole host of government leaders and scientists who became noted in other countries. D. H. Dufour, the Dutch scientist and engineer, was a graduate of the École Polytechnique, as were the Italian scientists Plana and Botto and a number of Belgian political leaders like Theodore Teichmann, minister of the interior after 1831. Poles, Portuguese, Swiss, Rumanians, and Americans, along with other western Europeans, attended the school on a regular basis, with Germans forming the largest foreign group in the first half of the nineteenth century. Among the most famous German graduates of the École Polytechnique were the future scientists Alexander Humboldt and Justus Liebig.

It was only a matter of time before similar schools were established elsewhere—in Prague in 1806, in Vienna in 1815, in Stockholm in 1825, throughout Germany in the 1820s and 1830s, in St. Petersburg and Copenhagen in 1829, in Liège and Ghent in 1835, and in Zurich in 1848. During this entire period, only the English lagged behind in the area of technical education. They did not establish a school of mines until fifty years after the French had done so, while such technically oriented schools as Owens College, Manchester, and University College, Liverpool

---

[1] J. T. Merz, *A History of European Thought in the Nineteenth Century*, 4th ed., 4 Vols. (Edinburgh: W. Blackwood, 1923), I, 110–11.

had to do without firm governmental support until the last thirty years of the century.

The French continued to provide Europe with scientific and engineering leadership right up to 1870. Mining engineers from France like Antoine-Marie Heron de Villefosse helped to improve mining techniques in the Harz Mountains of Germany. Another French mining engineer, Alphonse de Betancourt, rose to become chief of the Russian Corps of Engineers. French engineers were active in Egypt from 1800 on, capping their efforts in that country a few decades later with the building of the Suez Canal. At one time, more than a hundred of them were assisting nine European countries, a number of Latin American states, and the Ottoman Empire with plans for railway development.

The practical achievements of European engineers stand, along with the great medical discoveries of the era, among the finest accomplishments of the century. And even without a system of formal education, British engineers still made notable achievements. They were responsible for the invention of the steam-engine, the slide lathe, the piledriver, and the gas generator. John Buddle was able to ventilate mines by lining shafts with iron castings. James Fox improved some of the earliest planing machines, while Henry Maudsley was able to accelerate the development of machine engines by means of a number of technological innovations. In Switzerland, Hans Caspar Eschel operated one of the most sophisticated machine-tool plants in all Europe. In the Ruhr, Franz Dinnendahl and Fritz Harkout were among the early builders of factory machinery.

Discoveries in chemistry largely involved the application of chemicals to industrial processes. The result was the rise of a group of industrial chemists, of whom the German Carl Duisberg was perhaps the most prominent. Duisberg worked for the German chemical firm of Friedrich Bayer and Company, with its headquarters in Elberfeld. Motivated by Duisberg's discovery of three new dyes, the company decided in 1890 to invest millions of dollars in research. The investment paid off. The work of Duisberg and his trained staff enabled the company to move quickly into the production of such varied items as medicines, ointments, and photographic equipment.

The process of synthesizing, at first done mostly in laboratories, accelerated production in any number of areas, including textiles, alkalis, and fertilizers. Soda, perhaps the most important of chemical products, was now being synthesized in greater quantities. The French chemist Nicholas Leblanc first synthesized it by combining limestone, charcoal, and sodium sulphate under heat, and the Belgian Ernst Solvay improved the process by passing carbonic acid through a solution combining ammonia and salt. There were, of course, numerous other discoveries. By the 1860s, the Norwegian Alfred Nobel was manufacturing dynamite from nitroglycerine, and the first plastic substance, one of the truly great achievements of modern chemical synthesis, was produced as early as 1865 by the Englishman Alexander Parkes.

The electronic industry was just as dependent on research as the chemical industry. The industry began in the 1830s, when electricity was first successfully conducted over long distances, but real development had to wait until the 1860s, when the Italian Antonio Pacinotti and the German Werner Siemens simultaneously developed the dynamo. For the first time, electrical power could be concentrated with enough intensity to drive engines, wheels, and turbines. The growing applications of electrical energy also made possible a convenient form of home lighting, a discovery credited to both the Englishman Joseph Swan and the American Thomas Edison. Toward the end of the century, the Italian electronics engineer Guglielmo Marconi sped the process of communication by discovering, evidently along with the Russian A. S. Popov, electromagnetic waves. Their combined experiments made possible one of the outstanding inventions of the time, the wireless telegraph.

Mechanical engineering, already responsible for the development of machine tools, matched the continuous advances in chemistry and electronics with new automotive inventions. The internal combustion engine was first built in both France and Germany during the 1860s. The first plant established to produce the new gasoline engine was founded outside Cologne by N. A. Otto and an associate. They were quickly joined by Gottlieb Daimler and Wilhelm Maybach. By 1885 there were several German firms producing four-cylinder motor cars. A decade later, the German manufacturer Karl Benz was producing an inexpensive model called the Velo, a car that cost only £100 [2] and could travel up to 12 miles an hour. In the meantime, the French firm of Panhard and Levassor secured a patent from Daimler and immediately went into full-scale production. In fact, France emerged as the leading manufacturer of motor cars in Europe in 1900.

If the upper middle class had expanded production as never before in European history and contributed to the steady decline in the cost of such basic items as food, clothing, and household utensils, the professions also did their share to improve the quality of life. Medical discoveries, engineering feats, and scientific exploits all made a strong impression on people who were now convinced by visible evidence that progress, real material progress, was actually taking place. From their discoveries and efforts, the professions grew economically prosperous— not rich, but well above the remainder of the society in income. An economic· and educational gulf separated them from the mass of men.

---

[2] Little more than the equivalent of 500 American dollars of the time.

The professions joined the bankers and businessmen as part of the new elite, even if at a somewhat lower economic level. The Industrial Revolution would eventually reward everyone, but it benefitted some far more than others. The upper reaches of the middle class, the business and professional elements, appeared to be in the same position as the great magnates and prosperous gentry of the past, socially dominant, economically advanced, and politically prominent.

The Bourgeois Elite

The passing of aristocratic society was one of the most distinguishing features of the early part of the nineteenth century. Among the very first to notice this change in elites were the artistic and intellectual communities. The age of patronage was over; the more imaginative elements within society were now independent. For many of them, the disappearance of aristocratic society was a loss. Not only was there massive criticism of the new bourgeoisie and its doctrines of acquisition and personal restraint, there was a clear attempt by many artists and writers to romanticize the past, to make it better than it was in order to have it contrast all the more with the new industrial society and the factory system. In almost every endeavor, but in particular in literature, music, and political thought, criticism was heavy and the atmosphere pessimistic.

Many authors saw something forbidding, even destructive, in the emerging values of bourgeois society. Two great French novelists, Stendhal and Balzac, were both convinced that middle class morality, with its emphasis on emotional restraint for the sake of economic success, would be destructive of personality. The English social critic Thomas Carlyle declared in ringing terms that man had lost his soul and that materialistic doctrines were creating a psychological disease of such proportions that it could only be described as a social gangrene. Carlyle, who loved the era of kings, bishops, and aristocrats, never mentioned its poverty.

For Karl Marx, the new age was also devastating. The triumphant bourgeois capitalist was, to him, the carrier of social injustice and the cause of society's poverty. The materialistic doctrines of the bourgeoisie, he contended, had alienated the worker and reduced most economic effort to discomfort and dissatisfaction. Instead of looking to the past, however, he sought salvation in the future. For conservative political thinkers, such as the Frenchmen de Maistre and de Bonald, the institutions of the past had been merciful because they had held change in check. Both were convinced that change, now a commonplace, would be too much for man and would only bring out his worst aspects.

Disliking the present, a large number of social critics, especially in the first part of the nineteenth century, began to romanticize the past. Sir Walter Scott transformed society's vision of the medieval knight from that of a warrior to that of a benefactor. English Romantics like Wordsworth and Shelley contributed mightily to this idealistic vision of the past. Wordsworth glorified the nobles and peasants of old and the more natural setting of agricultural society, all of which he contrasted with the sordid materialism of the middle class and the ugliness of the factory system. Wordsworth's dislike for the industrial bourgeoisie may be compared with Shelley's contempt for capitalism and his indictment, somewhat misplaced, of industrial society as the cause of massive poverty. Among the German romantics, Richard Wagner used his music to glorify Europe's former way of life, to extol the aristocrat and artisan, and the past's search for honor and identity, while his colleague, Friedrich Schlegel, repeated the theme heard elsewhere that bourgeois pedantry and restraint did injury to the growth of personality.

The Romantic era supposedly gave way after 1850 to a more realistic age, but the new literature was just as idealistic and critical as that which had come before. From Dickens to Flaubert to Hugo to Chernyshevsky, the new realism took on the growth of bourgeois society and again found it wanting, this time in human values. But the new era did have its defenders. In England, many agreed with Andrew Ure, one of the more popular writers of the 1860s, when he glorified the up-lifting character of industrial society. The city, he declared, was better off than the countryside—just compare the condition of the urban labor force with the poverty in the countryside. Defending the new upper middle class, he wrote:

> From the documents published by this unexceptionable tribunal [The English Poor Law Commission] it appears that, but for the renovating influence of its manufacturers, England would have been overrun ere now with the most ignorant and depraved race of men to be met in any civi-lized region of the globe. It is, in fact, in the factory districts alone that the demoralizing agency of pauperism has been effectively resisted, and a noble spirit of industry, enterprise, and intelligence called forth. What a contrast is there at this day between the torpor and brutality which per-vade very many of the farming parishes, as delineated in the official re-ports, and the beneficent activity which animates all the cotton-factory towns, villages and hamlets.[3]

Many on the Continent would have agreed that the factory system being created by the upper middle class did represent steady improve-ment over the past. And they also would have subscribed to the com-ments of yet another bourgeois apologist, H. Byerley Thomson, of Uni-versity College, London and Jesus College, Cambridge, who insisted that

---

[3] Andrew Ure, *The Philosophy of Manufacturers* (London: Cass, 1967), p. 354.

the existence of the professions, the second most influential layer of bourgeois society, gave to modern industrial society a definite tone and polish. "The importance of the professions and the professional classes," he wrote in 1857, "can hardly be overrated, they form the head of the great English middle class, maintain its tone of independence, keep up to the mark its standard of morality, and direct its intelligence." [4] In a sense, of course, both apologists and critics were right. The triumph of the higher reaches of the middle class did represent an economic victory of sorts for the remainder of society. The critics served to remind the new elite of the dangers inherent in excessive materialism and of the fact that the masses were just as deserving as they were of a decent standard of living, education, and freedom from unexpected economic disaster.

One of Carlyle's most telling criticisms of the new bourgeois society of the nineteenth century was that it tended to reduce everything to what he called "the cash nexus." What he meant, of course, was the modern way of defining both status and acommplishment in terms of acquired wealth. To a large extent, Carlyle was right. With wealth adding up at the top and income growing among the masses, social position was increasingly being gauged by just how much money a man could make. The bourgeois elite not only had economic resources, but the means of shielding themselves against financial disasters such as depressions and inflation. Incomes at both the business and professional levels proved this point. In England, a man was often said to be personally worth £1,000 to £10,000 or £100,000 while in France the banks often described a man as either a first-rate or a third-rate credit, a rating that might determine a man's social standing and his opportunity for self-advancement as well as his ability to receive credit. More than ever, it seems, prestige was now associated with wealth. Among French prefects in the 1870s, family income indicated that these top administrators were definitely drawn from the *haute bourgeoisie*. Of 88 prefects, 14 had annual incomes of 40,000 francs a year, 31 had annual incomes of 30,000 francs a year, and the bottom 43 could count on 20,000 francs each per year.[5]

Great personal fortunes were to be found everywhere. By way of illustration, in Germany the Friedrich Diergardt family invested 60,000 talers, Quirin Croon was able to muster over 100,000 talers, and Wilhelm Prinzen put up another 55,000 talers.[6] It is obvious that impressive wealth had accumulated at the top of bourgeois society.

---

[4] W. J. Reader, *Professional Men* (New York: Basic Books, 1966), p. 1.

[5] The franc at that time was probably worth about $1.50 in current American purchasing power.

[6] A taler was roughly worth about $1.67 in 1850 American money.

The capital resources concentrating more and more in the hands of the upper middle class were never matched by the professions; still, they too were compensated at a level unmatched by the remainder of society. Factory managers in Austria in the early part of the nineteenth century, middle managers in effect, normally earned seven times as much as their workers. Typically, they received yearly incomes of 700 florins and above at a time when their workers were averaging about 110 florins per year. Higher civil servants in Great Britain later in the century might expect to earn up to £400 a year, with special assignments adding anywhere from £50 to £200 to their base salary. In Prussia, high-ranking civil servants might expect annual salaries of 14,000 to 17,000 marks a year, whereas university professors had to be content with yearly salaries of about 6,500 marks. British physicians in the late nineteenth century might expect to receive in the neighborhood of £300 to £400 a year, while a study of the income of Berlin doctors at this time showed that half of them were averaging less than 3,000 marks a year, considerably lower than the salaries paid civil servants and professors.

The bourgeois elite of Europe lived in a way that was still reminiscent of their ancestors in the eighteenth century. However the age was described, as Biedermeier or Victorian, there was a definite style to the lives of the business and professional elements. Housing was still luxurious, either in the form of homes or apartments. Lace, tapestry, and heavy mahogany furniture was everywhere in vogue. Whether it was the west end of London or the inner city in Vienna, work, comfort, and prayer, usually in that order, regulated the lives of the prominent. Servants were common. Women were expected to stay at home and contribute to the raising of the children, who were normally groomed to take a place in the upper reaches of society. Meanwhile, the city continued to offer the affluent its inducements in the form of concerts, theaters, and shopping.

Diet, always the special preserve of the well-to-do, continued to be varied and good. Good nutrition contributed to what the British liked to call "energy," that distinctive characteristic of the leaders of society. Longevity continued to be a feature of this class. A random sampling of middle class types showed that the British prime minister William Gladstone lived to be eighty-nine; his Italian counterpart at the turn of the twentieth century, Giovanni Giolliti, to eighty-six. Louis Pasteur died at the age of seventy-three, James Watt at eighty-three, the French political cartoonist Honoré Daumier at seventy-three; the French journalist Adolphe Thiers at eighty, and the French political leader François Guizot at eighty-seven. They outlived the general population by a good thirty years.

10

The Rise of the Masses

By the middle of the nineteenth century the rough outlines of Europe's new industrial and largely urban society were just coming into focus. The fact that the upper reaches of the middle class were about to replace the two levels of the aristocracy as the most prominent elements within society was now self-evident. While these two elitist elements were changing places, a different kind of metamorphosis was occurring lower down in the social order. The passage of political, economic, and social power from one group to another was not all that unique; Europe had seen changes in dominant classes before. The truly distinctive feature of nineteenth-century society was the way in which it transformed the masses from a passive into an active element by means of a rising standard of living.

Under the aristocracy, the masses had been for all practical purposes mute and powerless. The spread of industry and technology raised them up as never before. This is not to say that poverty in Europe had been eliminated, but by the end of the century the lower middle class, the working class, and peasantry would all have made significant advances. Illiteracy, poverty, bad diet, poor sanitation, lack of longevity, unhealthy working conditions, and bacterial diseases were all being controlled by a society bent on improvement. The process was steady, although its pace did not satisfy many critics. By the end of the century the average European was now living 50 years, a significant gain over the 28-year life expectancy of 1800.

The new society, with its emphasis on material gain, was from the beginning a progressively materialistic society within which one's social standing was largely determined by income—in other words, by one's occupation and status. This had been much less true of Europe's older agricultural society, in which one's position was determined by birth and in which so much of the population lived below the poverty line. Opportunities for employment and gain had been so few that the masses of people had had to be content with rigid social stratification. By contrast, the new society was by its very nature mobile. It is estimated that up to one-third of the population changed its social position, and its economic fortunes, each generation during the nineteenth century. Movement up the social scale to the very top was, however, difficult, for the upper middle class was already manned by those with established wealth. Toward the end of the century, the professions did open up to the especially ambitious. Most, however, had to be content with the move from the countryside to the city, from agriculture to factory work, or—with educational assistance—from the peasantry to the lower middle class.

The masses never really made history prior to 1848. They had for long centuries been made passive by both disease and malnutrition. Our conception of the past is largely based on an analysis of what magnates, merchants, master artisans, and peasant proprietors said and did. Industrial society and the wage system changed all that. For Europe's rising standard of living in the nineteenth century was carried along by an improving wage system. Throughout the century wages rose an average of 3 percent annually, with real wages, the more important criterion because it takes into account purchasing power, more than doubling after 1850. In the more advanced industrial states, the situation was often better: Real wages in Great Britain increased by 45 percent between 1870 and 1890; in Germany, real wages rose by 60 percent between 1884 and 1914. This meant a rising standard of living that broke the pattern of the past that had condemned a full 85 percent of the population to a subsistence level. Now the masses were gaining economically, nutritionally, educationally, and politically. They made their presence known and demanded even more improvement and even greater social security. And, as the masses broke with poverty, they too divided socially according to occupation and income: they were lower middle class, working class, or peasant. Unlike the past, when divisions were largely a matter of either class or caste, of inherited wealth or bare subsistence, social distinctions were now marked to a significant extent by differences in income. Material distinctions, based on effort and occupation, had replaced the hereditary caste distinctions of birth and custom.

The Coming of Mass Society

While the profits of the upper middle class were rising on the average of 4 to 6 percent a year, the classes of the new mass society were also gaining socially and economically. Urban society was reshaping the social order. The lower middle class lived on, but it was composed of entirely new elements. The artisans were still there, forming a declining portion of the shopkeeping class. For a while they were still prominent, especially in the old commercial centers like London, Paris, Berlin, Rome, and St. Petersburg, but after 1870 they were definitely on the wane. Taking their place as the new shopkeeping element in society were the small retail outlets that progressively characterized every city and town. The consumer products of the factory system had to be sold, and they were increasingly being distributed by grocery, clothing, and hardware stores.

Other layers of the lower middle class were also formed. Clerical workers in both industry and government grew over the course of time to become the largest element in the lower reaches of the middle class. Foremen in the factory system achieved lower middle class status, and so did most preprofessionals such as teachers and nurses. The lower middle class certainly regarded itself as part of the great European middle class, and perhaps it was socially. But economically it was much closer to those below it in the social order, making it, from a sociological point of view, an integral part of the mass.

The working class was to be the largest group that the Industrial Revolution would produce. It would form by 1900 a slight majority of the overall population in the more advanced industrial states in Europe. From the beginning, the working class was divided into skilled, semiskilled, and unskilled elements, so it is practically impossible to speak of this class as one. The skilled, especially in the metallurgical and chemical industries, were rewarded with very high wages from the onset of the Industrial Revolution. Industry literally could not have survived without their talents. The semiskilled, a group that rose in really large numbers somewhat later and that was closely related to mass production techniques, was adequately compensated. The unskilled in the textile and mining industries as well as in transportation and municipal work benefited least from industrial change. For industry tended to reward out of all proportion those who had vital mechanical skills to the detriment of those without specific abilities or talents.

The formation of new lower middle class and working class elements in the city drained the countryside of its peasant population, since the vast majority of urban immigrants were of peasant origin. What they were seeking in the city were new economic opportunities; the land was either no longer supporting them, or supporting inadequately. The shrinking peasant population was, then, still a third element within that very large social group which can best be described as the mass of men in industrial society. The middle peasant was by the last half of the century on the verge of extinction, squeezed out by economic forces. The peasant proprietor did survive, his ability to work the soil undiminished. Now, however, he was progressively a truck farmer. He produced more highly specialized crops—fruits, vegetables, and poultry—in place of the grain and root crops of a previous era. The landless peasant was still on the land, and still, it seemed, in large numbers. His plight had hardly changed. In fact, he seemed almost lost in a society that more than ever rewarded productivity and skill and tended to forget those who had nothing to offer except manual labor.

Through the nineteenth century, most mass elements were absorbed into the wage system characteristic of industrial society. The only exceptions were the petty bourgeois shopkeepers and the peasant proprietors, both of whom continued to depend on profit. Otherwise, most lower middle class occupations, along with the various levels of the working class and agricultural laborers, were now included within a wage system that pretty much determined one's standard of living. Actually, profit levels were so marginal for shopkeepers and peasant proprietors that they tended to either limit or force, relatively speaking, an actual decline in the standard of living of these two elements.

For Europe's 6 million lower middle class shopkeepers before 1914, profit levels never rose above 4 or 5 percent on turnovers close to 10,000 nineteenth-century American dollars, the equivalent of $400 to $500 a year. Whether it was Dublin, Toulouse, or Prague, most shopkeepers were above the subsistence level. What they were able to draw in was enough for today, but there was no guarantee of tomorrow, especially during depressions like those in 1873, 1891 and 1907, when sales on already marginal volume could and did decline. By the same token the fall in basic agricultural prices after 1870 could not help but shrink income for the peasant proprietors and ultimately make them déclassé. Peasant proprietors began to lose their lower middle class status and fall into the lower class, especially after abundant imports of food from abroad steadily reduced agricultural prices. In England the decline was gradual, prices falling 8 percent between 1880 and 1909. The prices of cereal crops fell the most, but even meat prices declined, an indication that the market for this commodity was, at long last, being satisfied. The continuous fall in farm prices eventually harmed countries with large peasant populations like France, Denmark, and Poland. The shopkeepers and peasant proprietors were not necessarily suffering, but their way of life was limited by inelastic opportunities in the market.

Meanwhile, those levels of mass society subject to wages were experiencing a steady rise in income. Clerical workers in the lower middle class and skilled and semiskilled workers gained quite a bit faster than unskilled laborers in the city and countryside. The gains were real, primarily because while prices of the luxury goods purchased by the middle class rose, the cost of basic items like food and clothing, such a large part of working class budgets, declined.

The growth of the clerical class was one of the outstanding features of the late nineteenth century. Clerical help, in the form of order clerks, accountants, and bookkeepers, was needed in both government and industry. These people were absorbed into the wage system, with opportunities for advancement that were simply not there for other lower middle class types like shopkeepers. In the British civil service, salaries for clerical workers were graduated from £80 a year to start up to £200 a year, with triennial increments of £15.

Most factory workers could also look forward to steadily rising wages. Among skilled workers such as calico printers in the textile industry, pressers in the shipbuilding industry, and puddlers in the iron industry, wages could rise as high as £250 a year, incomes that brought some of them close to the professional level. Semiskilled workers, often described as second-hands in the Sheffield steel industry, earned approximately two-thirds of what a skilled worker could command, and the same was true later on of assembly-line workers in the automotive and electrical fields. For the unskilled, wages remained marginal. In industries like mining, transport, and textiles, where a large percentage of the work force was gathered at the beginning of the Industrial Revolution, wages were often low. Average wages for members of the Austrian working class around 1900 were in the neighborhood of 900 kronen a year. That was just subsistence. Farm labor was also in this economic category, some 3 million German agricultural laborers making prior to 1914 what amounted to marginal incomes.

The rise in the European standard of living for more and more of the masses over the course of the nineteenth century transformed life. Food became more plentiful and was in greater abundance. The luxury foods that had been consumed by the few in the eighteenth century had now become available to all. This was especially true of the vegetables and meats that were adding so dramatically to height and stamina. With declining food prices, the masses had more left over for other things. For example, in France only about 60 percent of average income in 1890 was being spent for food; in the past it had been 75 percent. Clothing improved. The mass production of cottons, woolens, and linens brought a fairly decent wardrobe within the reach of nearly all for the first time. This was particularly true of cottons, the price of which fell 50 percent in France from 1873 to 1896. Housing was perhaps the only area where there was as yet no real change. As the urban population grew, housing failed to keep up with demand. Private capital simply ignored building because there was such a low level of profit. Not until public housing was introduced in the twentieth century was the problem solved in the cities.

Improvements in the way of life of the average European brought into being a popular culture. Because housing was so crowded, outside activities flourished. Music houses sprang up in England, as did *kellers* all over central Europe. Novelettes and adventure stories appeared, bought by those who were now able to read. In the 1890s, walking became a popular pastime, as did bicycling. The prize-ring and the rat-pit provided some entertainment, but mostly of a brutal type. In addition to the amusements that were beginning to soften existence, there were other signs and signals that the masses had arrived as a social force. The legitimization of the trade unions, beginning in Austria in 1867, allowed both industrial and agricultural workers to push for further reforms. Mass education helped to banish illiteracy. In Belgium, an excellent example, the literacy rate climbed from 55 percent in 1870 to 86 percent in 1900. Beyond this, universal manhood suffrage made the lower class a political force to be reckoned with. And helping to guarantee the economic gains through wages were the social security systems Germany introduced in the 1880s and England after 1906. Social security in the form of unemployment, sickness, accident and survivors benefits helped to guarantee that the rising standard of living of the working class would not be lost to misfortune. All in all, the masses in industrial society in 1900 were a different group from the peasant masses of the preindustrial era.

The Petty Bourgeois Occupations

The rise of an urban economy played a major role in determining the size and function of Europe's new lower middle class. The old petty bourgeoisie of preindustrial times tended to fade away. The master artisans diminished in number by the turn of the twentieth century, many of them disappearing and others losing status and prestige as the process of change continued. For example, tailors and shoemakers in the city of Prague became little more than lower class repairmen; shoes and clothing were now being mass-produced. The same was true of peasant proprietors. Because of falling agricultural prices, peasant proprietors in northern Italy, their incomes declining slightly each year after 1880, began to sink socially and economically into the ranks of the lower class.

Replacing the old petty bourgeoisie was a new class coming into existence in response to the needs of industrialization. The lower middle class under industrialism developed several layers over the course of the nineteenth century and became the largest element in the middle class. By the end of the era of social transformation, they would constitute about 25 percent of the general population, in comparison to roughly 3 percent for the upper middle class and 7 percent for the professions. The first level of the new lower middle class to arise was the shopkeeping element that retailed food and manufactured items. Then the administrative needs of industrial society began to create new occupations. Both industry and government developed huge bureaucracies, the lower levels of which were staffed by a growing army of clerks. And finally, as industrial society grew more sophisticated, it created a demand for preprofessional types—teachers, nurses, foremen, lab technicians, and factory inspectors. All these elements were, of course, urban-based and gave to the cities, especially the old commercial centers, a highly middle class character rather than the working class atmosphere like that which permeated the predominantly industrial towns.

At every level, the lower middle class was the product of intense social mobility. To some extent, the class was formed from elements that had previously been part of the elite and had now become déclassé. But in the main the lower middle class rose from lower down in the social order. The shopkeeping element was largely drawn from either the peasantry or factory workers. The amount of capital needed to set up a shop was not great. In England it could be done with £300, in Austria with 2,000 kronen. Of course, stocks were limited, turnover was small, and profits could be so low that bankruptcy often threatened. The marginal existence of many shopkeepers was the cause of great insecurity.

The French city of Toulouse may be taken as characteristic. At the turn of the twentieth century, Toulouse had a population of some 200,000. It had its own class of tobacco store owners, café proprietors, butchers, bakers, delicatessen operators, plus stationery, furniture, hardware, clothing, and shoe stores. As early as 1900, some of them were threatened by bigger outlets, especially department stores, which took away a portion of their business.

The opening up of other levels of the new petty bourgeoisie really had to wait until the expansion of public education. The growth of higher education during the first half of the century for business and professional elements was not matched by new educational opportunities for the masses until after 1870. After that date, free secular education brought into existence a trained force of clerical workers who would soon begin to staff the new commercial and governmental bureaucracies as file clerks, accountants, order clerks, recordkeepers, and so forth. The industrial center of Barmen in western Germany amply illustrates the tendency on the part of industry to multiply the number of white collar workers. In the textile industry, Barmen's most important in 1907, there were already 1,750 white collar workers; in metallurgy there were 696; in construction, 517; and in the chemical industry, another 170. Meanwhile, in the Siemens empire, the number of clerks being hired was steadily reducing the proportion of clerical workers to factory hands. It had been 7 to 1, 2,540 to 360, in 1890; by 1912 it was less than 4 to 1, 44,378 to 12,502. Moreover, with the expansion of banking, insurance, commerce, and industry during the nineteenth century, the total number of clerical workers employed in France in the private sector of the economy expanded from less than a million in 1866 to over 2 million in 1913.

Besides these growing opportunities in the private sector, governments were also opening up white collar employment as never before. In Great Britain, a statistical department was added to the Board of Trade in 1832. Factory inspectors were first employed in 1833, poor law commissioners in 1834, superintending registrars in 1837, school inspectors in 1839, and health officers in 1848. The growth in this area was even greater toward the end of the nineteenth century. By 1909, Germany employed almost 1.2 million people in government service, the vast majority of them in clerical positions. The same was true of Italy's nearly 320,000 governmental officials prior to 1914. The process continued unabated. A full 40 percent of those gainfully employed in The Hague, the capital of the Netherlands, would eventually be employed as office workers, mostly in government positions. Through the course of the twentieth century, 50 percent of the new jobs created in London would be clerical positions. To a large extent, they represented growing government employment, although the private sector also contributed to the total. And there was, prior to 1914, a certain pride associated with being a clerk, especially if the position represented social advancement. The Englishman Benjamin Battleaxe noticed this when he asked:

> But how comes it, if the pay is so miserably insufficient, that so many seek it; that clerks make their sons clerks; that warehousemen and farmers act similarly; and that the cry is "still they come"? Is it not because clerks are

socially gentlemen—treated as such, and allowed to dress as such? Clerks like officers in the army and navy, or like clergymen, have a position as well as a salary. They pride themselves on that position.[1]

In point of fact, clerks were never in the same social category as army officers or clergymen, and neither were teachers, but both occupations did carry prestige and pride. Teaching, like clerking, became a viable occupation only after the year 1870 and only after the introduction of free secular education, primarily at the elementary school level. In 1884, within just twenty years of the educational reforms of Alexander II, Russia had more than 18,000 primary and secondary schools. England introduced free public school education in the 1870s, France in the early 1880s. All over Europe, the idea of educating the masses was becoming generally accepted. By the middle of the nineteenth century, the English factory-inspector and spokesman for the working class, Leonard Horner, could write, "The day is happily gone by when it was necessary to debate the question, whether the low orders should be educated at all." [2] The Germans accomplished this by means of the *Volksschule* (the people's school), a term that truly describes the social orientation of the emerging system. The great emphasis on elementary education brought with it a corps of teachers. Increasingly trained at normal schools, the ranks of public school teachers expanded to nearly a million by the 1890s. By that decade, the Austrian Empire had 44,000 elementary school teachers; England and Wales, 101,000; France, 143,000; Germany, 120,000; and Italy, 51,000.

The growth of preprofessional occupations such as clerking and teaching was just the start; other career possibilities were also opening up. Three of these jobs exemplify the growing variety of new opportunities—foremen, lab technicians, and factory inspectors. According to the English social reformer Charles Booth, foremen personified "the summit of working-class life." Actually, they were very much lower middle class, having often risen from the working class. Foremen who worked efficiently for the Krupp works were rewarded handsomely. Johann Scheurmann was a fine example of the advances that a really good worker could make within the factory system. Of peasant origin, Scheurmann began work as an unskilled laborer but wound up as foreman, his salary upon retirement three times as great as it had been when he began working in 1833.

Later on in the Industrial Revolution, the chemical industry began

[1] David Lockwood, *The Blackcoated Worker* (London: Unwin University Books, 1958), p. 30.

[2] Carlo M. Cipolla, *Literacy and Development in the West* (Baltimore: Penguin, 1969), p. 70.

to develop research facilities. Here, lab technicians, like those eventually working for the great Swiss chemical firm CIBA, found themselves engaged in all types of research, including work in physiology, hygiene, and bacteriology. Equally as significant for society was the work of factory inspectors like the Englishman Leonard Horner, who lived during the first part of the nineteenth century. Extraordinarily diligent, he did much to point out the need for well-guarded machines and sought to cut down on the abuse of the labor force.

As large as the lower middle class grew prior to 1914 and as dependent as it was on salaries and promotions, it rarely organized. It considered itself different from the working class, even though in income it was actually much closer to the factory working class than it was to the upper reaches of the middle class. Socially it was middle class, and many members of the petty bourgeoisie considered it unprofessional to engage in trade union activity. As a result, an organization like the French Federation of Catholic Clerical Workers, which included some 30,000 French clerical workers in the 1910s, was a rarity. It had been in existence for almost thirty years in 1914, yet it could only attract a tiny portion of the clerical working element concentrated in the French capital. Moreover, organizations like the National Union of Bank Employees in Great Britain would have to wait until the 1920s and 1930s to develop a broader base. Only then did the idea of organization begin to catch on among white collar workers in Europe.

Under industrialism the lower middle class became less of a propertied class and more a part of the universal system of wages and salaries. Incomes at this level of industrial society were often less than those received by skilled factory laborers. In fact, if anything the Industrial Revolution blurred the economic distinctions between the lower middle class and the upper reaches of the working class. In addition, the new European petty bourgeoisie was progressively being separated from the other levels of the middle class. The wealth accumulating in the hands of the business and professional classes was carrying them further and further away from the bottom levels of the bourgeoisie. With economic distinctions fading as a sign of their bourgeois status, the new European lower middle class tried to distinguish itself outwardly as much as possible from the lower classes. Although their diet was no better, the petty bourgeoisie did spend heavily on clothing, housing, and—whenever possible—education, all in an attempt to look and appear different. Even voting patterns showed that the lower middle class thought and acted differently. In England, shopkeepers and clerks voted for the Liberal party, in Austria for the Christian Social party, and in Russia later on for the Kadets. Rarely if ever did lower middle class districts go over to the Laborites or Socialists, new working class parties that sprang up after 1889.

The Lower Middle Class
under Industrialization

The two largest groups in the lower middle class were the shop-keepers and the clerks, constituting between them the real heart of this new class. Retailing had always been a part of city life, but its character changed dramatically during the course of the nineteenth century. The earliest retailing in Leeds in England, a typical town in this respect, had come in the form of artisan shops—tailors, shoemakers, and woodworkers —places in which the artisan lived, worked, and sold. There were other retail outlets in Leeds largely dependent on imports for supply, such as wine and brandy shops and stores that sold china. But even in 1800, before the full impact of large-scale production, these shops accounted for no more than 100 of the 300 outlets in the city. The shops opening up next began to retail the expanding supply of foods now available. For example, after 1800, the number of Leeds butcher shops increased five-fold. Even exotic foods were now being retailed, as one public announce-ment indicated: "Martha Peale begs leave to acquaint her friends and the public . . . she intends to sell Coffee, Tea and Chocolate; also Snuffs." [3]

With the growth of manufacturing, the expanding shopkeeping class would eventually include those selling mass-produced shoes, cloth-ing, and furniture. During the first half of the nineteenth century, the shopkeeping class sold mostly to the more privileged and well-to-do ele-ments in Leeds. Retailing among the working class was usually done in the streets by lower class hucksters. In the latter half of the nineteenth century, these hucksters began to disappear from the streets as the work-ing class, its purchasing power expanding, started to buy in the shops. The shopkeeping class supported itself fairly well in Leeds until the appearance in 1902 of a department store, the first of many large retail enterprises that would take business away from the shopkeeper.

The actual variety of small retail outlets during the nineteenth century was not all that great, for the vast majority of them still dealt with the basic consumption items—food, clothing, and household goods— articles that still constituted the bulk of purchases made as late as 1900. In the food trades, grocers were the principal distributors. Most grocers in Vienna carried a variety of products including coffee, tea, sugar, spices, dried and fresh fruits, and some vegetables. In London, household deal-ers stocked such items as soap, starch, oil for lamps, paints, brooms, and

---

[3] W. G. Rimmer, "Leeds and Its Industrial Growth: Retailing," *Leeds Journal,* No. 26 (1955), p. 380.

mops. For the most part, butchers in Leeds would buy, kill, and dress the meat they dealt in. Bakers in places like Paris continued to supply the general population with different types of breads, for in spite of the addition of fruits, vegetables, and meats to the general diet, grain continued to be a staple.

There were other types of stores; clothing stores, for example, were often divided into drapers, who dealt in the heavier clothes; mercers, who sold the lighter fabrics; and haberdashers, who retailed items such as threads, tapes, and wrapping materials. Tailors, ubiquitous up to mid-century in places like Prague, began to give way after that to clothing stores specializing in ready-made items. Bootmakers and shoemakers were still common, but by the end of the century they were becoming mere repairmen, especially as shops and department stores began to retail manufactured boots and shoes. Finally, there were ironmongers who sold plumbing fixtures and fittings and furniture dealers who distributed less expensive furnishings such as tables and chairs.

While shopkeepers were surviving, clerks were emerging as yet another lower middle class element, often with far more opportunities than those available to the shopkeeping class. Many shopkeepers in Great Britain in 1900 were averaging only £100 a year in income. In 1909, 46 percent of all British insurance clerks were making more than £160 a year; in banking, it was 44 percent; in the civil service, 37 percent; in local government, 28 percent; in industry and commerce, 23 percent; and on the railways, 10 percent. These figures may be compared with average working class earnings of around £75 a year. They show that the so-called black-coated worker was generally better off economically than either shopkeepers or workers.

Not only were incomes potentially greater among clerks than they were for shopkeepers, but there were also opportunities for advancement and higher salaries. By 1871, B. G. Orchard of Liverpool could already distinguish two types of clerks, those who would experience social mobility and had a real chance for middle management positions, and those who would be forever frozen in the position in which they started. He declared:

> £150 and £80 point to two distinct classes, distinct in their education, business prospects, and various other things, but chiefly in the social usages which custom has made the framework of their daily life. Each sum may be taken as a test of a class. Those in banks, insurance offices and other public companies, who, while living on their salaries, reside in a fairly genteel neighborhood, wear good clothes, mix in respectable society, go sometimes to the opera, shrink from letting their wives do household work, and incur, as unavoidable, the numerous personal expenses connected with an endeavor to maintain this system. At twenty-eight years of age

they receive about £150 and hope to reach £350 or more. . . . below them and forming a much more numerous body come the young men (if in many cases well read, well mannered and religious) who still are not in society, place little value on gloves, lunch in the office on bread and cheese, clean their own boots, and are not alarmed by the prospect of doing without a servant when married, of lighting the fire each morning before they go out, and of never entering a theatre or buying a bottle of wine. These are they whose salaries, averaging £80, are unlikely ever to exceed £150.[4]

It is probable that clerical workers had a greater sense of security than did shopkeepers. Shopkeepers were overly dependent on market conditions, whereas clerical workers could count on steady, if not spectacular, wages. When periodic depressions struck as they did on a major scale in 1847, 1873, 1891, and 1907, shopkeepers found themselves with shrinking profit margins. Clerical workers did not have to face these exigencies. Not only were their positions often protected by a system of seniority, but they rarely had to worry about layoffs. Moreover, clerical workers in both government and industry were usually privileged in still another way: they had pensions for their retirement years, something shopkeepers did not have. Siemens, in a typical attempt by a private firm to attract the loyalty of its workers, introduced a welfare program in the 1870s covering both white collar and factory workers. The program was rather extensive: Not only did it provide for pensions upon retirement, it also granted benefit payments to widows and orphans in the case of a worker's death, plus family allotments in the event that a clerical worker fell ill. Payments, by the way, were higher to clerical workers than they were to factory hands. Moreover, practices of this kind spread to other industries as well. The British civil service began to pay pensions to civil servants in 1834 and expanded the practice by means of a legislative act in 1859. After this, civil servants could pretty well count on pensions as a regular part of clerical employment everywhere on the Continent.

Petty bourgeois status did not provide all the amenities of middle class life, but for many such a position within society represented an advance over what their parents or grandparents had known. Many shopkeers were either one generation or two removed from peasant origins, and many clerks were the sons of either factory workers or peasants, so that the petty bourgeois occupations, even before they became more or less hereditary, did represent a distinctive way of life among the masses. Such people were much more genteel, it was thought, than men who worked with their hands in the factories or on the land and who constituted Europe's most numerous class, the manual laborers.

[4] Lockwood, *Worker*, pp. 27–28.

The Formation
of the Working Class

The largest social class spawned by the Industrial Revolution was the working class. Eventually this class would be more and more identified with the factory element, but in 1900 factory workers probably formed little more than 50 percent of this whole group. Other types of employment, including mining, transportation, municipal employment, and dock work would therefore have to be included in this category. The working class was not so much divided by occupation as it was by skill. The fate of factory workers, for example, varied so greatly under industrialization that it is virtually impossible to speak of them as a single group. They were divided into skilled, semiskilled, and unskilled elements, with the economic difference between the skilled and unskilled so great that it really produced two very different groups with two very different sets of interests.

One illustration may suffice to suggest the disparity. In 1892, in the rolling mills of Prussia, highly skilled heaters were making 6 marks a day, while unskilled dressers were earning only 2. The difference over the course of a year was gigantic in terms of standard of living. The percentage of low-paid unskilled labor was the greatest at the beginning of the Industrial Revolution, because both miners and textile workers fell into the unskilled category. Their numbers, however, declined proportionally as the Industrial Revolution intensified and as the metallurgical, chemical, and electronic industries grew, for these three industries required skills.

An examination of wage rates in most countries undergoing industrialization shows an overall tendency for real wages, that is purchasing power, to go up. On a statistical basis, wages rose continuously. In the coal fields of the Saar, the wages of miners rose from 386 marks in 1850 to 729 marks in 1869. The daily wage rate for iron and steel workers in the Krupp works at Essen increased from 1.25 marks to 2.86 marks during the same period. What was true on an industrial scale was also true on a national level. For France as a whole, wages for all working class families between 1870 and 1910 improved by 75 percent, in Belgium it was 80 percent, and in Prussia it was close to 90. But if one analyzes these figures, it becomes clear that the gains being made by skilled workers were outdistancing those of the unskilled. In Paris, the wages of skilled workers by 1902 had risen to over 2,500 francs a year, the semiskilled were up to 2,000, and the unskilled had not gotten past 1,350. The same situation existed in Austria, where skilled metallurgical workers were making 2,500 kronen a year as compared to the general working class average of 900 kronen just after the turn of the twentieth century. And what was true of capitalist countries before 1914 was equally the case in Soviet Russia in the 1920s, where skilled metal workers earned four times as much as the unskilled. The difference here was between 580 kopecks an hour and 140. The skilled were obviously favored because industry could not have perpetuated itself without their highly specialized knowledge and ability.

Skilled workers were, in terms of greater and greater numbers, progressively characteristic of the latter three stages of industrialization, which means they first came into real prominence with the growth of the metallurgical industry. In the textile industry, only calico printers were really considered skilled; mechanical weaving and spinning was work that required much less attention and much less concentration. In the iron and steel industry, skilled workers in the factories of Sheffield, Essen, Graz, and Ekaterinoslav were almost always identified with some of the later stages of factory production. Among the most talented here were puddlers, formers, and forgers. In the tool and die industry, better known in England as engineering, the moulders, smiths, turners, and platers who made the machines of the new industrial age were always among the better paid workers.

In Le Havre, for a long time the principal center of the shipbuilding industry in France, laborers working as platers, riveters, and caulkers were absolutely vital to the production of new steel shipping. It is obvious, then, that the metallurgical trades were as dependent on highly paid skilled labor as the textile industry was upon the unskilled, low-paid worker. In the rising chemical industry of the last part of the nineteenth century, skilled workers with at least a measure of knowledge about the mixing of chemicals and powders were indispensable to the industrial process. Men working with mechanical filters, chemical baths and certain fertilizer and powder combinations, like those in the German chemical industry, all required what amounted to preprofessional knowledge. The same was true of certain technicians in the electronics industry, which was just springing up in the 1890s.

Life could be exceedingly comfortable for skilled workmen. They could be secure in the knowledge that industry was indeed highly dependent upon their skills. For this reason, Russian metallurgical workers in the 1890s were conscious that their wages would continue to rise. Not surprisingly the workday for skilled labor in Austrian industry first fell below ten hours for metal workers. By the same token, a representative sampling of twenty-two workers in the German iron and steel industry showed that all but one of them expected and got annual increases in wages. Because skilled workers were compensated at such a high rate, they often had incomes above those of the lower middle class, and on occasion approximated those of some middle middle class elements.

The generally favorable position of the skilled workman in the nineteenth century was summed up in the following way by one observer:

> The home of a steady, skilled and fortunate [workman] would bear comparison with the lamented yeoman of old times. Mutatis mutandis, the conscious wants are about as well met, and there is therefore progress, . . . Unstinted food, clothes of the same pattern as the middle class, when house rents permit, a tidy parlour, with stiff, cheap furniture, which if not itself luxurious or beautiful is a symptom of the luxury of self-respect, and an earnest of better taste to come, a newspaper, a club, an occasional holiday, perhaps a musical instrument—these represent the nineteenth century equivalent to the yeoman's pony, shining pewter, bits of ancestral oak, and homespun napery. . . . The prosperous operative is better off in comparison with the unprosperous middle class man than ever before.[5]

Destined to join the skilled workman as a member of "the comfortable working class" was the emerging class of the semiskilled. Semiskilled workers had first made their appearance in the metallurgical industry of the first half of the nineteenth century. In the tool and die industry, they held down a variety of positions as less well trained coremakers, fitters, turners, strikers, slotters, planers, and platers. In the iron and steel industry, they functioned as second-hands, doing puddling, smithing, fitting, and drawing. In most instances their wages were pegged at about two-thirds of that skilled labor. Later on, toward the end of the century, the number of semiskilled workers in industry expanded sharply. The automotive and electronics industries were almost totally dependent on them. As assemblers they were vital in those industries that required the gradual and progressive assembly of parts in order to produce a finished product. They were also to make an appearance in the chemical industry. Beyond this, much of the labor force in Birmingham and Paris, two of Europe's better-known automotive centers, would eventually be semiskilled. And in time, electronics workers in Berlin, rubber workers in Milan, and chemical workers in Vienna would also fall into this category.

The semiskilled could not reach the level of the skilled, but they could often approximate the way of life of the higher reaches of the working class. They could enjoy better diets, improved housing, and growing wardrobes. The same could not be said for the unskilled, whose low wages during the nineteenth century sometimes left them outside the general picture of economic improvement. The number of unskilled workers performing rather unsophisticated tasks in the textile industry

---

[5] Sidney Pollard, *A History of Labour in Sheffield* (Liverpool: University of Liverpool Press, 1959), p. 105.

or doing manual labor on the docks or in the mines was great. The textile industry, a labor-intense area, grew so rapidly all over Europe that it initially became dependent on a huge reservoir of relatively untrained personnel. In fact, giant textile centers like Manchester, Lille, Barmen, and Lodz seemed to some to symbolize the Industrial Revolution. Great Britain had 500,000 textile workers in 1850, by 1880 Switzerland had 90,000, and by 1900 Austria had 250,000. Textile workers also participated in the nearly annual pay raises that characterized the nineteenth century, more slowly at the beginning than at the end, and never to the extent of the skilled and semiskilled.

A recent study of wage rates by Frances Collier for spinners in the cotton factories of Lancashire in the early 1800s revealed an extraordinary pattern. Wages advanced consistently upward in the factories, maintaining themselves in spite of economic downturns and depressions. Still there were many hardships at this level, as these factory hands, usually in combination with their wives and children, worked collectively for bare subsistence, about £50 a year. For all its drawbacks, this type of employment was at least relatively steady, something that was not true for those artisans working as independent craftsmen outside the mills. By the latter part of the century, conditions even for unskilled factory workers had improved, as Wolfgang Köllmann has shown in the case of the textile workers of the German industrial center of Barmen. Between 1887 and 1910 average weekly salaries had risen from 15 to 21 marks, pushing the bulk of the textile workers of Barmen above the level of subsistence.

If textile workers experienced a rather uneven fate in the age of social transformation, first flirting with and then rising above the poverty line, their position was significantly better than that of manual workers, the most common of whom were miners. Mining provided a great deal of employment, especially for the unskilled. As early at 1830, tiny Belgium had 30,000 coal miners working 300 collieries, while Great Britain had 250,000 miners by 1850. Decade after decade, mining continued to provide employment for manual laborers, in particular for unskilled peasant labor. By 1906, Germany, with an expanding mining industry, had 570,000 miners, 511,000 of them in the coal fields. Wages in mining often lagged behind the general rise in prices. For example, in Great Britain wages for miners during the whole of the period from 1800 to 1900 rose only 60 percent, a figure that left British miners below the level of subsistence.

The economic fate of European miners reflected the general condition of all those working outside the factory system. The real cause of the improvement in living standards at this time among the members of the working class was significantly rising factory wages. It was outside the factory system that there was poverty—among artisans, miners, dockers, and general laborers. Because their incomes often failed to keep up, it was they rather than factory workers who were the real losers during the nineteenth century. The new society did not reward manual labor or lack of skill. Poverty for the bottom one-third of the population, mostly the laboring poor, was by the end of the nineteenth century closely identified, as it had been in preindustrial society, with lack of both skill and training.

Wages, of course, were already climbing steadily before trade unions were finally legalized toward the end of the nineteenth century. Still, the organization of the factory working class in particular went a long way in sustaining the already well-established trend toward an annual increase in income. Unions were first permitted to organize in Austria in 1867, then in the Netherlands in 1872, and after that in England in 1876. France relaxed the prohibitions against workers' organizations in the 1860s, but did not lift them completely until 1884, and Germany did not do so until 1890. As a general rule, the trade unions never enrolled a majority of the workers in any industry; overall membership figures remained relatively low. In this respect, France was probably typical. The ruling national organization, the Federation of Bourses, had grown by 1901 to encompass sixty-five separate craft and industrial unions, with 782 local organizations. Total trade union membership in France reached 100,000 by 1886; by 1892 it was 400,000, by 1905, 780,000, and by 1912 it had peaked at a little over 1 million. This figure, though impressive, actually represents only a small portion of the total labor force in pre-World War I France.

The British and German trade unions enrolled up to a quarter of the work force in some industries, while other countries like Italy and Russia were even further behind France, Russia because the unions were not allowed to organize fully until 1905. All of this meant that trade unionism before 1914 was still somewhat weak. The Austrian unions give a good illustration of what unionism was and was not capable of in this period. In the middle of the 1890s, the unions had enlisted only 6 percent of the miners and an equal percentage of the metallurgical workers, while only 7,000 out of Austria's 400,000 textile workers were unionized. A decade later, the unions had enrolled 12 percent of the total number of workers, and one out of every four metallurgical workers. But because of their low enrollment, the unions hesitated to be too daring; they concentrated more on collective bargaining and less on strike activity. Only the more powerful unions could really afford to take that avenue to achieve success.

The vast majority of Europe's expanding working class population was of peasant origin. Some factory workers came out of the guilds, especially the metallurgical workers, but the bulk of the new working class was definitely of rural origin. For most, both factory work and manual labor represented an improvement in their station, although manual labor was much more of an economic dead end. Whether of artisan or peasant origin, workers adapted differently to their new way of life. Young miners and textile workers appearing before parliamentary committees in England sometimes seemed more impressed by the fact that meat had been added to their diet than by the hard conditions surrounding their work. When the Norwegian Folk Museum began to collect depositions from factory workers of recent peasant origin, it found that many were genuinely grateful to those who gave them employment. Again, many of them commented on the improvement in their diet once they left the land.

This feeling that things had improved, if only somewhat, may well have been the basis of working class acquiescence. Many observers have commented on how factory workers seemed to accept bad working conditions. To the middle-class humanitarian Minna Wettstein-Adelt, the sight of girls in the German textile industry happy in the midst of working conditions that to her seemed unwholesome was indeed difficult to understand. Many workers did accept hard work and poor working conditions without rancor or complaint. For the less docile, the factory offered its opportunities. Many artisans, especially those in the metallurgical industry, found that their guild training helped them to achieve high-paying jobs. In the later stages of the industrial revolution, particularly in the metallurgical, chemical, and electronics industries, there was a clear chance for advancement for some. For the ambitious, the possibility of moving up from unskilled to semiskilled to skilled positions was always there. If factory labor had its compensations, manual labor outside the factory did not. It was difficult to adapt here because the work was so physically punishing and because the rewards were meager in comparison with those in industry.

The Condition of the Laboring Classes

Most of the speculation about the working class during the Industrial Revolution ignores the conditions out of which the vast majority of factory workers actually emerged. Europe's peasant population in the eighteenth century was, in fact, far more miserable and unhealthy than her working class population in the nineteenth century, despite the harshness of working and living conditions for many workers. And there were obvious injustices. If social justice means the abolition of poverty and the elimination of the worst economic abuses, the nineteenth century did not attain this ideal. But things did improve, and the growth of a social consciousness during the nineteenth century did much to focus attention on the need for even more improvement than that being provided by rising wages.

The most marked and most obvious improvement of the nineteenth century was in dietary patterns. The proportion of grain in the diet was progressively reduced by the growing consumption of other foods. Germany around 1900 may be taken as an example of the changes in eating habits that rising income could and did produce. In 1909, skilled workers were actually spending slightly more on food, 58 percent of total income, than were the unskilled, who allotted about 53 percent of their budgets for food. The fact that the skilled spent more on meat probably accounts for the difference between the two groups. For the whole of Germany by the end of the century, meat consumption was soaring. In 1883, the average per capita consumption of meat was about 30 pounds a year; by 1913; the total was well above 100. The addition of meat to the working class diet was surely an advance over the peasant diet of the eighteenth century, which was virtually meatless. But other new foods were also being added. Vegetables, primarily root crops but also some of the leafy type, were being consumed along with dried fruits.

To eat well became one of the symbols of a higher standard of living within the working class, just as it had once symbolized upper class existence almost exclusively. Indeed, the impression in the industrial center of Sheffield was that workmen did not stint when it came to food. One observer insisted:

> It was he [the brawny broad-shouldered man of the forge] who buys the early peas, the winter salads, the first asparagus . . . and it is the aristocrat of labor—the workman who earns his three or four guineas a week, and *spends it all*—that carries off the fastest capon, the plumpest goose, and the biggest turkey the market affords.[6]

Such diets were, of course, only within the reach of the skilled factory worker; others would have to settle for less. The unskilled, in particular, had to depend upon a diet based on bread, potatoes, and cheap meat. This was an improvement over the past, but hardly provided really good nutrition. One French metallurgical worker complained that the very sight of potatoes made him sick.

The question might legitimately be asked, how much better off was the average worker of the late nineteenth century as compared with the

[6] Pollard, *History,* p. 108.

peasant of the past? Carl von Tyska's exhaustive study of 1914 [7] has gone a long way to answer this question. After comparing consumption rates in France, England, Spain, Belgium, and Germany, von Tyska concluded that the average working class family in these countries in 1909 consumed 109 kilograms of meat (50 percent beef, 40 percent pork and 10 percent lamb), 35 kilograms of butter, 28 kilograms of other fats, 392 eggs, 437 kilograms of potatoes, and 504 liters of milk.[8] All in all, this was a rather significant departure from the diet of the eighteenth century, which was overwhelmingly dependent on bread.

While the major breakthrough for the working class was in the area of food consumption, an examination of working class budgets also shows increasing expenditures for clothing. With food taking between 50 and 60 percent of income, there was enough left over in most instances for clothing. Indeed, by the end of the century, working class elements were spending about 10 percent of their incomes on both work and dress clothes. Falling prices for manufactured cloth helped. In Great Britain, the production of cloth tripled between 1884 and 1914, creating a situation like that in France, where the price of cotton goods fell by half between 1873 and 1896. In the German industrial center of Chemnitz, the typical working class family with three children between 1890 and 1903 purchased on a yearly basis the following items of clothing: 1 man's suit, 6 women's blouses, 1 girl's garment, 6 stockings, 6 men's shirts, 1 skirt, 6 socks, 1 cotton blouse, 1 child's suit, 16.25 meters of cotton cloth, 1 flannel blouse, and 3 pairs of children's shoes. Obviously, these families would have to make do with shoes and clothing lasting from one year to the next, but again they had more than the peasant population of the past. The remainder of family income went for shelter—rent, fuel, and lighting—with next to nothing left over for savings. Only the skilled had high enough incomes in the nineteenth century to be able to save.

Eating habits and dress were changing, but the problem of housing remained unresolved through most of the nineteenth century. Many peasants, it is true, had left inadequate and unsanitary housing; it actually represented an improvement when they no longer had to live with their animals. This was certainly true of Irish peasants entering London in the last half of the eighteenth and early part of the nineteenth centuries. But many peasants simply traded the unhealthy conditions of the countryside for the equally unhealthy conditions of the city. Neither city nor countryside had sanitation, and the urban areas compounded the problem by

[7] Carl von Tyska, *Löhne und Lebenskosten in Westeuropa im 19. Jahrhundert* (Munich: Duncker & Humblot, 1914).

[8] A kilogram is equal to 2.2 pounds, and 10 liters equals 2.64 gallons.

overcrowding. Some scenes were nothing short of atrocious. London lodginghouses, which sometimes packed twelve to fifteen persons to a room, represented one of the worst abuses of the day. Because housing was so dear, increases in rents could take away from money needed to purchase basic commodities, like food. Moreover, housing was nearly always cramped; somehow there were always more people than there were rooms. In places like Berlin, Breslau, Leipzig, and Gorlitz in Germany, this usually meant under the best of circumstances two or three to a room. Not even skilled labor could buy itself out of this particular dilemma. In Munich in 1895, for example, 35 percent of all skilled factory workers were living in small units with only one heated room. Of all the cities of Europe, Vienna in 1900 had one of the worst records for overcrowding, with 43 percent of the city's population living in apartments with only one or two rooms.

The deteriorating effects of overcrowding were at one point summed up so succinctly by the English social reformer Lord Shaftesbury that his words seem to apply to the whole of the century. He wrote:

> The effect of the one room system is physically and morally beyond description. In the first place, the one room system always leads as far as I can see to the one bed system. If you go into these single rooms you may sometimes find two beds, but you will generally find one bed occupied by the whole family, in many of these cases consisting of father, mother and son; or of father and daughters; or brothers and sisters. It is impossible to say how fatal the result of that is. It is totally destructive of all benefit from education. It is a benefit to be absent during the day at school, but when they return to their homes, in one hour they unlearn everything they have acquired during the day.[9]

The only thing that Lord Shaftesbury forgot to mention was that the one-room system originated in rural Europe and had been just as characteristic of the past as it was of the present.

The worst abuses of the Industrial Revolution involved working conditions. Even those employed in the more advanced industries suffered, for not even the high wages in the metallurgical and chemical industries were enough to reduce the hazard of respiratory illness. Metal specks and chemical fumes were a constant threat to health and helped to perpetuate tuberculosis as the working class disease of the nineteenth century. Both inside and outside the factory system, evidence of pollution was everywhere. In 1897, the French observer J. Huret described what the industrial town of Le Creusot, a major iron and steel center in east central France, could be like during the height of an air inversion:

[9] E. Royston Pike, ed., *Human Documents of the Age of the Forsytes* (London: Allen and Unwin, 1969), p. 178.

The streets of Le Creusot are bathed in sunlight, and yet the atmosphere is far from pleasant; the sun is accompanied by a haze of dust and smoke and it is impossible to breathe, a smell of sulphur gets in the back of the throat, and a blinding stinking smoke hangs over the streets. The fronts of the houses are black, everything one touches is dirty; the persistent noise of machines can be heard everywhere.[10]

The district government of Ekaterinoslav in the Ukraine reported similar conditions in the Russian iron and steel industry. Commenting about working conditions in the rolling mills, it reported that "the air in these work places is insufferably hot," and that the workmen are asked to "endure incomparable heat and burn," [11] enough to exhaust most of them.

Air pollution was also a constant threat to health in the German textile industry. As Minna Wettstein-Adelt reported in 1893, "tiny flakes of the twisted wool fill the air, settle on dress and hair, and float into nose and mouth, the machines have to be swept clean every two hours, the dust is breathed in by the girls." [12] If significant air pollution remained a continuous health problem in most industries, it was to take its most ominous form in the coal mines. The typical miner of the Donbass, again in the report of the district of Ekaterinoslav, was "an emaciated, understrength figure with a sickly-pale colour to his face and bad eyesight." [13] Miners almost always suffered from poor eyesight. How this condition arose has been described by a Ruhr miner, one Max Lotz. Remembering the situation in the pits, he explained:

The visual nerve becomes overly strained because of the flickering of the gasoline lamp, that eternal flickering of the small light in front of his eyes. The lamp always has to be quite close to the work and many miners consequently look into the flame of the weather lamp as they set or stand, while not at work. . . . A trembling of the pupils forms in the eyes of many miners. At first it is not noticeable but it gradually becomes stronger. Where this eye ailment reaches a certain stage the stricken person becomes unable to work in the pit any longer.[14]

The existence of the working class could be made uncertain by two other factors; one was accident, the other unemployment. In either case, the result was the loss of employment without compensation. Factory work always had its hazards. According to one estimate, 100,000 industrial

---

[10] Pollard and Holmes, *Documents*, II, 326.

[11] Pollard and Holmes, *Documents*, II, 324.

[12] Pollard and Holmes, *Documents*, II, 322.

[13] Pollard and Holmes, *Documents*, II, 325.

[14] Peter N. Stearns, ed., *The Impact of the Industrial Revolution* (Englewood Cliffs, N.J.: Prentice-Hall, 1972), p. 159.

workers lost work in 1900 due to on-the-job accidents. Most of them were not serious, but some 10,000 accidents a year did lead to disability or death. Mining accidents were even more frequent. In Great Britain alone in 1849, 756 miners lost their lives. Then there was unemployment. In 1849, the French mining industry had an unemployment rate of 18 percent; in the 1860s, the same industry had a marginal rate of only about 4 percent. The most serious threats to factory employment during the period before 1914 were the economic depressions of 1847, 1873, 1891, and 1907, which pushed dramatically upward the average European unemployment rate of 5 percent. The passage of factory acts, regulating hours and conditions of employment, plus growing pressure in favor of social security legislation were all attempts to remove the insecurity that still surrounded the modern system of wages. When the Austrian Trade-Union Commission called in the 1890s for unemployment, survivors, old-age, and accident insurance, it was obviously insisting that whatever still made life insecure in modern industrial society should finally be cleared away. The rise of comfortable lower middle class elements, along with the emergence of a working class now demanding better wages and conditions, should not obscure the fact that there was still a peasant population left on the land. True, the peasantry was declining in both numbers and influence, but it was an integral part of the European mass.

The Survival
of the Peasant Proprietor

Before the nineteenth century was over some 80 million peasants would have left the soil and migrated to the cities, which were being filled by displaced rural elements. For example, 867 out of every 1,000 new inhabitants in Budapest after 1880 were migrants; the figure for Stockholm was 734, for Prague it was 700, and for Amsterdam and Brussels it was 502 and 489, respectively. The middle peasants, crushed by the burdens of commercial capitalism, led the movement from the land, to be followed by large numbers of landless peasants. Surviving in the wake of mass migration were two distinct peasant elements. Peasant proprietors continued to live on, sometimes on less land and often with an income that failed to rise at the same rate as that of some of the newer urban elements. The result for the peasant proprietor was a relative decline in both social prestige and economic position. The landless still remained at the bottom of peasant society; their numbers never significantly diminished, it would seem, because those who still clung to the idea of a rural existence tended to remain on the land even if it meant living at a subsistence level.

After 1880 and the fall in world agricultural prices, the peasant proprietor often survived as a truck farmer specializing in garden crops such as fruits and vegetables, and poultry products. Most peasant proprietors were forced to turn in this direction because grain and meat, now being introduced on a massive scale from abroad, would have been either unprofitable or impossible for them to raise. In 1876, the first refrigerated ship carrying Argentinian beef docked in the port of London, the beginning of what was to become mass importation. A year after this event, the grain crop failed for four continuous years, 1877 to 1881. Europe turned almost permanently to foreign sources of wheat, primarily the United States and Canada. Denied both these agricultural possibilities because of foreign competition, the peasant proprietor now made a go of things by growing specialty crops and commodities. But as before, he was not a farmer in the modern sense; his holdings were much too small for him to achieve that elevated level of agricultural production. Rather, he often had to make do on less land than before, in this case because of subdivision. The increase in the size of peasant families, with more sons living to adulthood, meant a continuous process of inheritance that divided and subdivided the plots of peasant proprietors as never before.

Subdivision of the land unquestionably reduced the effectiveness of some peasant proprietors. The result could in extreme instances be economic failure within one generation or two. The process could be so accelerated that it reached ridiculous proportions, as in the famous case of the commune in the Loire River valley of France when 5,000 acres of land were eventually reduced by inheritance to some 48,000 plots. Still, the peasant proprietor hung on in a number of areas where holdings were sufficient to support his old way of life. In places like England, northern Ireland, the Low Countries, Scandinavia, western Germany, Bohemia, Upper and Lower Austria, northern Italy, and Hungary, there was still prior to 1914 a steady, functioning class of peasant proprietors, surviving as their forebears had on a specialized diet. On units of slightly under 30 or over 40 acres of land, the peasant proprietor could still maintain the standard of living he knew in the past—a good diet, a comfortable home, furnishings, and now formal education. He could have all this even if the larger society no longer saw him as an essential part of the middle class.

The characteristic response of the peasant proprietor to difficulty was improvement. Often enough after 1872, he was helped by government and by the growing system of agricultural education. By the early 1800s, France had more than 100 secondary schools in her large towns teaching courses in agronomy. With the introduction of mass education, most villages in England and Germany taught courses in agriculture. Beyond educational opportunities, peasant proprietors were willing to learn new methods. The new agriculture was very intense, both the rate of growth and crop yields being highly dependent upon soil preparation, in particular the massive use of the new chemical fertilizers. The peasant proprietor was helped in still another way. Farming was not mechanized yet, but agricultural machinery was being used with greater frequency, sometimes in conjunction with draft animals, sometimes not. Seed drills, vital to the new agriculture, were seen more often, and so were threshing machines, which took much of the labor out of planting and harvesting.

When and where the peasant proprietor was able to keep his holdings intact, his income usually rose slightly prior to 1914. But though he sometimes got more, the peasant proprietor could not match the gains of either lower middle class elements or even some working class elements in the city. As a result, his income did decline in relation to that of others. Beyond this, there were numerous threats to the stability of peasant income. After 1880, grain prices for wheat, barley, and oats fell so precipitously in England that those crops were deserted by many. In Germany in 1914, the production of rye, the oldest European staple, was in some areas down to one-quarter of what it had been in 1880. Dutch and Danish peasants specializing in butter and pork were relatively safe up to 1895, but after that date, butter was imported into Europe on a massive scale and after 1905, pork and bacon from abroad began to intrude on the European market in an unprecedented way. Many peasant proprietors in Austria, after they had managed to get away from grain, had gone over to the production of eggs—economical, as it turned out, on relatively small plots. But the importation of eggs was again a major blow, the number of eggs coming into Europe increasing by 300 percent after 1890.

In order to protect themselves from dramatic fluctuations in income caused by changes in the market and foreign competition, some peasant proprietors began to join together in cooperatives. Rural cooperatives were organized to buy, sell, or provide credit. By 1886, organizers inside France had succeeded in creating a peasant organization, the UCSAF, the Central Union of French Agriculturists, designed to support traditional peasant life in the countryside. The organization, which by 1914 had 10,000 locals and 200,000 members, engaged in the cooperative buying of fertilizer, seed, and agricultural machinery. By World War I, some 750,000 French peasants were enlisted in cooperatives of one kind or another. In Denmark, cooperative dairies were the first such organizations to be founded. They were established in the 1870s primarily to market butter, but by 1900 there were 942 of them wholesaling almost every kind of dairy product. More common than cooperatives formed for purchasing and selling were savings associations. The vast majority of peasant proprietors were in need of credit, and cooperative banks were able to provide it. The so-called Raiffeisen cooperative banks in the German countryside were actually built around the accumulated savings of the peasantry. The banks, once they acquired sufficient capital, specialized in short-term loans, usually for five-year periods. In this way, many peasant proprietors in Germany were helped with credit as they shifted from one crop to another.

During the second half of the nineteenth century, peasant proprietors began to realize the degree to which their survival depended on protection against overseas competition. Almost everywhere in Europe, pressure from peasants or on their behalf lead to the establishment of at least partial tariff walls. By 1881, the French were excluding livestock, while Italy actually started to drive foreign wheat out of her national market in 1887. Germany made her first move against foreign agricultural products as early as 1879 and then proceeded to build her tariff walls even higher during the 1880s. By the 1890s, Austria, Hungary, Spain, and Russia, each with large peasant populations still on the soil, were all engaged in protection. Tariffs went a long way toward helping the peasant proprietor survive; he could not have weathered the competition with cheaper foreign producers. As a result, the peasant proprietor has been able to live on in the twentieth century, still subsidized and still an integral part of the European social order.

The Fate of the Landless Laborer

The landless peasant of the late nineteenth century was still a vital factor on the agricultural scene. His numbers were large. Even though some landless peasants left for the cities, there were always new recruits for this class. Those middle peasants who were bankrupted by crop failure, indebtedness, or depression and who could not bear to leave the land simply slid into the lower reaches of the peasantry, making a go of things thereafter as agricultural laborers. In the more advanced countries where the overall agricultural population was dropping, they were less numerous. Around 1900, there were only 2 million of them in Germany, and only 750,000 in Great Britain. But they existed on a much larger scale elsewhere. There were an estimated 3 million of them in France and Italy, respectively, while Hungary and Rumania had about a million and a quarter apiece.

It was obvious by 1914 that landless peasants were still a majority of the peasantry and that they could survive only by offering their labor for sale. A few at this level leased land as tenants, but their numbers were now really quite small, only about 5 percent of the total in Germany. The overwhelming majority made their way as hired agricultural laborers. The 2 million German agricultural workers around World War I made their living in slightly different ways. Some of them did work at specialized tasks, as vine-growers, milkers, and household servants. Most, however, did field work, and over a million lived on great estates as a permanent workforce. Another 800,000 worked as migratory laborers, a large portion of whom in eastern Germany were actually landless Polish peasants desperately searching for employment. In southern Spain, agricultural labor normally planted and harvested the grain and root crops grown on the large estates. Here, as was frequently the case elsewhere, the average laborer worked only about half the year, the rest of the time being inactive and without an income. If he did not make enough at harvest time, he might not survive until the following spring without public charity.

By the twentieth century, the wage system was being accepted by agricultural laborers. This had not always been the case, for prior to 1900 wages had often been paid in kind. In east Prussia, agricultural laborers in the past had been given a certain percentage of the crop in the hope that this would increase their productivity. But this system waned as it did elsewhere in Europe, giving way to the payment of wages. Such wages were generally low, leaving this particular element of the peasantry with the lowest standard of living of any group in society. The condition of English agricultural laborers may be taken as typical of what was happening elsewhere. Between 1795 and 1850, wages rose a bare 15 percent. Toward the 1870s farm labor in Britain did begin to organize and to force up wages, but the rates were still so low that the agricultural laborer was, in fact, the worst fed of all workers in the nineteenth century. In southern England, they often survived on just bread, with occasional bits of cheese or bacon, potatoes, and some tea. Meat, being consumed almost everywhere else in the nineteenth century, was still unknown at this particular level of English society.

The description of peasant life among those who owned no land whatsoever seems to fit the underdeveloped eighteenth century much more than the economically advanced nineteenth century. But then, those without special abilities simply did not fare well in a society in which skill and training were rewarded most. Unskilled farm labor was just like unskilled manual labor in the cities, poorly compensated for strenuous physical effort. The sheer number of agricultural workers limited the wages that they could demand because there was an oversupply of those willing to work. Moreover, staple production on the great estates did not automatically mean a continuous need for agricultural labor. The great estates of Britain, Prussia, Hungary, and Russia, especially if they grew grain, needed labor only seasonally. As a result, employment was only seasonal in many parts of Europe and so was income. Farm labor in the more advanced countries, Britain and Germany, did organize, but it never successfully broke the cycle of poverty.

By 1914, the mass of men in European society had been integrated into the existing order as never before. Prior to the industrial age, the vast majority had never been truly able to participate actively in the social life of the time. The peasant masses had never benefited in any way from preindustrial society. As the nineteenth century drew to a close, the masses had been truly transformed. The bottom levels of society, the manual laborers of the city and the agricultural workers of the countryside, did not seem to have changed all that much from the urban poor and landless peasants of the previous age. Their standard of living had hardly seemed to budge. But though they were kept down economically, they could still vote if they pleased and were entitled to at least an elementary education. In this sense, they were better off than their forebears.

The failure of industrial society to reward this submerged third of the population should not obscure the fact that a rising standard of living, more material comfort, and sometimes luxury had become available for the first time to the majority of people, not just the rich and powerful. Even with the insecurity an overdependence on profit could bring, the petty bourgeois shopkeeper and the distinctly lower class peasant proprietor could still partake of the advantages that modern society had to offer—better diet, improved schooling, and the right to organize and have one's political voice heard. Far more fortunate were those tied to the wage system, particularly the wage system that was built on certain mental skills and that had a built-in elevator clause. For the lower middle class teacher, foreman, and clerk could progressively depend on a rise in salaries, just like the skilled and semiskilled factory worker. The key to advancing income for these mass elements was bigness. Big government and big business were always able to pay more, thanks largely to greater tax revenue and greater profit. True, the masses would have to organize in order to get it, but it was there to be had.

Prior to 1914, the fate of masses under industrialism had been uneven. Most were living above the level of subsistence; a substantial minority was still not. The growing affluence of industrial society in the twentieth century would solve the problem of the poor, too. For the glaring difference between Europe's agricultural and industrial society was its potential. Europe's agricultural society could never have solved the problem of poverty. There was simply not enough food, clothing, and shelter for everyone. In this sense, Europe before 1800 was an underproductive society. And even if the well-to-do had been expropriated and their fortunes redistributed, it would not have been enough to improve the lot of the many. Only industrial society, with its capacity for the large-scale production of food and commodities, had the potential for eliminating poverty within society. And the elimination of poverty was done without serious governmental interference; it was accomplished through the willingness of the many to learn the skills demanded by the new industrial society. Those who were left out, the manual laborers, would be helped in time by a forced redistribution of wealth, a welfare state system that would at long last solve Europe's problem of poverty.

11

Advances and Changes in Modern Society

The transformation of European society that resulted from industrialization gave people the idea that change was a permanent feature of life. So much had changed, and in so relatively short a period of time, that age-old attitudes of resignation and endurance seemed as antiquated as knee breeches and powdered wigs. The migration of millions upon millions of peasants to the cities meant an unprecedented and unforeseen shift in population whose effects were compounded and intensified by growing social mobility. Not only had millions changed their place of residence, but a large proportion of the population was moving up in the social order. Adding to the spirit of optimism and progress were mass emigrations from Europe to North America. One no longer had to put up with a bad situation; it was possible to pick up and move on in search of new opportunities. The fatalism that had reinforced the old social order had now given way to the conviction that self-improvement could bring a better future.

The mass movement of people during the nineteenth century was truly astonishing. Not only did some 40 million Europeans leave the Continent, a mass exodus for which there was absolutely no precedent, but more than twice that number were involved in the internal migration from country to city. The result in Europe was the rise of two types of cities, expanded traditional commercial centers and new industrial towns. The greatest of these were metropolitan centers whose size could never have been imagined prior to the industrial age. In 1800, London with its 900,000 people and Paris with 600,000 were considered gigantic and unwieldy. Yet London would soon have a population of 9 million and Paris, 4 million.

Those who moved had a definite goal—an improved standard of living. This is exactly what the city offered. Not only were there more job opportunities, but there were larger supplies of food, better sanitation and health facilities, and greater chances for education and training. Indeed, the overall process of improvement in the nineteenth century was essentially an urban phenomenon; the city was the key to Europe's rising standard of living.

Urbanization

Urbanization in preindustrial Europe had been severely limited by the lack of agricultural surpluses. With food in such short supply, no more than 15 percent of Europe's 190 million people in 1800 lived in towns and cities. The extension of the food supply available to the cities, in combination with new job opportunities, led to the sudden growth of the nineteenth century. Population pressures in the countryside actually provided the cities with a host of new recruits. As the peasant population doubled during the century, a larger and larger proportion of the rural population was no longer needed in agriculture. Moreover, many peasants, tired of subsistence agriculture and low wages, simply picked up and headed for the city. Between mass migration from the countryside and natural increase in the cities, the size of the urban population began to swell. By 1900, western Europe was almost 45 percent urbanized, and eastern Europe 25 percent. This meant that 130 of Europe's 400 million people had now been absorbed by urban society. And still the process went on. It continued until the latter part of the twentieth century when Europe, both west and east, finally emerged as a society 85 percent urbanized.

The leading countries in the development of urbanization were, of course, those with the most mature industrial economies—Great Britain and Germany. England, in combination with Wales, is often said to be

the first urbanized country in Europe because by 1890 a full half of her population was living in cities and towns of 20,000 people or more. Over the course of ninety years, from 1800 on, England's population had expanded by some 20 million, of whom 85 percent had been absorbed by growing urban areas. Germany, her industrial revolution rolling after 1850, achieved urban status in 1900. Germany's rural population remained static at 26 million after 1871. All the gain in population after this went to the cities until, at the turn of the twentieth century, the urban and rural portions of her population were equal. Other countries also underwent urbanization at a pace not too much slower than that of England and Germany. By 1900, Belgium was 47 percent urbanized; Holland, Austria, and France, 33 percent; Italy, 25 percent. Russia, way behind, was still only 15 percent urbanized, although that figure is somewhat deceptive, since she did have nearly 20 million urban dwellers, the third largest total in all of Europe.

These urban dwellers lived in two types of cities: the old commercial centers, and new industrial towns. Old urban areas like London, Paris, Rome, Berlin, Vienna, and St. Petersburg continued to grow. Vienna was a typical example; its population rose from 600,000 in 1857 to 1,350,000 in 1890 and then peaked at around 2 million just prior to the outbreak of World War I. The rise of great metropolitan centers during the nineteenth century was impressive: London had a population of 4.5 million by the end of the century, Paris 2.5 million, Berlin 1.5 million, and St. Petersburg a little over a million. But the characteristic city of the nineteenth century was the middle-sized industrial town.

Manufacturing was, of course, the great source of population increase. Once an industry was successfully planted in a town, it tended to expand almost automatically, and very often the growth rate was a standard tenfold factor. This was true, for example, of Sheffield, Barmen, Graz, and Lodz. Barmen's rising population after 1809 was a reflection of yet another process—the tendency of industrial towns to accelerate growth by means of the progressive addition of industry. Barmen began the nineteenth century as a small town in the Wupper Valley of western Germany with a population of 16,646. A century later, with the steady expansion of both textile mills and chemical factories, the population was 169,214.

The gravitational pull being exercised by commercial and industrial centers drew immigrants in great numbers from nearby areas. Most cities grew so fast that immigrants soon far outnumbered the native-born. For example, in Stockholm 75 percent of all those added to the city's population in the 1880s and 1890s were migrants, most of whom came from surrounding rural areas. The change was so dramatic that French newspapers in the 1850s and 1860s complained that the area around Paris was becoming depopulated. One study of 420 immigrants entering London in 1881 showed that 166 had traveled less than 23 miles to get there, another 121 had come from within 52 miles of the city, and an additional 61 migrants had originated within a 90-mile radius of the metropolis. Those who traveled longer distances were helped by the existence of rail facilities. But even with this option, the typical nineteenth-century migrant moving in the direction of one of the industrial towns went only a distance of 30 or 40 miles. By heading for the nearest city, the average peasant migrant was able to maintain ties with his home village and so soften the impact of the move.

Right up until the 1870s, preindustrial cities maintained older types of economies and offered jobs in commerce or in the guilds as they always had. The Industrial Revolution did not at first touch them directly; it was only later that manufacturing establishments would attach themselves to traditional commercial centers. For developing alongside the older centers was a second set of cities, almost totally dependent on industry. Many of these were often confined to a single specialized industry. In a number of instances, however, these separate industrial towns began to grow into one another and form enlarged manufacturing areas known as industrial complexes. The Rhine-Ruhr complex is a prime example of this phenomenon, as is the area around Lille in northern France, some of the contiguous manufacturing centers of northern England, and the Ukrainian industrial complex in Russia.

The Rhine-Ruhr industrial complex in western Germany developed stage by stage during the course of the nineteenth century, beginning with the discovery of coal in the Ruhr Valley. Up to mid-century, most of what would become the great industrial cities of the area were little more than towns or villages. Many, like Oberhausen, had about 15,000 people, and none had more than 60,000 in 1871, not even Essen, the center of the Krupp iron and steel works. But as coal was mined in greater and greater quantities, the iron and steel industry began to give economic life to the area. While metallurgical production was developing in industrial towns like Essen, Dortmund, and Mülheim, textiles were being encouraged in nearby Krefeld and a chemical industry was being founded in Barmen and Leverkusen. In every instance, these towns grew into middle-sized cities of 200,000 to 400,000 people where the majority of those gainfully employed were occupied in factory work. It is little wonder that peasants headed for the cities of the Rhine-Ruhr industrial complex, for by the end of the nineteenth century, the area already had nearly a million jobs in mining and manufacturing.

The development of Russia's Ukrainian industrial complex followed a similar pattern. Urbanization in Russia, outside of Moscow and what used to be St. Petersburg, tended to concentrate on certain key industrial sites. As in the case of the Rhine-Ruhr complex, the great manufacturing centers of the Ukraine grew up before and after World War I in response to the discovery of coal, this time in the mineral-rich Donets Basin. It was only a matter of time before an iron and steel industry based on such cities as Zhdanov, Kramatorsk, and Konstantinovka would come into existence. These towns and cities developed populations in the nineteenth and twentieth centuries ranging from about 100,000 to 500,000 people. The chief means of employment in these industrial cities was factory labor. Eventually, 55 percent of the jobs in the city of Zhdanov were in the iron and steel industry. The figures for the total number of gainfully employed in Kramatorsk and Konstantinovka were even higher in the twentieth century. In these two metallurgical centers, 65 percent of the jobs were filled by those working in factories. Between mining in the Donets Basin and manufacturing in the surrounding industrial centers of the Ukraine, hundreds of thousands of jobs were created before 1914 and several million after 1928, when Russia began to industrialize even more extensively than before. Just as in the case of the Rhine-Ruhr, the placement of industry in the heart of the Ukraine attracted thousands of peasants from surrounding areas, each in search of greater economic opportunity.

In the course of time, industry was to become the characteristic feature of every European city, for toward the end of the nineteenth century, large-scale manufacturing finally began to attach itself to the great commercial centers of Europe. This meant that by the 1860s and 1870s, industry was locating itself in cities like London, Paris, Berlin, Vienna, and St. Petersburg. If anything, the addition of industry to the burgeoning economies of Europe's major preindustrial centers spurred the expansion of their populations even more, to the point where they were now becoming truly gigantic. Berlin picked up an electronics industry; St. Petersburg, metallurgical facilities; Vienna, chemical industries; and Paris, automotive assembly plants. London after 1860 was typical in the way that it developed factory industry. The first major industry to locate itself in London featured the manufacturing of lighter metallurgical products, so that in time London was producing elevators, refrigerators, automotive parts, scales, stoves, and meters. By the 1880s, London had an electronics industry specializing in the production of lamps, irons, switching gear, and then radios. Finally, just prior to World War I, London became a major automotive assembly center.

Although the cities were able to absorb the flow of population from the countryside and provide the overwhelming mass with employment and improved diet, they could not help the migrants in every way, housing being the most conspicuous lack. Still, the pressure on the cities never became so great that it broke down the cities' ability to assimilate immigrants. During the period from 1858 to 1875, for instance, the cities of Germany took in migrants at a rate of increase of 3.2 percent per year. After 1875, the rate was even lower, only 1.6 percent. What these figures suggest is that the flow was both continuous and steady, but never staggering in terms of overall numbers.

Those who left the countryside to make the short-distance move to a city usually settled permanently once they got there. Census data for London in 1881 shows that 80 percent of those born in the city remained there, while in Vienna the census of 1890 proved that 85 percent of the native-born Viennese population had stayed in the city. As might be expected, those who did penetrate the city were young. A special study done of the migrants entering Frankfurt in the early 1890s revealed that the average age of the immigrants was twenty-two. Generally speaking, it was the younger peasant who was leaving the land, but somewhat surprisingly, women left more often than men. In England and Wales, 104 women moved off the land for every 100 males; in Scotland it was 108, and in Ireland 104. Evidently these women were looking for economic opportunities as domestic servants or factory workers. Those opportunities were definitely there: The German census of 1890 showed that the larger the city, the less the degree of unemployment. Even more, the class of urban poor in these cities was at long last beginning to disappear.

The city had marked effects on the expanding population within its confines. As an example, the marriage rate among the urban population was much higher than it was in the countryside. Studies done on Stockholm and rural areas surrounding it show this to be true from 1851 on. The increase in the marriage rate in the cities was the direct result of the city's younger population and the fact that healthier types in the cities were now more willing to take on the responsibilities of married life. What is more, the birth rate in the cities was actually higher than it was in the countryside. Rural poverty had always limited the number of live births. Since the city improved standards, especially in health and stamina, it was inevitable that the birth rate would be higher. Closely tied to this fact was evidence proving that people in the mining and industrial areas of northern France, southern Belgium, and western Germany normally outlived those in the immediate rural areas around them during the late nineteenth century. All of this suggests, of course, that the great urban breakthrough in diet had a much more profound effect on population than had previously been suspected. Indeed, diet may very well have been at the center of Europe's rising standard of living, higher birth rate, and increasing life expectancy.

Social Mobility

Social mobility was a characteristic of nineteenth-century European society. The mass movement of individuals up and down the social ladder after 1800 was in striking contrast to Europe's static preindustrial society. The population movement off the land and into cities was made even more dynamic by growing commerce and industry, which in turn spurred social growth and initiative. But those who did achieve a new and often higher status in society did so only by coming to terms with the new industrial age. Aristocrats who clung to an old way of life, artisans who insisted on pursuing handicraft industry, or peasants who were unable to adjust to market agriculture were all eliminated. Upward mobility was only possible for those willing to accept bourgeois ways. Many peasants, willing to do this, rose in urban society to achieve either a working class or a middle class position.

Since what one did for a living became the way in which individuals were distinguished from one another, social mobility was almost always defined by occupation and skill in the new industrial age. The conversion of peasants into factory workers was the most common type of occupational mobility. Later, the tendency among factory workers was for the son to follow the father, so that the class by 1900 began to take on a distinct hereditary character. There was to be occupational change for the majority of factory workers in the twentieth century, but it was to be the result of automation, which reduced the need for unskilled labor while greatly expanding the number of skilled and semiskilled jobs in industry. In other words, most factory workers improved themselves without leaving their class. This does not mean that there was no further upward mobility, for a significant minority of the sons of factory workers did penetrate the middle class during the late 1800s and early 1900s. In fact, successful movement up the social ladder was most likely to be accomplished by the sons of factory workers. The factory was essentially an upper middle class institution; it operated in the precise and workmanlike manner demanded by its owners. Those who absorbed the order and discipline of the factory and passed it on to their sons guaranteed their sons a chance in middle class society. After all, in a real sense, they were already prepared for it.

This fact is borne out by a number of studies done in Europe before 1914, in particular in Germany, showing that the working class was indeed the jumping-off place for the middle class. By far the most extensive investigation ever done of social mobility prior to 1914 was conducted by the German trade unions in the late 1920s. Its findings on white collar workers reflected social movement both before and after World War I. The data collected from this study of some 90,000 individuals working in middle class positions revealed that 24 percent of the males questioned had clear-cut working class backgrounds. What is more, among those who were thirty years of age, 32 percent came out of the working class, indicating that movement upward into the various levels of the middle class among the young was now even more pronounced.

These findings parallel earlier research on social mobility done in both Germany and England. For example, in 1906 it was reported that 30 percent of the workers employed in the Krupp works in Essen for thirty years or more had sons who had left the working class and taken up middle class occupations. A similar pattern could be detected among immigrant families in Karlsruhe over several generations. It was discovered that 25 percent of the grandsons of peasant immigrants to this German city now held lower middle class positions within society, while another 15 percent had attained professional status. This remarkable prewar record of social mobility was matched by the truly astounding discovery in 1912 that two-thirds of the owners, directors, and managers in the cotton mills of Lancashire had begun their careers as clerical workers or factory hands.

Not everyone experiencing social mobility moved up, either socially or economically; for many it was a downward plunge. The artisan class more often than not wound up members of the new factory working class. This group was especially conspicuous in the German factory system. In some instances after 1890, a significant minority of factory workers had fathers who had been either self-employed or had worked in nonmanual middle class occupations. Some were evidently artisans, others just victims of the vagaries of fortune. Evidence of downward mobility can be found elsewhere. In Rome after the turn of the century, a full 22 percent of all manual workers had fathers who had held middle class positions. The clerical element in England was known to contain a number of business and professional people who had failed to make it in the higher reaches of the middle class and who now had to settle for petty bourgeois positions.

Social mobility during the course of the nineteenth century shaped the nature of mass society. It led to the dissolution of older social groups and the rise of new mass elements. In the more prosperous economic groups, social mobility was also significant in reshaping the bourgeois elite. It is true that many business and professional elements were already well established long before the Industrial Revolution. Still there were some, entrepreneurs and managers mostly, who were able to penetrate the upper middle class. If others did not go this high, at least they might aspire to a professional status in society. This process, often described as elite mobility, was obvious at certain points during the era of social transformation. For example, the well-to-do elements in Parisian society rose from 2.4 percent of the city's total population to 3.7 percent between 1820 and 1847. And this happened while the city itself was growing in population. In England, the number of men in the upper reaches of the middle class enjoying yearly incomes of £5000 or more increased four times between 1801 and 1851. In the middle of the century, most of Germany's leading industrialists were from the lower reaches of the middle class.

The number who could penetrate the upper middle class was, of course, proportionately quite small. What is more, this area of the middle class, after taking in some recruits, tended to close up very quickly, largely because the amount of money needed to maintain oneself at this level of society was extraordinarily large. For those who wanted to experience elite mobility, the next best thing to business achievement was professional status. The professions expanded largely in response to new educational opportunities. In Holland, the expansion of the educational system by 1919 allowed a number of mass elements to move up into the middle middle class, but after this date upward mobility leveled off and then came to an end. Those lower down in the social order could also hope to attain a civil service or a managerial position in countries like England and Germany if they had the educational background or if they were promoted through the ranks.

Considering how long Europe's preindustrial society was in existence, it is surprising how quickly it was transformed by economic change. Within two generations, the older society was disappearing and a new industrial order was taking its place. The process of change was so fast that by 1914 in the more highly industrialized countries, the new social order was beginning to take on a permanent character. After several decades of change, social mobility was actually coming to an end. The upper reaches of the middle class had expanded and become hereditary within a few decades of the beginning of the Industrial Revolution. No sooner had this group closed off than the professions opened up, thanks to the expansion of higher education, but here too the period of growth and addition was comparatively short-lived. By 1914, the professions were also becoming hereditary. Even before this, the business and professional elements were more than able to guard their privileged position because they alone had easy access to higher education and thereby to the dominant positions in modern industrial society.

Social mobility was also eventually to slow among the masses. The situation had been dynamic for many decades; the lower reaches of the middle class added one new stratum after another during the century. First there were shopkeepers, then clerks, then preprofessionals. As each new layer emerged, lower class elements were encouraged to try for a higher social position. At the same time, there were internal shifts within the working class. Manual workers had an opportunity to enter the factory system, which continued to grow right through the twentieth century, especially as the chemical, electronics, and automotive industries expanded even further. There was increasing movement within the factory system as well, as the unskilled received more and more formal training and began to move into the categories of skilled and semiskilled labor.

All this dynamism belied the fact that the age of social change was coming to an end by 1914. Social mobility, especially in the west, was slowing. Many positions within society were once again becoming hereditary, particularly after social mobility had actually been achieved. Once the various classes began to fill up, the new hereditary character of European society became more and more discernible. Opportunities for advancement were steadily being cut down as one social group after another began to settle in place. For change is not a permanent feature of industrial society; it is only a characteristic of eras of transition—in this instance, the historic passage of Europe from an agrarian to an industrial society. Once the transition neared completion, Europe's social classes would begin to take on a distinctly hereditary air, with sons following fathers at the same social and economic level, just as in preindustrial society.

As it turned out, however, the era of social change was not over. It might have come to an end except for the social and economic consequences of World War I, which caused so much loss of life that society was to a degree churned up all over again.

Mass Migration

The shift of Europe's rural population into the cities represents just one of the mass movements of the nineteenth century; the other was overseas migration. After 1820, some 40 million Europeans would choose to leave the Continent. For the most part, those who left were artisans and peasants displaced by economic change. They were either masters or journeymen trying to save their old way of life, or middle or landless peasants seeking to survive in another area of the globe. Either way, those who left tended to be individuals who were losing their former identities because of social and economic changes that benefitted others. There was, then, an element of misfortune involved in overseas migra-

tion, with the majority of immigrants coming from the poorer classes. In fact, it may be argued that the United States, which took in the vast majority of these people, actually acquired a peasant population for the first time.

The distinctly lower class nature of European emigration that drained off parts of the artisan and peasant class began in the late 1810s and continued throughout the century. The first wave of emigration, lasting into the 1850s, came predominantly from northern Europe and featured the exodus of English, Irish, and Germans. The numbers leaving during the first half-century did not involve more than 3 million, small in comparison with the truly massive waves of the last half of the century, which involved tens of millions of people. Assistance to emigrants was, generally speaking, the exception, although some British migrants, both English and Irish, did make it to Canada and the United States as a result of philanthropy. More interesting than the aid itself were those who were encouraged to leave in this manner. A few yeoman farmers, better off than most, were encouraged to settle along the Canadian side of the St. Lawrence River, but the vast majority who left in this way were poor and indigent. For example, in 1823 a small group of 568 Irish peasants were aided by the Reverend Peter Robinson, whose main concern seems to have been to rid some of the local districts of their paupers. Among others given the opportunity to settle in North America were individuals described by sea captains as "street-urchins" and "girl-arabs." Still others receiving help were "destitute laborers, ejected tenants and poor cotters" from Ireland. Some of the English helped over in the 1830s were listed as former shopkeepers and shoemakers. So, while there were some yeomen and artisans involved in the movement out of the British Isles in the 1820s and 1830s, not even assisted emigration hid the fact that those leaving had a definite lower class and peasant background.

The most spectacular outburst of emigration, involving more than a million people, came as a result of the Irish potato famine of the middle and late 1840s. There had been smaller waves of Irish emigration before this time: By 1827, 20,000 Irish peasants a year were emigrating, and by 1838, the figure was above 30,000. Those leaving were largely evicted tenants unable to meet their annual rents. They could make the trip from the north of Ireland to the United States for as little as £5. From the start, those who left were primarily from Ireland's huge class of landless peasants, those who had previously survived as tenants or, in some cases, agricultural laborers. Sprinkled among them were some artisans, but, in the main, it was the Irish peasantry that was deserting the land and leaving for England, Canada, and the United States. When the potato, the agricultural staple, was destroyed by blight starting in

1845, famine struck. Hundreds of thousands emigrated in the belief that "poor Ireland's done" and "the country's gone forever." From 1847 to 1854 some 200,000 Irish peasants a year emigrated, deserting the land and the system of tenantry that had been the only way of life the bulk of them had ever known.

The sudden rush of Irish peasants to North America eventually matched, numerically, the somewhat slower movement of German emigrants to the New World that had been going on at a much steadier pace. German peasants who emigrated were moved less by disaster than by inducements. Stories circulated widely in the peasant villages of western Germany that America was abundant in food. It was said that peaches and apples rotted in Ohio for want of anyone to eat them, that farmers often left enough ungleaned grain in their fields to feed a parish. They understood that common laborers ate meat daily and that it was even possible for an ordinary worker to buy a whole pig for himself. In the unsophisticated world of the German peasant, struggling year in and year out with subsistence, such stories might well have been an inducement to emigrate.

Reinforcing the exodus of German peasants was the desire of younger sons for land. Thanks to better nutrition, more peasants were living and inheriting, and peasant plots were becoming smaller and smaller. Many middle peasants in Germany were now willing to leave in the hope of being able to obtain land in the New World. Adding to their woes was the loss of income resulting from the decline of the domestic system in the rural areas of the Rhineland, Westphalia, and Hesse, plus a succession of crop failures. The result of all these pressures was increasing emigration by middle and landless peasants.

Beginning in the 1830s, the German peasantry, joined by some artisan elements, began to emigrate, more than half a million of them before 1845. The movement was facilitated by cheaper and cheaper means of transportation, first sailing ships and then steamships. German emigration reached a high point during the middle part of the century. Between 1852 and 1854, half a million Germans left the country, a flood of outward-bound migration previously surpassed only by the mass exodus of Irish after the famine. Those who were leaving now were distinctly lower class. For example, in 1853–54 the bulk of those emigrating from Pomerania were apprentices, agricultural laborers, or shepherds. During the early 1880s, still other German peasants were driven to emigrate by the failure of the grain crops. Once again disaster was the prelude to another mass migration, as some three-quarters of a million Germans, mostly peasants, left their native land.

The last great movement of peasants from western and northern Europe was the German migration of the early 1880s. After this, those leaving the Continent came in overwhelming numbers from southern and eastern Europe, primarily from Italy and the Slavic countries. Italian migration, which began in the 1880s and reached a floodtide after 1900, tended to draw the poor peasant population of southern Italy from the land. Whole areas of Campania, the Abruzzi, Calabria, and Sicily were depopulated as a result of the removal of almost 4 million Italians to such areas as the United States and Argentina. Italian emigration never had peak periods; rather, it was a steady flow of about 100,000 per year prior to 1900 and then about 200,000 annually after the turn of the century. Those leaving were, again, distinctly of peasant and artisan origin. The American Consul in Naples, F. L. Dingley, watched this movement closely, and his comments give a good insight into the basic sociological character of this movement. Dingley's 1890 official report included the judgment that "about eighty-five percent of the emigration from Italy to the United States comes from southern Italy. . . . From eighty-five to ninety percent of the Italian emigration is the peasantry from the land; the rest are tailors, shoemakers and carpenters." In part, Dingley's judgment was based on his analysis of a group of Italian emigrants sailing from Naples on the English steamship *Britannia*. After interviewing this group, he reported, "I was able to find among these 1,075 emigrants not one dweller in an Italian city; all were peasants originally in Italy." [1]

Emigration from the Slavic areas of Europe in the last half of the nineteenth century was really quite pronounced. More than 4 million people left Russia, in the main Poles, Ukrainians, and Jews. Among the Poles and Ukrainians, the great majority were from the poorer peasant classes. Predominating among those listed as emigrating from the Ukraine were agricultural laborers, tenants, and middle peasants. Among Polish emigrants leaving the Russian-ruled part of Poland around 1900, a full 56 percent were landless peasants who had previously worked as agricultural laborers. Of the overall total of those included in the study, only 10 percent had owned land. Jewish emigration from Russia, which reached the hundreds of thousands by the late nineteenth century, differed from the general character of European migration, for these people were urban rather than rural in origin. In this sense the Jews were unique, for everywhere else the rural pattern held. For example, elsewhere in eastern Europe, the 1.5 million Slavs, primarily Czechs, Slovenes, Croats, and Serbs, who emigrated before World War I were overwhelmingly of peasant origin.

The motive behind most of this movement out of Europe was plainly economic. Consul Dingley, who had a persistent interest in emi-

---

[1] F. L. Dingley, *European Emigration* (Washington, D.C.: U.S. Government Printing Office, 1890), pp. 216, 223.

gration and its causes, interviewed others embarking from the port of Bremen in Germany for the New World. He came across the same story over and over again—the emigrants, in this case Hungarians, were leaving in the hope of finding greater economic opportunity. One of the Hungarians commented to Dingley, "I go to Cleveland to work in copper works; my brother is there; he makes four times the wages he could in Hungary. I was a farm worker in Hungary. I shall send for my family as soon as I get money enough to pay their passage." Still another added, "I go to join my son who is in Pittsburgh where he makes $1.50 a day— four times the wages in Hungary." [2] Yet another young Hungarian girl told Dingley that she had made the equivalent of $7 a year working for the family of a Hungarian nobleman, but was now emigrating because she heard that she could make the same amount in the United States in just two weeks. These stories, like those about food, probably encouraged emigration more than any other single factor.

The Rising Standard of Living

The most pervasive change that the nineteenth century produced was in dietary patterns, for it was the improving level of nutrition that lay at the heart of Europe's rising standard of living. There were so many changes during these decades—the mass shift of population from the countryside to the cities, emigration overseas, the growth of industrialization, increasing social mobility—that it would have been easy to lose sight of the major victory over poor nutrition. The change in diet that so improved the quality of life at this time helped, along with advances in public health and sanitation toward the end of the century, to make existence much more tolerable for the average European. Dietary change was a continuous feature of nineteenth-century life. The first major shift came as the potato began to supplement grain. Then more nutritious foods such as meat, milk, vegetables, and fruits were added to the diet. Standards of cleanliness and public health also improved during the century; the use of soap on a wide scale along with vaccinations and modern systems of sewage disposal all progressively liberated the European population from the scourge of bacterial and viral disorders.

The doubling of the population during the first half of the nineteenth century can be directly traced to the addition of the potato to the basic peasant diet. It is true that the cities of Europe absorbed excess population in the second half of the century, but the population explosion began as a rural phenomenon. As an example, the population of

2 Dingley, *European Emigration*, p. 257.

rural Pomerania in Germany rose faster than that in many urban areas between 1816 and 1849, a pattern statistics show was just as true of Norway, Russia, and other areas in Europe. In more precise terms, this meant a decline in infant and childbirth mortality in rural areas and a growth in longevity. What the potato did was to give to the rural population vitamins A, C, and E. With those vitamins, the body was better able to fight off the invasion of bacteria. Now the young infant had at least some protection against such childhood diseases as diphtheria, while his parents had a better chance of warding off cholera and typhus. A classic example is the disappearance of typhus among the Irish peasantry after the potato became a staple in their diet. The disease reappeared in 1847 only after the potato crop had failed twice and the peasantry had lost its immunity as a result of famine and poor nutrition.

The greatest nutritional gains came in the cities, where food existed in greater abundance and quantity. It was here that meat, milk, fruits, and vegetables were added to the diet on a truly grand scale. The addition of protein from meat made for a much stronger and more energetic population. Meat also provided such vital minerals as iron and potassium, to say nothing of more of the B vitamins. Milk did much the same thing, adding calcium to the diet, complementing the amount of protein already in the body, and strengthening the total of B complex vitamins in the system. Fruits and vegetables gave a higher blood-sugar level, which automatically meant more energy, plus the disease-fighting vitamins A, C, and E. Eating patterns all over Europe toward the end of the century revealed a trend to better nutrition. By the turn of the twentieth century, Italians, to take one example, were already consuming large quantities of vegetables and fruit. There was still grain in the Italian diet, but now it was being complemented by other foods. In Rome, average consumption of meat was up to 88 pounds a year by 1893. In the working class center of Turin, in the north, the unskilled were consuming 28 pounds of meat a year, the skilled 50. These figures do not, however, compare with England and Germany. In England by this time, the poorest elements in society were already averaging close to 60 pounds of meat a year, while in Germany the national average for meat consumption was already over 100 pounds per person per year.

The addition of more calories, proteins, vitamins, and minerals to the basic diet was bound to have some conspicuous results. The most obvious of all was the decline in infant mortality, as better nutrition went a long way toward eradicating the previous cause of death among infants, organic failure. By 1902, infant mortality rates had fallen to about 14 percent in France and 16 percent in Prussia, a real gain over the past when half of the children had failed to survive. Rates of life expectancy were also going up thanks to better nutrition. In 1840, in all of western Europe, the average male was living to be thirty-eight, the average female forty-one. By 1910, those figures had jumped considerably: the average male now living to be forty-nine, the average female fifty-two. The rise in nutritional standards during the nineteenth century sharply curtailed the rate of childbirth mortaility and created a situation in which women were now outliving men. Better nutrition also meant, of course, a declining death rate. Statistics for the German industrial center of Barmen reveal a pattern characteristic of all of Europe. From 1858 to 1910, the population of Barmen grew from 45,000 to 169,000, yet during the same period the death rate fell from 26 per 1,000 inhabitants each year to 17.

There was other evidence to indicate that the population was better off biologically. The average European had, over the course of the century, grown considerably in stature, so that as of 1900 males averaged 5'8" in height, while females were about 5'2" tall. The history of World War I also suggests that the population was better off nutritionally. All told, almost 60 million men served in the armed forces of the various European countries between 1914 and 1918. Many of them saw combat duty in the trenches whose conditions were truly appalling. Yet most of them escaped disease. In a previous era, disease would have taken a terrible toll, but there were no major epidemics during World War I. At the end of the war, in 1918 and 1919, the general population was struck by an epidemic of influenza that took some 2 million lives. The epidemic caused this much death only after segments of the European population had been left undernourished toward the end of the war as a result of rationing. Only when the food supply was actually cut back did portions of the population weaken and become susceptible to attack from this viral disorder.

While health was being improved all over Europe by rising standards of food consumption, other factors also contributed to an improvement in the physical character of life. Cleanliness was becoming a much more important consideration. Soap, in such short supply prior to the nineteenth century, was becoming plentiful and easy to obtain at retail outlets. The growing acceptance of cotton clothing also contributed measurably to rising standards of personal hygiene, largely because cotton goods were so much easier to clean than woolen or linen garments. Beyond this, the rise of the chemical industry meant the production of ammonia and other cleaning agents used increasingly by the general population.

The major impediment to a cleaner urban environment prior to the second half of the nineteenth century had been the lack of an adequate water supply. Most municipalities could supply their citizens with only 10 or 12 gallons of water per person each day. The supply of water was usually so short that there was never enough for flushing human waste from the city. Vienna, with an advanced sewage system, was an exception. It was only after 1850 that metal and clay conduits could be produced cheaply enough to supply industrial centers such as Manchester and ports like Liverpool with an adequate water supply. Another contribution to improvements in public health after the 1880s was the introduction of vaccination, which by late in the century had become commonplace.

Credit is often given the sanitary and medical breakthroughs of the nineteenth century for Europe's rapid rise in population. For the most part, however, these innovations came so late and touched the masses in such a marginal way that they do not really account for the improvement in the physical character of life that made population growth possible. Evidence is now accumulating that the death rate really began to fall in areas such as England, the Low Countries, and Scandinavia in the eighteenth century as a result of improved agricultural yields and dietary advances. During the course of the nineteenth century, higher nutritional standards spread to other countries as the food supply multiplied and as the variety of food was measurably increased. All of this suggests that the conclusion of some recent observers, Thomas McKeown and R. G. Record, who in 1962 insisted, "The fact that mortality fell rapidly from the time when nutrition improved, and when there is no reason to believe that exposure to infection was reduced, seems to us to provide good grounds for regarding diet as an important factor," [3] is accurate. As knowledge about nutrition increases, it may not be long before nutrition is recognized as perhaps the most important factor supporting Europe's rising standard of living during the nineteenth century.

[3] Thomas McKeown and R. G. Record, "Reasons for the Decline of Mortality in England and Wales during the 19th Century," *Population Studies,* I (1962), 115.

Part Three

European Society after World War I 1914-1939

World War I devastated Europe, disrupting its economy and creating a decade of social instability. The mighty economy that had produced the greatest industrial powers in the world was by 1918 close to breakdown. The serious dislocation caused by the massive loss of men, material, and capital during World War I had a shocking impact on society. After decades of continuous growth, Europe in 1918 was no longer in a position to support the material expectations of a large part of its population. Most seriously hurt were the members of the lower class, especially the working class. Caught between unemployment and inflation, the overall purchasing power of the working class declined. This led in turn to shrinking profits and opportunities for the middle class, since their livelihood now depended to some extent on the ability of lower class elements to buy. The result was working class discontent that manifested itself in the form of strikes and riots.

The material deprivations caused by World War I, distressing in themselves, were nothing in comparison with the suffering caused by loss of life and injuries. The fighting between 1914 and 1918 cost Europe almost 36 million killed, missing, and wounded. All levels of society were affected. Junior officers with business and professional backgrounds were slaughtered in large numbers in the bloody trench fighting; so were talented peasant proprietors and skilled members of the industrial labor force. Actually, the majority of those who died in combat were of peasant origin, because the various European countries began at one point to exempt certain skilled workers from the draft. France withdrew machinists from the army in 1915 and Great Britain exempted shipyard workers in 1916. They were needed in industry. Still, Europe wasted some of the most talented elements in its society, whose loss once again set in motion the process of social mobility as the survivors tried to fill the positions left vacant.

Europe, both west and east, groped its way back from the serious economic and social dislocations caused by the war. It was not until 1926 that the European economies, including that of the Soviet Union, regained 1914 levels of production. As the economy stabilized once more, so did the social order. Working class discontent ebbed, and profits began to grow again. Then Europe was hit by still another devastating economic crisis, the Great Depression. After five years of expansion, the economy suddenly contracted in 1931, just as it had in 1918. This time there was unemployment on an even wider scale, purchasing power declined even more precipitously, and profits and opportunities shriveled up all over again. The working class had been most seriously hurt in the economic aftermath of World War I, but the Depression touched all levels of society. Among those most frightened and disturbed were the members of the middle class. The petty bourgeoisie, distrustful of working class demands and tending to blame the upper reaches of the middle class for their difficulties, turned to fascism. Hitler moved to the center of German political life with the backing of a frightened lower middle class.

The economic ups and downs of the interwar period threatened what had been a rising standard of living. The era of steady gain before 1914 had created hopes and expectations of more at almost every level of society. World War I and the Great Depression dashed those hopes. The rise and then decline in the standard of living, which occurred not just once but twice in the interwar period, led eventually to louder and louder demands for economic security. The result was a determination after World War II to achieve greater social justice and to ensure economic progress for all by means of an expanding system of welfare state legislation. Once introduced, the system helped to eliminate many of the insecurities that between 1919 and 1939 had caused massive social unrest.

12

The Economic
and Social Consequences
of the War

World War I took a staggering amount of money to finance. General estimates place the value of war goods, such as guns, uniforms, and airplanes, at something like $331 billion. This is what the various European governments paid out just for the production of materièl. An additional $273 billion was spent on military salaries, crop subsidies, and loans, at a time when the gross national product of the United States was estimated to be around $50 billion. The Allies and the Central Powers resorted to two techniques in order to accumulate the money needed for the war. One was taxation; the other was borrowing.

Great Britain quadrupled its tax revenues from 1914 to 1918; France increased her taxes by about 60 percent; and taxes in Germany during the war tripled. Both France and Russia introduced the income tax in an attempt to raise revenue. The result was to dry up the sources of middle class capital available for immediate and long term investment. Heavy taxation also affected the lower classes, particularly in France.

The general population found the price of consumer items shooting up because the government, to finance the war, had levied a heavy turnover tax on basic commodities. In fact, the turnover tax, which affects those with lesser incomes most, was France's principal source of war revenue. Besides taxation, all countries involved in World War I resorted to borrowing. Government on both sides literally forced their own banks to loan them money in exchange for treasury notes. These notes carried a promise to pay at some future date, but had the ultimate result of drying up deposits and other sources of capital in the banking system. By resorting to excessive taxation and heavy borrowing, the wartime governments of Europe absorbed much of the capital in society and used it to pay for the cost of noncapital goods—that is, war materials. The result was a desperate shortage of capital for recovery after 1918.

During World War I there was an unparalleled loss of human life. All told, 9 million men were killed in the fighting, another 5 million were reported missing, 7 million were permanently disabled, and yet another 15 million were wounded more or less seriously. Russia, Austria-Hungary, France, and Germany all lost more than a million men killed. Russia alone had taken some 3.5 million casualties by the early part of 1917, at a time when she was already too exhausted to continue the war. France, her population already small in comparison with neighboring Germany, lost 1.5 million men dead and another 750,000 permanently disabled. The Battle of Verdun in the early part of 1916, which cost the Germans 300,000 dead and the French nearly a half a million casualties, was typical of the slaughter. In the wake of artillery and machine-gun fire, in the words of the military historian Cyril Falls,

> The landscape assumed a lunar aspect, an unending succession of shell craters, some immense. The woodlands were reduced to a debris of tangled, shattered boughs and stumps. Here and there rotting bodies of men and horses protruded from the churned and tortured soil. As the weather grew warmer the stench of carrion became more disgusting. Troops left long in this inferno appeared to age. Their eyes sank in their heads; their features became drawn.[1]

Conditions were no different along the eastern front. The American war correspondent John Reed, reporting from Serbia, described the same sights: "A smell of decaying bodies and neglected filth was in the air." Describing the aftermath of a battle between Serbian and Austrian forces, he wrote: "All of this country has been burned, looted, and its people murdered. Not an ox was seen, and for miles not a single human

[1] Hanson W. Baldwin, *World War I* (New York: Harper & Row, 1962), p. 77.

being lived." [2] It was from this kind of devastation that Europe would somehow have to recover in 1918.

The Dislocation
of the European Economy

The destruction caused by World War I, coupled with the national antagonisms that developed afterward, seriously disrupted the European economy. Before 1914, goods, services, and capital had passed fairly easily from one country to another, and one economy had reenforced another. All this ended in 1918, as each country in Europe tried to recover by means of independent effort. The two countries that suffered the most serious dislocations were France and Russia. France's main industrial areas along the Belgian and German borders had been ravaged by years of warfare on the western front, while Russia's industrial establishment had collapsed as a result of World War I and the revolution that began in 1917. Germany's industrial plant, by contrast, was still very much intact as of 1918, but its wealth was soon to be drained off by British, French, and Belgian demands for reparations. Only the British and Italian economies remained relatively strong, although both now were burdened by indebtedness and a serious lack of investment capital, the universal problem of the postwar period.

France's industrial and agricultural production had been severely reduced by German occupation of her northern and eastern departments. The war in the west, largely fought on French soil, had taken 70 percent of her coal and 80 percent of her iron ore. Even worse, 80 percent of her prewar textile and metallurgical facilities had been located in areas where the brunt of the fighting had taken place. And a full 15 percent of her agricultural land had been cut off from production by the fighting. It is little wonder that in 1918 the franc was a very unstable currency. Matching France's predicament was the paralysis affecting Russian economic life. When the railway system collapsed in 1917, the industrial centers automatically shut down, largely because coal, iron, and cotton from the Ukraine, the Caucasus, and Turkestan were no longer reaching them. By 1918, industrial production in Russia was down to 5 percent of what it had been in 1914. The paralysis in industry continued through the civil war, which lasted from 1918 to 1921, and was accompanied by declines in agricultural production and then crop failures.

[2] John Reed, *The War in Eastern Europe* (New York: Scribner's, 1916), pp. 88, 55.

But all the major European powers were faced with severe strains on their economies. Although the German economy emerged strong, its industry untouched and its agriculture still productive, the French, backed by the British, tried to make the Germans bear the cost of French economic recovery. The Western Powers demanded reparations of $33 billion, in cash and in kind, and then at the Versailles peace conference the French and British went a long way toward depriving Germany of the resources she needed to pay that bill. They took from Germany much of her coal, most of her merchant marine, and a great deal of her railway rolling stock.

With France desperately searching for capital to rebuild, the Russian economy paralyzed, and Germany about to go under as a result of runaway inflation, British goods were unable to find a market on the Continent. As a trading nation, Britain had depended on the profits from Continental markets. Now those markets were no longer there, and other overseas markets were being lost to the two new industrial powers, the United States and Japan. All these problems might have been solved by more capital, but a large portion of Europe's capital reserves had been eaten up during the war by war production and taxation.

As far as the general public was concerned, the immediate consequence of these economic strains was a rising inflation. Prices spiraled upward in an unprecedented manner, cheapening savings, jumping costs, and depriving many of any real gain in purchasing power. The production of so many noncapital goods during the war, items like artillery and rifles, made most other industrial and consumer goods dear. The result was a rising inflation that began early in the war and climbed steeply after 1918. As wartime production came to an end and as capital for reinvestment virtually disappeared, industry began to contract. By 1920, there had been a 39 percent cutback in German industrial production from prewar levels; in France it was 34 percent and in Italy 26 percent. Falling industrial production fed unemployment and inflation. Compounding the problem was a precipitous decline in agricultural production for Europe as a whole. Production fell 27 percent, the result of a shortage of labor, farm machinery, and fertilizer, all of which drove the prices of agricultural goods up.

Prices rose unchecked until 1926, when the European economy finally began to stabilize. In the meantime, developments in Italy provide an excellent illustration of what was happening all over Europe. The wholesale price index rose feverishly from 1913 levels. If 1913 is taken as a base of 100, then by 1915 prices had nearly doubled to 184.7. By 1918, they had almost doubled again to 412.9 and by 1920 they stood at 590.7, nearly six times what they had been before the war. Wages, meanwhile, failed to keep up, advancing only fourfold to 403.1 by 1920, which meant that the Italian working class suffered a decline in real wages during the war.

The recovery from the economic dislocations caused by World War I was slow, the pace limited by a severe shortage of capital, although all the major countries had regained 1913 levels of industrial and agricultural production by 1926. In Great Britain, overseas trade revived and income from shipping expanded sufficiently for the economy to begin to grow again. The loss of skilled manpower during the war was another factor contributing to economic decline, with per capita productivity in Great Britain, as elsewhere in Europe, falling after 1918. But by 1926 Great Britain and the other European countries had solved this problem by means of job retraining.

France revived, with tremendous effort, after 1920. Selling in foreign markets, France's trade increased fivefold, bringing the capital needed to revitalize the war-ravaged economy. After a disastrous inflation that nearly bankrupted her, Germany was given a huge lift by the infusion of $5 billion in American loans that soon stimulated her flagging economy. Inflows of capital increased production, eliminated unemployment, and added to purchasing power. Italy under Mussolini and Russia under Lenin both followed the same policy, but instead of depending upon private sources, Europe's first Fascist and Communist states stimulated industrial recovery and growth by means of significant government investment. The pace of European revival might have been faster had capital moved across national boundaries as it did before 1914, but this was not to be the case.

Industrial and agricultural production, after a decade and a half of serious dislocation, once again stabilized by the mid-twenties, and when they did so did the social order. World War I and the economic woes that followed it had had a very disturbing effect. The precipitous rise in prices, unemployment caused by demobilization and industrial slowdowns, the failure of wages to keep up with prices, and the general economic insecurity of the times left many members of the working class both discontent and angry. Compounding the social unrest of the times was renewed social mobility as peasants continued to leave the countryside and as upward mobility continued to exist in the cities. Europe still seemed a society in flux.

Social Pressures
in the Postwar Period

The two decades from 1919 to 1939 were years of turmoil in Europe. The economic instability of first the war and then the Depression affected both working class and middle class elements, and the result was massive social unrest. The period after 1918 was characterized specifically by a great deal of working class discontent. Union membership rose sharply as the working class began to unite in protest against economic conditions like inflation and unemployment, both of which were direct contributors to a decline in purchasing power and a lowering of the standard of living. The protests lasted from the mid-1910s to the mid-1920s, subsiding only as industry stabilized and employed increased.

Through all the social upheaval following the war, industrial society itself was undergoing a series of internal adjustments. The rural population continued to move to the cities, encouraged by the number of positions to be filled because of war losses. The factory system continued to grow, especially the chemical, electronics, and automobile industries, all of which called for more and more skilled and semiskilled labor. Factory workers finally became the largest element in the working class. Economic opportunities in the middle class also opened up, especially at the middle middle class and lower middle class levels, where vacancies created by the deaths among junior officers during World War I were most conspicuous.

In the period prior to 1914, the working class in Europe had shown a real tendency toward docility. Most workers had not joined unions or participated in strikes. Periodic outbursts that took the form of general strikes like those in Belgium in 1893, Sweden in 1902, Italy in 1904, and Russia and Austria in 1905 were sporadic and short-lived. The European working class was simply not radical in an age of rising wages and improving standards of living; what radicalized the working class was economic deprivation, rationing, taxation, and inflation, all of which threatened its standard of living. Then there were strikes and demonstrations, greater organizational efforts, and a shift in voting in the direction of the Labor, Socialist, and Communist parties. Spontaneous protests were a characteristic of the last months of the war; popular protest against the economic sacrifices caused by the war lay behind a series of strikes that convulsed Austria, Germany, and France during January of 1918.

This first wave of protest began on January 13, 1918, in Vienna. Opposing both the war and the reduction of the flour ration, workers struck in Vienna, Graz, Linz, Budapest, and other key industrial centers. Within two weeks, 400,000 workers in Berlin were out on strike. The strike spread to the Ruhr and other parts of western Germany, eventually causing a million workers to walk off their jobs. In the same month, January, workers went out in Lyons, St.-Étienne, and Paris. Some of the most serious disturbances actually came a year later in Italy. Working class demonstrations got out of hand, frightening the middle class. De-

manding an end to rising prices, Italian workers struck in the hundreds of thousands in June and July of 1919. The strikes largely hit the textile, metallurgical, and railway industries; some factories were seized and some shops looted. Strike activity lessened after this but remained a potent device for expressing working class discontent, the British general strike of 1926 being a prime example. During that strike millions of workers left their jobs in support of the demand of the miners for increased wages.

Two of the most conspicuous consequences of postwar working class restlessness were the growth of trade union membership and increased labor representation in the various European parliaments. The size of the British and German trade unions doubled to well over 4 million in each case. Trade union membership in France, organized politically by the Catholics, Socialists, and Communists, increased to 1.5 million. Meanwhile, the Italian unions were enrolling an equal number. Success at the polls came to political parties representing the interests of the working class. By 1928, the Socialists and Communists had 25 percent of the popular vote in France, the Socialists winning 1.7 million votes in the elections of that year and the Communists a little over a million. In the general elections of 1929 in Great Britain, the Labor party emerged with more than 8 million votes, while Socialist candidates in Germany could count on the regular support of some 7 million voters. The growth in trade union membership coupled with an increased political influence indicated that the working class was becoming a more powerful force than it had been prior to 1914. But it was not strong enough or powerful enough to overcome some of the economic factors, such as inflation and depression, that contributed so mightily to its insecure position in the interwar period.

Working class expressions of discontent after 1918 may have disturbed the European social order, but they did not alter it. For society was already taking on a hereditary character, with sons succeeding fathers in the most advanced industrial states at most levels of society. There was a major renewal of social mobility in this era, but it was now a case of replacing the losses created by World War I and of rounding out a society about to become both mature and stratified. Evidence of growing social stratification, present before 1914, became conspicuous after 1918, especially in the more advanced industrial societies. In truth, two apparently divergent trends were now noticeable, social mobility existing side-by-side with stratification.

The peasantry continued to move off the land and penetrate the cities. Economic pressures, both old and new, were keenly felt at this particular level of society. Purchasing power among French peasants, for example, declined by 28 percent between 1913 and 1933. In Germany, in spite of massive Nazi propaganda extolling the virtues of agricultural life, the size of the peasantry continued to shrink. The movement off the land was conspicuous in eastern Europe, especially in the Soviet Union, where rapid industrialization drew more than 7 million peasants into the cities of Russia between 1928 and 1932.

The seemingly perpetual migration of peasant elements into the cities made Europe, of course, even more urbanized than it had been before World War I. The city still provided opportunities for the peasant, but now, except in the case of Russia, which was experiencing massive social mobility, movement up the urban social order was becoming more difficult. At best, most peasants could find employment in the new automobile factories of Paris, the chemical works of Vienna, or the new iron and steel centers of the Ukraine. They expanded the size of the factory working class in society, but for most of them mobility came to an end right there.

As early as 1900, the majority of factory workers in Europe were the sons or grandsons of factory workers. The growing hereditary character of this social class would soon overtake the recruits just entering the factory system. In Sweden, the percentage of those following their fathers at the level of manual labor at this time was about 65 percent; in Denmark, it was near 75 percent. In places like France, Germany, and Switzerland, the range of retention appears to have been about 72 percent. There was still the possibility of social movement within the factory working class, but not outside it. As industry grew more sophisticated, largely through technological change, the increased demand for skilled and semiskilled workers opened up highly paid jobs at a rapid rate, but these were to remain in the working class category.

Movement up the social ladder from the working class to a middle class more stable than ever before was very often achieved by the sons of those in the upper reaches of the working class. The passage was frequent enough in the interwar period to add an important minority of men of lower class origin to the European middle class. Social mobility, then, did not come to an end, but it affected a proportionately smaller part of the population. Those who did penetrate the middle class entered a class that was already solidifying.

The upper levels of the middle class were difficult, but not necessarily impossible, to reach. Selective studies done in Germany after World War I showed that 80 percent of the university professors, judges, and top-ranked civil servants in certain cities came from the higher reaches of society. A similar examination of highly paid members of the administrative elite in Great Britain in 1929 showed that only 7 percent were of lower class origin. In the Netherlands and Sweden, both of which escaped the human losses suffered by others in World War I, bourgeois society was even more stratified by the interwar period. If the bourgeois elite was already formed, the only mobility of major proportions at this level was horizontal. Social movement was becoming more conservative in nature; it was interoccupational, that is, between occupations rather than between major social groups or classes.

The position of the lower middle class after World War I was made very unstable by the war and the economic downturns that came later. Many men of lower middle class origin had an opportunity to penetrate the officer corps in Germany toward the end of the war, only to have their careers shut off by the drastic reduction in the size of the armed forces in 1919. Ambition could also be seriously stifled by circumstances. Thousands of German doctors and lawyers, a substantial number of whom were of lower middle class origin, were unable to set up practice because of declining economic circumstances in the late 1920s. Meanwhile, profits for shopkeepers in Italy fluctuated dramatically, leaving this element of the lower middle class badly shaken in the years immediately after World War I. Similarly, many clerical workers in administrative centers like London, Brussels, and Rome found their marginal savings wiped out by the inflation of the post-1918 period.

The uncertain nature of life in the lower middle class made movement into this particular level of the bourgeoisie less attractive to the various levels of the working class and often slowed their resolve to move up the social ladder. Extensive studies done in Sweden during the interwar period show the slowest rate of social mobility occurring between the upper reaches of the working class and the bottom levels of the middle class. And what was true here was also characteristic of what was happening in other countries. Within the lower middle class, the response of clerical workers in government and industry to economic threats was white collar unionism. The Central Association of Commercial Employees began to organize in Austria, while the Federation of French Civil Service Unions had 300,000 members by 1927. Great Britain had a number of such organizations, including the National Union of Clerks, the National Association of Local Government Officers, and the Bank Officers' Guild, all with tens of thousands of members by the 1920s. In the 1930s, the Public Employees' Central Organization, with 175,000 members, was founded in Sweden.

While social mobility was slowing in western Europe, in the Soviet Union it was proceeding at a greatly accelerated pace. For almost two decades there was massive movement up the social scale as Russia underwent rapid industrialization. But the final outcome of that process was exactly the same as it was in the west, the formation of a new middle class society that began to take on a conspicuously hereditary character by the late 1930s.

Russia, of course, had in pre-World War I times developed both business and professional elements. But they, along with the old aristocracy, had been chased out by the revolution of 1917. When the Bolsheviks, most of whom were from the well-to-do middle class, took over, they began a massive program of upward mobility. Hundreds of thousands of workers and peasants were given positions of responsibility in the new middle class they were creating. The Communist Party housed these new middle class elements in government, industry, and the armed forces. The majority of those who improved their position were from the working class. By 1929, nearly 62 percent of the Party's membership was drawn from the working class; the remainder came from the peasantry and lower middle class elements of czarist times.

Of those being raised up, about 85 percent had less than an eighth-grade education. Only 11 percent of those who had been industrial workers remained in the factory; the majority assumed positions of administrative responsibility in the civil service, trade unions, industry, the army, and the national police. They were, of course, rewarded disproportionately, the difference between top and bottom in Soviet society being the 2,000 rubles a month paid to administrators and the average working class wage of about 100 rubles a month. Once in positions of power, the new Soviet middle class sought to perpetuate its privileges, power, and wealth from one generation to another. And this is exactly what happened in Russia from the late 1930s on: as social mobility slowed, stratification grew, and the system began to show an increasingly hereditary character.

13

The Impact
of the Depression

The long-term causes of the Great Depression, which struck Europe in 1931, were the same as those that had dislocated the economy in 1919, lack of capital and the decline of purchasing power. Once again, capital was in short supply and the consumer market limited. The depression itself actually began in the United States, causing a severe drop in the American gross national product, from 100 percent in 1929 to 68 percent in 1931. The European economic recovery of the late 1920s had been built to an important extent on the middle class American luxury market. This was particularly true of French exports. As the American market collapsed, china from Limoges and Bavaria, lace from Calais, toys from Nuremberg, watches from Switzerland, linen from Ireland, and cloth from Britain all lost their major markets. Britain also suffered because much of her post-World War I recovery depended on shipping profits. And the carrying trade declined, especially as tariff walls began to go up after 1929, limiting the total volume of products being moved.

There were, of course, other factors affecting the European economic scene. The fall of world agricultural prices because of overproduction reduced income primarily in the agricultural states of eastern Europe. Their ability to purchase industrial products declined as did the ability of some of the colonial areas to absorb manufactured products from the European continent. Declining markets for manufactured goods in the United States, eastern Europe, and the colonies overseas meant a decline in profits, the shrinking of capital resources, and a growing reluctance to invest. The result was the economic depression of 1931: important cutbacks in industrial production, a major decline in the gross national product in most countries, and a precipitous fall in purchasing power. By 1932, the gross national product in Germany was down to 80 percent of what it had been before; in France in 1936, it was down to 79 percent.

The fundamental problem with the European economy in the interwar period was its periodic shortage of capital for investment, the inevitable consequence of declining profits. Those profits had become overly dependent on the production of luxury goods and on a middle class consumer economy, both in Europe and abroad. The sale of industrial goods could have been sharply increased inside Europe if the working class and the peasantry had had more purchasing power. The products of industry would have found a much wider market among a much larger portion of the European population, the demand for manufactured goods would have been maintained, production would have been kept up, and profits and capital supported to the point where reinvestment was both natural and inviting. What the Depression proved, if anything, was that the economic life of Europe was now more than ever dependent on the standard of living and purchasing power of the lower classes. Somehow they would have to be given more. It was limited markets that created much of the economic chaos of the interwar period.

In the meantime, of course, all levels of European society were dislocated. The upper reaches of society were harmed just as much as the various lower strata. Profits within the upper middle class and incomes for the professions shrank. Shopkeepers, always dependent on marginal incomes for survival, were badly hurt. Workers suffered massive unemployment. No one was spared after 1931; the skilled, semiskilled and unskilled were all tossed out of work. In Europe as a whole, 15 million workers were unemployed during the Depression. The worst situation of all existed in Germany, where in 1932, 43 percent of the labor force was without work. And the Depression was a disaster for the peasant population. The fall in agricultural prices prior to 1931 had already reduced peasant income all over Europe. The Depression caused an even further decline in agricultural income, as the general public bought less.

The Middle Classes

The Depression had severe consequences for all levels of the middle class. Banking and business failures occurred on an unparalleled scale, wiping out, in the process, numerous personal fortunes. The economic crisis of 1931 began when the largest banking house in Austria, the Credit-Anstaltverein, with 70 percent of the country's banking assets, teetered close to insolvency. The bank had lost assets as its shareholdings dropped precipitously in value. English and German banks rushed in to help, but this move only drained British resources. The British pound, formerly one of the world's strongest currencies, depreciated in value, destroying more wealth, this time in Great Britain.

In Germany, the general banking crisis was compounded by business failures. For example, when Nordwolle, one of the country's largest textile manufacturers, collapsed, the Dresdener Bank had to absorb the loss. The bank survived, but other German banks like the Rhenische Landesbank did not. Between depreciation and bank failures, established wealth all over Europe, most of it belonging to the upper reaches of the middle class, was wiped out. When one of Rumania's leading banks failed in Bucharest, the cost to depositors was the equivalent of 15 million American dollars. The loss of the accumulated wealth of the upper reaches of society was matched by hard times for the professions. The economic downturn in Germany left 7,000 engineers without jobs. Thousands of doctors and lawyers in that country were unable to set up practices. By 1930 in Germany alone, 300,000 university graduates were competing for 130,000 positions. Meanwhile, middle-range civil servants in countries like Great Britain and Austria found opportunities for advancement curtailed. In Italy, the professions, seriously dislocated, were prominently represented during the 1920s in the Fascist party, just as they were among the Nazis in Germany in the 1930s.

For the more numerous members of the lower middle class, the Depression was an even more fearful experience. Shopkeepers, clerks, and preprofessionals were ranked socially in the middle class, but economically they were close to the working class. The petty bourgeoisie had already been through one crisis in the 1920s, and it had left scars. Even before the Depression, many members of the petty bourgeoisie were already becoming déclassé as a result of economic misfortune. In Germany, at least half a million former members of the lower middle class were working in the factory system during the 1920s. Social ambition during this era was also being limited; movement up the social ladder was being made impossible by declining revenues and fewer new administrative jobs in government. Clerical opportunities were difficult to find as most bureaucracies simply stopped growing.

The Depression compounded these difficulties. By 1933, retail sales were off 37 percent in the Netherlands, 34 percent in Italy, and 25 percent in Great Britain. Even worse, the decline in purchasing power beginning in 1931 forced down prices, contributing to a further loss of profits at the shopkeeping level. Nazi party propaganda in Germany took advantage of the situation to emphasize to this segment of the middle class that it was being caught between the capitalists above and the working class below, both of whom were said to be threats. The establishment of department stores worsened the crisis. For example, in Great Britain after 1931, no less than 500,000 small retail outlets had to compete with each other and larger outlets in a declining market. Economic pressures of this type in Germany and Austria often led to anti-Semitism, evidently because many small shopkeepers in cities like Berlin and Vienna were Jews. Many shopkeepers in Germany joined the Nazi party, constituting through the period from 1930 to 1933 a full 20 percent of the party's membership.

Militancy spread among clerical workers. The Nazi party in Germany, for instance, was able to attract a large number of white collar workers in both industry and government, many of whom showed a zest for extreme right-wing politics. Between 1930 and 1933 schoolteachers, public officials, and clerical workers formed a third of the membership of the Nazi party, which in combination with the shopkeeping element gave that party a distinctly lower middle class character. And militancy by white collar workers was not confined to central Europe. The Trade-Union Center for White Collar Employees in the Paris area, with 100,000 members, was involved in major strike action during 1937 and 1938. Their most spectacular strike took the form of a sitdown against the Parisian business house of La Soie that lasted for 155 days. Meanwhile, teachers, civil servants, and railway and bank clerks in Great Britain had to take pay cuts and suffered rates of unemployment varying from 10 to 25 percent. By the middle of the 1930s, pressure from white collar unions in Great Britain restored the cuts and an improving economic situation led to rehirings.

The Lower Classes

The Depression hit the working class and the peasantry with perhaps even more force than it struck the lower middle class. The working class, now more than ever composed of industrial workers, was undermined by both massive unemployment and a decline in purchasing power as industrial production for all of Europe except the Soviet Union fell by 20 percent in 1931 and then 29 percent in 1932. The majority of workers in most countries kept their jobs throughout the Depression, but the size of the unemployed group was still large. The country that was hit the hardest was Germany, with 40 percent of its labor force, 7 million people, unemployed in the winter of 1932–33. Unemployment in France, Italy, and Great Britain, which ranged between 15 and 20 percent, was not as great, but it also created social problems.

The peasantry suffered an even further decline, both socially and economically, as a result of the Depression. With consumption severely curtailed, prices for agricultural products fell disastrously, sometimes by 50 percent. Countries like France, Poland, and Rumania, with large peasant populations, now had to deal with another dislocated group.

The effects of the Depression were felt by the working class in every major industrial country except Russia. The most pressing problem was unemployment and its effect on the standard of living. In Germany, where unemployment was the most severe, food again became a subject of conversation. One observer recalled:

> Food is the great topic of conversation in Germany today. . . . It has replaced even reparations as the burning question of the hour. Where two Englishmen will, in nine out of ten cases, begin discussing sport, two Germans will ask each other why they and their families should go hungry in a world stuffed with food. Why German children should be suffering from rickets for the first time since the allied blockade? [1]

Homeless men were to be seen everywhere in Germany. There were also acts of desperation. A German observer noted, "I saw them—and this was the strongest impression that the year 1932 left with me—I saw them, gathered into groups of fifty or a hundred men, attacking fields of potatoes. I saw them digging up the potatoes and throwing them into sacks while the farmer who owned the field watched them in despair and the local policeman looked on gloomily from the distance." [2] Such scenes were extraordinary, but they did indicate the plight of many workers without jobs, who were usually left with only partial incomes.

Unemployment insurance programs were widespread enough in Europe to help at least a portion of the working class. In France, at the depth of the Depression, there were a total of 1.4 million unemployed, of whom only 500,000 received unemployment assistance, and that only in small amounts. The British, with a more advanced system of unem-

---

[1] H. H. Tiltman, *Slump! A Study of Stricken Europe Today* (London: Jarrolds, 1932), p. 32.

[2] S. B. Clough, *et al.*, eds., *Economic History of Europe: Twentieth Century* (London: Harper & Row, 1969), pp, 247–48.

ployment insurance, did better. Unemployment benefits by this time covered a full 63 percent of the labor force, and reserve funds were used to keep benefits flowing. Trying to care for the huge number of unemployed in Germany was a major problem, especially since there was so much more long-term unemployment there than elsewhere. For example almost 2 million workers receiving public assistance in 1932 had been unemployed for more than a year, and another million had not been able to find jobs for more than nine months. Still, Germany supported up to 90 percent of the unemployed with public funds or through private charity.

Governments trying to meet the crisis often created jobs in the form of various public works projects. By 1933, Sweden had a third of her unemployed working on several such projects. In Italy, major construction projects were started under government auspices. In the Netherlands, the government decided to drain the Zuider Zee. France virtually converted the building of the Maginot Line, a heavily fortified series of bunkers along her eastern frontier, into a public works project for the unemployed. At about the same time, Hitler solved the problem of mass unemployment by revitalizing Germany's war industry, a procedure that was finally followed, sometimes unwillingly, in some of the western states.

The working class, militant in the years immediately after 1918, responded to the Depression in a rather subdued fashion. Except for France, strikes and demonstrations were not all that frequent. The French trade unions themselves were growing rapidly. Membership jumped from 1 million to more than 5 million as the semiskilled and unskilled sought union protection for the first time. Labor unrest in France peaked in May of 1936 with some 1.5 million workers participating in sit-down strikes. The workers had been encouraged by the political success of the Socialists and Communists in the general election of 1936, and the strikes were a direct attempt to influence government policy. They indicated a growing emphasis on political action.

All over Europe, except in places like Fascist Italy and the Soviet Union, where it was impossible, the working class more and more sought a solution to its problems by political means. This changing attitude accounts for some of the major electoral successes scored during this era by the Labor party in Great Britain and the Socialists and Communists in Germany and France. In Great Britain, the Labor party won an important electoral victory in 1929. In Germany, before Hitler closed off the right to vote, the Socialists were receiving up to 30 percent of the popular vote and the Communists 17 percent. In 1936, the French Socialists became the largest party in the Chamber of Deputies by winning 2 million votes, and the Communists were not far behind with 1.5 million.

The fate of the working class in the Soviet Union, the one country to escape the impact of the Depression, was nonetheless the same as in western and central Europe. When Russia launched a series of five-year plans in 1929, she also inaugurated a program of rationing and heavy taxation to pay for them. The turnover tax, which in many instances doubled the price of such basic commodities as bread, meat, and cotton goods, fell heavily upon the working class, driving its standard of living down. Other sacrifices were forced on the working class as a result of the shortage of food brought on by the slaughter of livestock and the decline in the production that accompanied the process of collectivization. For different reasons, then, the working class in the Soviet Union met the same fate as other working class elements elsewhere in Europe.

The tensions of the interwar period, the result of serious disruptions in the standard of living of the working class under both capitalism and socialism, led for the first time to severe class conflict. The remedy was economic stability for the lower classes. The working class and peasantry just could not be subjected to periodic ups and downs in their standard of living without serious social consequences, but it was not until after World War II that European leaders would find a solution in the welfare state.

It is obvious from the events of the interwar period that the European peasantry had been hurt just as much as the working class by the economic vicissitudes of both 1919 and 1931. The basic problem for the peasant was that falling prices for agricultural commodities had seriously depressed income. In most of Europe outside Russia, prices began their downward plunge during the 1920s; the fall was only accelerated by the Depression. In France, the price of wheat tumbled by more than 50 percent between 1925 and 1935. In Germany and Denmark, all agricultural products fell in value by more than 40 percent during the late twenties and early thirties. Countries with large peasant populations were even harder hit because agricultural income was such a significant part of the gross national product. In Spain in 1924, for example, agriculture still accounted for 42 percent of that nation's income. When agricultural income collapsed, dragging down the whole economy, agricultural labor, already poorly paid, found itself either unemployed or unable to push wage rates up any further. The German government tried to solve the problem by settling agricultural workers on their own land. In the Soviet Union, its economy no longer fixed to that of the remainder of Europe, agricultural prices were kept up during the 1920s as part of the Bolshevik government's concessions to the peasantry. But after 1929, high quotas and low government payments for crops grown on the new collective farms of the 1930s severely reduced peasant income.

Most governments acted after 1931 to save agriculture from complete disaster. In the main, they tried to push up prices by one means or another, a move that helped the peasantry but increased the cost of food in the cities. High tariffs in countries like Great Britain, Denmark, and Poland guaranteed the domestic market for agricultural producers, but kept out cheaper foreign commodities at a time when the working class had less purchasing power. Governments also tried other devices in an effort to improve agricultural income. Great Britain guaranteed the price of all grains by means of subsidies. In Denmark, cattle and pigs were deliberately slaughtered to reduce the supply and shore up prices. The Danes, in fact, eliminated 40 percent of their pig herds in order to bring about a higher market price for pork. France subsidized the production of wine so successfully that prices for this basic commodity never did collapse. Government policies in this area were so successful that by 1938 prices were regaining 1929 levels in both France and Italy. The only exception to this general picture of improvement was the Soviet Union, whose government did not turn to a policy of price supports until the 1950s.

The Standard of Living

The economic impact of World War I and the Depression made life more uncertain for the masses than at any time since the beginning of the industrial age. Through the course of the nineteenth century, the various classes in Europe had steadily and for the most part smoothly improved their economic positions. Except for disruption in periodic downturns, life in the nineteenth century had had a rather certain character. The crises of 1919 and 1931 were disasters for Europe not only because they were unprecedented in scale, but because they robbed the social classes of Europe of their expectations. Most elements in society had come to expect improvements and a higher standard of living. Instead, they found themselves cut off from opportunities, and even worse, saw their standard of living decline. Social justice between the two world wars became less a matter of eliminating poverty than of guaranteeing that the individual's standard of living would not in the future be seriously undermined by disease, disability, death, or unemployment.

Even before 1914 European society was beginning to provide guarantees. Both Britain and Germany had extensive welfare state programs by the interwar period that helped to cushion the Depression in those two countries. Moreover, with food and clothing increasingly plentiful in peacetime, most European governments set out after 1918 to do something about housing, the major outstanding social problem of the time. Housing projects got underway almost everywhere. The Labor government in the 1920s in Great Britain pushed the development of public housing as its major contribution to social welfare. The municipal government of Vienna, under Socialist control after 1918, managed over the course of a decade and a half to build 50,000 new apartments and 8,000 individual homes, resettling nearly 180,000 people. In so doing, it cleared away some of the worst slums in pre-World War I Europe. In Sweden, the state had already moved into the field of housing beginning in 1904. By granting credit to buyers and then builders, the government encouraged private ownership. After the Depression, the state was once again active, this time in the distribution of rental subsidies. Sweden's national commitment to improved housing was matched by the French government both before and after World I. The main aim of French policy was to provide as much inexpensive housing as possible for the emerging working class.

What was particularly disturbing about the economic crises of 1919 and 1931 was the way in which they seriously disrupted previous patterns of consumption. In a number of instances levels of food consumption were reduced. For example, in Germany, average daily per capita consumption of food in 1913 had reached a high of 3,000 calories. During the inflation of the early 1920s, the total fell to 2,000 in 1921 and was only back up to 2,650 in 1924. More specifically, the average German was eating in 1927 only about three-quarters of the meat that he consumed in 1913. During the Russian famines of 1919 and 1931–32, the food supply was seriously curtailed. Later on, the Soviet government even admitted officially that the average Russian had eaten better in 1913 than he did in the interwar period. The French managed to maintain their national prewar average of about 120 pounds of meat per person per year through the 1920s, but they did so only by means of massive imports. These imports were made necessary by the destruction of some of France's best agricultural lands during the war. Consumption of food in most of Europe seems to have remained normal during the Depression, cuts being made in the purchase of other items such as clothing, furniture, cigarettes, and alcohol.

The economic uncertainties of the interwar period that forced many mass elements to accept a lower standard of living was bound to have a demoralizing effect on the population. Memories of the prewar period were still strong; as one member of the British working class remarked during the mass layoffs following 1918, "Nothing like this happened before the war." There was, besides this, the added insecurity caused by economic fluctuation. First the economy contracted after the war, only to expand again in the late 1920s; then it contracted again in 1931, only to revive again beginning in 1936. The peasantry responded somewhat passively, but the lower middle class shifted politically to the far right and the working class, further to the left.

The most obvious way of relieving economic want was to establish a system of welfare benefits designed to maintain a specific standard of living. Great Britain and Germany had already begun to do this before World War I. Through a combination of government support and social security taxes on employers and employees, both the British and German governments were able to support a number of programs. In both cases, workers were provided with pensions and unemployment benefits, plus provisions for income in the case of disability or ill health. In 1901, the German program added a unique feature by also providing for medical benefits. Very few countries had the economic resources or will to support similar programs prior to 1914. Austria did have a voluntary system of sickness and accident benefits, but it was weak in comparison with what the British and Germans were able to provide.

After World War I, both Great Britain and Germany improved their systems. The British extended unemployment benefits to the point where at least two-thirds of the labor force was covered by the time of the Depression. Germany, in the aftermath of a crippling inflation, passed comprehensive social welfare legislation in 1924. Welfare benefits were increased and made easier to obtain. Public assistance was guaranteed to all needy and destitute persons in the forms of food, clothing, shelter, and medical attention. Pensioners, invalids, survivors, and victims of inflation were all to be aided by means of what were truly described as social security benefits. Maternity benefits, unusual at the time, were added to the program's provisions and medical assistance made more readily available to the public.

The German example did not really become a model for the rest of Europe. Declining tax revenues and the need for capital for investment in the Soviet Union limited the impact of programs everywhere. France, however, did initiate a program of social security benefits in 1928 similar to those the British and Germans had set up before World War I. The concept behind the French program was spelled out in the preamble to the legislative act of 1928: "Social insurance covers sickness, premature invalidity, old age, death, and allows a participation in family and maternity allowances, and involuntary unemployment benefits." [3] The innovation in the French system was allowances for family assistance; the practice of giving family assistance based on income and the number of children originated with the French program of 1928. As wide-ranging as these benefits appeared to be, actual cash payments were small and the system was not extensive. It eventually covered only a minority of the unemployed in France during the depression of the 1930s.

[3] Pollard and Holmes, *Documents,* III, 531.

The Soviet Union was philosophically committed to the idea of social security. Article 120 of the Soviet Constitution of 1936 declared:

Citizens of the USSR have a right to material security in old age as well as in the event of sickness and loss of the capacity to work. This right is ensured by the wide development of social insurance of workers and employees at the expense of the state, free medical aid, and the provision of a wide network of health resorts for the use of the toilers.[4]

Actual benefits, however, often fell below subsistence, meaning that the system was, as in the case of France, inadequately funded.

This situation was not peculiar to Russia; many Swedes living on state pensions in the interwar period had to apply for poor relief because the pensions were so inadequate. Europe was clearly moving in the direction of a system of material security, but it was not until after 1945 that most states, both capitalistic and socialistic, came up with welfare benefits that would save the European masses from the violent economic fluctuations and the uncertain standard of living that they had faced in the period between the two world wars.

[4] Bernice Q. Madison, *Social Welfare in the Soviet Union* (Stanford, Calif.: Stanford University Press, 1968), p. 57.

Part Four

Contemporary European Society 1939 to the Present

After nearly three decades of turbulence, society finally began to stabilize after 1945. The stratification that was progressively characteristic of the European social order was often masked in those tumultuous years by wars and economic disasters, but it was nonetheless growing. It was obvious in Great Britain and Germany in the early 1920s and just as apparent in the Soviet Union by the late 1930s. Whenever and wherever industry matured, social classes took on a hereditary character. In spite of the devastation caused by World War II, this process went on unabated. All over Europe, both west and east of the Iron Curtain, industrialization divided society into the elite and the mass. Even if the process was not total or complete, it was apparent after 1945 that a mass element composed of the lower middle class, the working class, and small peasants had been formed.

Industrial society had produced wealth of a kind and proportion never before known. That wealth in turn made possible welfare state programs. But by providing extensive benefits, the governments of Europe, again both west and east, went a long way toward stratifying society even more. In an earlier age, individuals had to climb into a higher social group or class in order to receive greater economic remuneration. Now that was no longer necessary. Extensive economic benefits limited social mobility, checked personal ambition, and gave a conservative and stable character to modern industrial society. Welfare state programs may be seen, then, as the means by which the elites of western and eastern Europe not only raised the standard of living of the masses but reconciled the great majority in society to their continued leadership.

Social stratification after 1945, which increasingly left most people in the position in which they were born, was a sign that the era of social transformation was nearly over. It could even be argued that Europe was becoming as stratified after 1945 as it had been before the coming of the Industrial Revolution. Evidence of the growing hereditary character of society was everywhere. Generally speaking, only the elite penetrated the universities, leaving them, of course, with a monopoly on positions in business and the professions, while lower middle class, working class, and peasant status progressively tended to pass from father to son.

With society more castelike than at any time before 1820, entirely different challenges began to confront Europe. The conflict was now between the elite, which had a lot, and the masses, which had less, for economic gain. The masses were not helpless; they could and did exert pressure on the elite to gain concessions. In the west they were able to do this through unions and certain left-wing political parties; in the east, by passive resistance that encouraged government concessions. The European population no longer lacked for food, clothing, or shelter. Indeed, many members of the lower middle class and the lower classes were now buying items that in a previous age would have been considered luxuries, commodities like cars, appliances, and televisions. The problems now were not those of life and death, but questions bearing on the quality of life—the overconcentration of population in the cities, land use, public transportation, town planning, and environmental control.

14

The Coming
of the
Welfare State

Europe emerged from World War II just as exhausted as she had been in 1918. Once again, industrial production lagged behind prewar levels and agricultural production was seriously reduced. Not only were important parts of England, Germany, and Russia heavily bombed, but the human losses were again devastating. Probably up to 45 million people lost their lives in the conflict, half of them Russians. Twenty-five percent of Germany's industrial capacity had been destroyed by bombing. Russia was only able to produce, in 1945, 58 percent of what she had manufactured prior to the German attack. Coal production was down by 30 percent in Italy, and the figures for steel were about the same. European agriculture had a more difficult time reviving from the war. In 1946, food production was down a third from prewar days and in 1947 it was still off 25 percent, making rationing necessary.

And once again, Europe found itself in debt. Britain and the Continental countries owed the United States alone $9 billion in 1947. In spite of its economic difficulties, Europe made a relatively quick recovery from World War II by solving the problems that plagued it after 1918. The United States provided the west with capital in the form of Marshall Plan aid, and purchasing power was increased by means of redistribution of wealth in both western and eastern Europe.

Even with a dislocated economy Europe deliberately set out to redistribute wealth. In spite of reduced resources, countries like Britain and France moved quickly in the direction of increased social justice by creating and extending welfare state programs to the point where those at the lower socioeconomic levels of society would benefit most. Western Europe thus prevented the collapse of the standard of living that occurred on two occasions in the interwar period. Following their example, the Soviet Union in the 1950s moved in the same direction, measurably improving the standard of living of both workers and peasants by means of massive new government investment in social welfare. The loss of so much capital both in the form of war materials before 1945 and thereafter as a result of redistribution of wealth left Europe short of capital resources. The United States stepped into the void with Marshall Plan aid of $60 billion, which revitalized industry and agriculture in the west very quickly after 1945. In the Soviet bloc, which refused Marshall Plan aid, capital was initially used to finance recovery, and only later was there enough to begin the first massive redistribution of wealth to the masses in Soviet history. Once this happened, society stabilized in the west, in the Soviet Union, and soon enough in the new states of eastern Europe, with middle class elements in control everywhere and the masses at least partially satisfied by economic gain.

The Welfare State, West and East

The welfare state was based on certain fundamental ideas. In the first place, its aim was not economic equality, only the redistribution of wealth from the rich to those less well off to the point where a minimum standard was established for all. Its basic aim was to eliminate want, to see poverty disappear. Advocates of the welfare state felt that only the central government was in a position to eliminate poverty; the state was the means by which a redistribution of wealth could take place. The state could tax the more well-to-do, meaning the bourgeois elite, progressively, until there were enough resources to bear the costs of welfare programs. Among the wartime advocates of the welfare state was the English aristocrat Sir William Beveridge. The now famous Beveridge Report of 1942 signaled the beginning of Europe's total commitment to the idea of social security for all. In it, Beveridge called want "a needless scandal due to not taking the trouble to prevent it." His plan called for "a method of re-distributing incomes, so as to put the first and most urgent needs first," or as he described it somewhat more prosaically on another occasion, "bread for everyone before cake for anybody." Beveridge's report was, generally speaking, favorably received. The *London Times,* commenting on his ideas, responded by saying "Sir William Beveridge has succeeded in crystallizing the vague but keenly felt aspirations of millions of people." [1]

When the British Labor party was swept into office under Clement Atlee in 1945, it moved to introduce Europe's most comprehensive system of social security. Raising the taxes on the more well-to-do, the Labor government built up a system of national assistance based on both old and new concepts of welfare. The idea that the unemployed, the sick and injured, the disabled, the old, and survivors should be helped was perpetuated, with even greater benefits going to these groups. But Labor government went much further by establishing a national floor below which incomes were not to sink and by providing equal access to medical care for all based on a popular program of socialized medicine. All citizens would be protected by the old and new schemes. There were to be direct payments to both individuals and families whose incomes fell below a certain mean average established by the government. These payments, which first began in 1948, were complemented in 1968 by a program of family allowances that provided payments for each child under the age of fifteen. The National Health Program began in 1946 and guaranteed payments for care by general practitioners, for specialist services, hospitalization, maternity care, dental care, medicine, and home nursing.

The French, who had lagged behind both the British and the Germans in welfare legislation before World War II, suddenly came up with their own advanced program in 1946. The welfare state in France was the work of three left-wing parties, the M.R.P. (Christian Democrats), the Socialists, and the Communists, who together dominated postwar French politics for a number of years. The goal of the program was greater social justice, based as in the case of England on a redistribution of wealth and the elimination of poverty. Public demands for more "economic and social democracy" led to a spate of legislation in 1945 and 1946 that improved France's primitive system of social security benefits. Fairly generous payments were provided for widows, orphans, the sick, the injured and disabled. Unemployment benefits, weak under the old system, were greatly increased. And new features were added. Socialized medicine became a part of the French program, just as it was finding universal

[1] Maurice Bruce, *The Coming of the Welfare State* (London: Batsford, 1961), p. 273.

acceptance in the rest of Europe. One of the most generous features of the new system was the provision for family allowances. Based on child allotments, it provided for payments of 22 percent of minimum wages for the second child and 33 percent for each child thereafter.

European society was obviously forcing a transfer of wealth from the higher reaches of the middle class to the masses. Those who were part of the mass found their standard of living improved. Some programs went beyond the standard benefits provided by most of the schemes. For example, the Austrian program provided for maternity benefits at 100 percent of earnings, plus a lump-sum grant and provisions for nursing care. In West Germany, which after 1945 spent the highest percentage of its national budget for social welfare programs of any country in Europe, disability payments were extraordinarily high. In the case of total disability, a worker could receive income support above what he was actually earning when he was injured. In Sweden, to make sure that old-age pensions went far enough, the government provided a program of supplemental payments. In this way, the Swedish system guarantees that payments will keep up with the cost of living.

The social security system that developed in eastern Europe after 1945 consciously copied the program existing in the Soviet Union. The Soviet system, born in the interwar period, had been inadequately funded. Beginning in the 1950s and extending into the 1960s, the Soviet government, in an attempt to reconcile the general population to its rule, made major concessions in the form of welfare state benefits. Since everyone was expected to work, there was no provision for unemployment insurance, but otherwise, the system looked like those of western Europe. Socialized medicine was a prominent feature, as were disability payments at 80 percent of previous wages, and pensions, beginning at age sixty, paid at 50 percent of the worker's last yearly earnings. Maternity benefits were the most generous in Europe. In addition to pregnancy leave, the government paid a straight cash allowance at the time of birth, provided nursing benefits during the child's first nine months, and even guaranteed a sum for the child's clothing. Here, as elsewhere, the benefits contributed to a rising standard of living for the masses.

One of the chief arguments used against welfare state programs in the past was the high cost of maintaining them. From the time of Bismarck on, the system in most of Europe had been paid for with funds from three sources. The government paid for some of the expenses, and the remainder of the money came from a social security tax on employees and employers. The practice continued until after 1945, when government took over a higher and higher proportion of the costs, taxing the wealthy in order to get the money. In western Europe, more established programs are still supported by a social security tax of about 8 percent on wage earners, plus employers' contributions which average about 25 percent of the costs involved. But newer programs, like socialized medicine, have been paid for almost entirely by the treasury. In eastern Europe, the entire social security system is supported by the government; there is no social security tax on workers' salaries.

Maurice Crouzet, one of the more perceptive twentieth-century historians, has described these programs as "measures of social appeasement." And to a large extent they are. The various levels of the masses, the lower middle class, the working class and the peasantry, had to be helped; they had to be protected from economic disaster. It could be argued that the leaders of the western and Soviet blocs made these concessions in order to reconcile the masses to their rule. This was undoubtedly a factor, but so was a growing social consciousness that made poverty less and less acceptable. And the introduction of massive welfare state programs seemed to provide the social order with a stability it had not previously possessed.

Stratification and the Middle Class

Except for eastern Europe, where there was massive social mobility in the wake of Communist takeovers, the social order in Europe was starting to stagnate. This was especially true of middle class society. Studies done in the Netherlands show that. By the post-World War II period, better than 60 percent of the population occupied a stationary position within society. Whatever social mobility there was existed on the periphery of society, with slight drops in social station for those at the top and slight advances for those at the bottom. In the highest social and economic categories of the middle class in Great Britain, social mobility after 1945 was largely interoccupational, between and among groups at the same level rather than between classes. For example, 55 percent of the sons of doctors in Britain were being trained as doctors or in a profession with equal social prestige. In France, 60 percent of the higher civil servants in the postwar period came from 9 percent of the population. In the Soviet Union, ideologically directed toward a classless society, a study of displaced persons after World War II showed that doctors, scientists, and factory managers were considered by the majority to be a part of the country's new elite.

The basis of upper middle class and middle middle class control of European society, both capitalistic and socialistic, lay in the ability of these groups to monopolize the higher reaches of the educational system. Since the universities prepared the business, professional, and managerial elements in society for positions of leadership, it was almost

inevitable that these people would want to have access to higher education limited primarily to their own children. As a result, the numbers
of those entering the universities at the age of eighteen or nineteen between 1960 and 1963 were quite small. The percentage of those attending the universities in the Soviet Union, primarily the sons and daughters
of Party members, was only 7.3 percent of the age groups involved. In
Great Britain, it was 8.5 percent; in France, it was 13.8; and in the
Netherlands, 4.6. The elitest character of advanced education in Europe
was dramatically revealed in a 1967 study of those entering the French
university system. Only 4.6 percentage of the total were the sons or
daughters of peasants, agricultural laborers, or workers, whereas nearly
75 percent were the sons or daughters of businessmen or men in the professions. The remainder were lower middle class types trying to achieve a
higher social and economic status by means of a university education.

This accumulated evidence seems to back up the contention of the
contemporary German sociologist Ralf Dahrendorf, who pointed out,

> All mobility studies since [1954] confirm the conclusion that throughout
> society (with the deceptive exception of peasants, in whose case only one
> son can succeed his father) the most likely status of sons is that of their
> fathers.[2]

And what is true of society as a whole seems even more characteristic of
Europe's bourgeois elite. Primary evidence for this assertion comes from
two sources, West Germany and the Soviet Union. Among elite elements
in German society there was in 1955 an amazing degree of continuity
from one generation to another. This direct hereditary link has been
proved by studies showing that 60 percent of West Germany's political
leaders were the sons of political leaders, 60 percent of the country's high
civil servants had fathers in the same occupation, and 52 percent of the
postwar business leaders came from upper middle class banking or business families.

The bourgeois elite in West Germany is older, historically, than the
elite that had formed in the Soviet Union by the late 1930s but the Soviet
elite has been just as tenacious in holding on to its position. The growth
of a middle class elite, first in the Soviet Union and then in eastern
Europe, has been analyzed by one of the Communist leaders of the postwar period, the Yugoslav Milovan Djilas. At one time, Djilas stood next
to President Tito in the Yugoslav party hierarchy, but he fell from
favor with his insistence that the Communist takeovers in eastern Europe
produced a new middle class just as dominant as the elites that had been

2 Ralf Dahrendorf, "Recent Changes in the Class Structure of the European
Societies," *Daedalus*, No. 93 (1964), 239.

thrown out. Industrialization, he argued, was the key in the Soviet Union to the creation of what he called "the new class," the new middle class. The Party in Russia rose to a position of social and economic dominance as a result of administrative talent, a process we have already seen at work in nineteenth-century Europe. Writing in the mid-1950s, Djilas insisted:

> Without their special role as administrators over society and as distributors of property, the Communists could not transform themselves into a new [middle] class, nor could a new class be formed and permanently established. Gradually, material goods were nationalized, but in fact, through its right to use, enjoy, and distribute these goods, they became the property of a discernible stratum of the party and the bureaucracy gathered around it.

The Party, according to Djilas, was the new middle class, and the man who pushed the development of that class was Stalin. Djilas went on:

> While the country was being industrialized, Stalin began to introduce considerable variations in wages, at the same time allowing the development toward various privileges to proceed. He thought that industrialization would come to nothing if the new [middle] class were not made materially interested in the process, by acquisition of some property for itself.[3]

Once the new Soviet middle class, made up of Party, government, economic, and military officials, plus scientists and members of the professions, came into existence, its wealth and privileges were perpetuated by legislation. Wealth was perpetuated in the upper reaches of Soviet society by reducing the inheritance tax to a mere 10 percent. An unprogressive income tax taxed the highest incomes in society at maximum rate of 13 percent. As of 1950, incomes in the Soviet Union of better than 60,000 rubles a year were common, and much of it was kept, chiefly because income tax rates were so low and so favorable to the middle class.

Movement up the social ladder continued to be a feature of modern industrial society but it was now only a marginal experience. Most countries, moreover, had by this time virtually institutionalized upward mobility by means of competitive examinations. Those in the higher social and economic groups, with decided cultural advantages, tended to do the best. But these examinations, as for example in the case of Sweden, did detect talent at the lower reaches of society as well. The individual was usually rewarded with a scholarship and soon passed into the upper reaches of society. Some of the best elements in European society do get to penetrate the upper classes in western and eastern Europe through education.

[3] Milovan Djilas, *The New Class* (New York: Praeger, 1957), pp. 49, 55–56.

The lower middle class now exists as a separate and distinct group, still isolated socially and economically from the higher reaches of bourgeois society and still struggling to distinguish itself from those who work with their hands. During the middle part of the twentieth century, the lower middle class expanded to the point where it now constitutes about a quarter of the European population. The growth within this group took place not among shopkeepers but among white collar workers. The number of independently owned shops in western Europe has tended to remain the same. France is a case in point. There are now about 700,000 shops in France. In the period from 1954 to 1960, the number of shops declined by 35,000, then increased by 11,500 with the growing prosperity of France in the 1960s. In an effort to preserve this social group, several countries in western Europe, in particular Denmark and West Germany, have made it government policy to save small businessmen from extinction whenever possible. The real economic threat to this level of the petty bourgeoisie, of course, comes from supermarkets and department stores, both of which continually take away a larger and larger portion of retail trade.

The most dynamic group within the lower middle class in recent times has been the clerical element. Their numbers have grown as both government and industry have continued to expand their operations. Nationalized industry and socialized agriculture in the Soviet Union and most of eastern Europe has brought into existence a large class of white collar workers. A whole army of government workers functions in the Soviet capital—an estimated 600,000 within the various offices and ministries. The International Labor Organization confirms the same trends in western Europe, where white collar employment has until recently been increasing sharply. By 1960 in Sweden, 35 percent of those gainfully employed were in white collar positions, most of them clerical. The same figures, which obviously include the smaller business and professional groups, hold true for a host of other countries, including Belgium, Austria, Great Britain, and West Germany. It now appears, however, that this dynamism has slowed and that the last major push of social mobility has come to an end.

Increasingly faced with a static position, the lower middle class has organized as never before. In Great Britain, unionization is now widely accepted as both imperative and important by this group. Among the leading occupations to organize at this level were the National Union of Teachers, with 220,000 members; the Civil Service Clerical Association, enlisting another 148,000; the National and Local Government Officers Association, which includes some 230,000 men and women; and the Railway Clerks Association, with 91,000 members. In West Germany there are nearly 700,000 white collar workers affiliated with the German

Trade Union Federation, and another 450,000 organized into independent unions.

For a few, the lower reaches of the middle class still represent a place from which to move up socially and economically. Outside of those from privileged business and professional backgrounds, students at universities are most likely to be petty bourgeois. When the French opened up their university system in the 1960s, it was largely the lower levels of the middle class that were admitted for the first time. But social advance for most petty bourgeois elements is not really a possibility. The fact that the lower middle class is organizing in defense of its rights is an admission that it is being held in place both by circumstances and by growing social stratification. The petty bourgeoisie remains in its old, uncomfortable position, unable to identify with the bourgeois elite above it or the working class and peasantry below it.

Stratification and the Lower Classes

The size of the European working class has grown since 1945, just as the peasantry has been reduced in numbers. Here, then, there was still some semblance of mobility in the postwar period, even though working class status was now being more and more inherited. More than ever, factory workers constituted a definite majority within the working class, but other elements were still there. In the Soviet Union, Europe's greatest industrial power, there were by the early 1970s nearly 28 million factory workers. Except for some of the small countries of eastern and southern Europe, industry everywhere provided the greatest amount of available employment. In the Rhineland-Palatinate in West Germany, 46 percent of those gainfully employed worked in industry; in the Paris Basin it was over a third.

While industry continued to grow in importance, producing even more factory jobs, agriculture—peasant agriculture in particular—declined. In the most advanced industrial states in the west, Britain and West Germany, the agricultural portion of the population was down to 5 percent; in the Soviet Union it was 40 percent, the lowest it has ever been. The lower classes, whether they lived in the city or in the countryside, shared in Europe's rising standard of living. They did not, it is true, have nearly as much as the middle classes, but they were certainly not in want.

Since 1945, the internal composition of the working class has changed somewhat, in line with the growing sophistication of European industry. A greater premium than ever is now placed on skilled and semiskilled labor, primarily because the newer industries require workers with much greater skills. Expanding industries, especially the electrical, chemical, and petrochemical industries, require a work force radically different from the untrained men of the early stages of the Industrial Revolution. Older industries, like those producing steel, have not increased their employment figures to any significant degree. For example, even though steel production almost doubled in Europe between 1952 and 1967, the number of steel workers increased by only 10 percent. Employment gains were, however, noted elsewhere. As car production after World War II shot past 2 million a year in France, companies such as Renault, Peugeot, and Citroën more than tripled the size of their work forces. Moreover, most French factory workers, like those elsewhere in Europe, found themselves employed in giant industrial works, for large-scale industrial enterprise was now commonplace. Two-thirds of the factory workers in the Soviet Union, for example, were employed in plants with a thousand or more workers.

The continued growth of industry into the middle of the twentieth century only exaggerated the previous differences among the skilled, the semiskilled, and the unskilled. In those countries with more advanced industrial establishments, the skilled continually outdistanced the unskilled in earning power. In the Soviet Union, differences in income have steadily increased. In the Russian textile and metallurgical industries, skilled workmen were earning nearly four times what the unskilled could hope for. In the rubber industry, the wage differential had increased to almost 500 percent. The same trend was obvious in a number of British industries. By 1951, skilled factory labor was not only drawing away from the unskilled in wages, it was widening the gap between itself and the semiskilled.

This evidence emphasizes the key role skilled labor has played in the history of the Industrial Revolution, a role that it played once more in eastern Europe after 1945. Yugoslavia was among several east European states to begin industrializing in the 1950s. In fact, during that decade Yugoslavia had the highest rate of industrialization of any country in the world. Like the Soviets in the 1930s, the Yugoslavs discovered that the pace of industrialization was overly dependent on skilled factory labor for success. As a result, differences in income designed to encourage the most skilled elements began to appear. One study of a Yugoslav factory manufacturing metal cables showed that the skilled were making 35,000 dinars a month while the unskilled, in this establishment of 3,500 workers, were receiving an average 20,000.

Trade unions serve entirely different functions in Europe's two industrialized societies. In the west, they are a pressure group; in the east, they serve an administrative function. Whether organized by Catholics, Socialists, or Communists, the trade unions of western Europe have been primarily concerned with the elimination of grievances, with higher wages and better working conditions. Socialist unions like the Dutch Federation of Trade Unions and the Catholic Workers' Movement in the Netherlands may be divided ideologically, but they are in agreement on what they want from employers and the government. Communist, Catholic, and Socialist unions in Italy all cooperate, largely because in most factories, as in the Fiat works in Turin, all are represented on the plant's labor committee. In order to present a united front to management, the unions must get along with one another. The same holds true within the British Trade Union Congress, which is the overall organization for some 8 million workers. But there are so many locals in most British plants, twenty of them, for example, in the Vickers aircraft works in Manchester, that cooperation at the local level is necessary if successful negotiations with management are to be conducted. Trade unionism is also a characteristic of the labor movement in eastern Europe, but in most of these countries unions do not have the right to strike and exist primarily to administer various social programs such as housing, plant meals, and sports programs. Still, these unions can and do function as interest groups. For example, the Polish unions in the early 1970s forced the government to grant both factory and shipyard workers a major increase in wages.

Rising wages continue to be a permanent feature of industrialization in its most advanced stage. With very few exceptions, the growth of industry has produced an increase in both real wages and purchasing power. Again, the experience of the countries of eastern Europe after 1945 shows the same pattern. Real wages in East Germany and Czechoslovakia, both of whom had a manufacturing tradition, rose by about 4 percent a year during the 1950s. In the former agricultural states of Poland, Hungary, and Bulgaria, industrialization pushed factory wages up nearly 8 percent a year. Improvements in real wages in the east were, of course, matched by rising purchasing power in the west. Between 1954 and 1964, factory wages in France, Italy, and Belgium increased by 40 to 50 percent. And expanding purchasing power, especially for skilled factory workers, brought into existence in both east and west a new social type, in the affluent worker. In spite of his lower class status, this worker very often has a middle class income that allows him to emulate middle class ways in housing, clothing, vacations, and other amenities. It is a way of life that in a former age would have been thought impossible for a factory hand.

Europe's contracting rural population continued to live on after 1945 either as small peasant proprietors or agricultural workers. In eastern Europe, the landowning peasantry almost disappeared in the wake of collectivization in such countries as East Germany, Czechoslovakia, and Bulgaria, and most of the peasants became agricultural laborers. Only in Poland and Yugoslavia did a landowning peasant class survive the Communist takeover. In the west, peasant proprietors, averaging 25 acres apiece, and agricultural workers could still be found on the land, but their numbers were shrinking. During France's postwar industrial boom, 90,000 French peasants a year deserted the land. In spite of a declining agricultural population, yields shot up as never before. More and more countries in the west increased their self-sufficiency. Great Britain, with only 5 percent of its population in agriculture, doubled production of feed grains and dairy products within twenty-five years. Yields were improving because agriculture was now completely mechanized and fertilizers were being used more and more. In the east, Russia's collectivized agriculture would finally begin to produce huge yields in the 1970s for the same reasons.

Most peasant proprietors after 1945 enjoyed a comfortable standard of living even if they did continue to drop below urban groups in purchasing power. Only in places like western France, southern Italy, Spain, and Portugal did peasant proprietors have a really difficult time surviving. Some marginal producers were, however, supported by the Common Market. In order to lessen the flow of rural migrants to the cities, the Common Market deliberately kept marginal peasant holdings alive by means of subsidies.

Europe's rural population after World War II was largely composed of agricultural laborers, the bulk of them in the Soviet Union. In places like France, a relatively large class of agricultural laborers still exists. Many of them vote for Communist candidates, very often to protest their position as part of a social class with the lowest standard of living of any group in western Europe. Collectivization in the Soviet Union created one of the largest groups of agricultural laborers anywhere. Their standard of living remained depressed for several decades, but beginning in the late 1950s, the government made a deliberate attempt to improve their lot. Ever-increasing government payments for fixed quotas added more and more income to the collectives. In 1964, the government decided to include the peasantry in the social security system. These changes, coupled with new educational opportunities in the countryside, have gone a long way toward raising the standard of living of a full 40 percent of the Russian population. All the various strata within the European social order were, of course, living at a higher level by the 1970s. That elevated standard of living, which at times reached the point of affluence, is the product of urbanization and industrialization, the two forces which over the course of a century have entirely reshaped the nature of European life.

15

Contemporary Society

Modern European society is, of course, vastly different from European society in the eighteenth century. By the postwar period it had taken on characteritics that now appear to be permanent features. For one thing, the long struggle with poverty is now virtually over. The standard of living, both west and east, is one of the highest in the world, and a combination of wages and welfare has created an economic floor below which most Europeans can no longer fall. Massive housing projects, to replace the dwellings destroyed in World War II and to guarantee each family sufficient living space, have eliminated the last of the great social problems inherited from the past.

With food, clothing, and shelter in adequate and even abundant supply, most Europeans can now look to another level of existence. The majority can go beyond the purchase of basic consumer items to the acquisition of luxuries. The quality of life in Europe has been improved by the existence of both entertainment and amenities. From soccer to the movies, most Europeans can punctuate their work week with diversions of some sort. In addition, the growth of a consumer market based on the purchase of commodities such as automobiles, motorcycles, electrical appliances, televisions, and radios indicates that the wealth of industrial society has, to some extent at least, spread to the masses. Affluence, once the monopoly of the elite, has percolated down through all social levels.

The key to a continually rising standard of living and the growth of affluence lies, of course, in a healthy economy. The countries of Europe have learned that economic isolation like that practiced in the interwar period either slows or stymies growth. As a result, the tendency after 1945 has been for Europe to unite in economic blocs designed to spur growth on an international basis. Economic interchanges, like those that grew up naturally in nineteenth-century Europe, have become a part of the European Economic Community, also known as the Common Market, the European Free-Trade Association, and the Council for Mutual Economic Assistance, more widely known as Comecon. The international and integrated approach of all three blocs has facilitated the exchange of men, money, materials, and services and has further aided the growth of the various European economies.

An advanced economy has always been the product of the city. Even in the eighteenth century, the city was always more prosperous and economically more viable than the countryside. What was true then is even truer now that Europe has emerged as an essentially urban society. But a high level of prosperity does not mean that Europe has no problems; urbanization has created its own difficulties—overcrowding, public transportation, land use, and town planning. As serious as these concerns are, they do not have the character of some previous problems. There is a difference in kind between not having enough to eat and not being able to find a comfortable or convenient way of getting to work. The first is debilitating, the second aggravating. That difference symbolizes the change from preindustrial to industrial times, from physical trials to psychological and spiritual concerns.

The Standard of Living

In the past, Europe's standard of living was largely defined by its ability to provide the population with adequate food, clothing, and shelter. In the eighteenth century, the majority lived below the level of subsistence. By the end of the nineteenth century, they had been raised above it, a result of the economic advantages provided by industrialization. By the last half of the twentieth century, food, clothing, and shelter were all secure enough that Europeans could begin to forget that they had once known poverty.

The cost of food continued to decline, taking a smaller and smaller percentage of the family budget. The cost varied from a high of 50 percent of net income in the Soviet Union to 22 percent in Denmark. In Italy, it was 39 percent; in Great Britain, 25. Not only did the relative price of food decline, but the nutritional content of the diet was at an all-time high. True, the older staples, grains and potatoes, still remain a significant portion of the diet in some areas. In countries such as Sweden, Switzerland, and the United Kingdom, they have been superseded by fruits, vegetables, and meats, but not in the less well developed nations. For example, in Rumania the population still eats nearly 400 pounds of grain per capita a year, compared with only 75 pounds of meat. But in countries like France, the amounts consumed are almost equal, nearly 175 pounds of each a year. From the point of view of nutrition, West Germany had by 1967 the best balanced diet in all of Europe. High in proteins, vitamins, and calories, it was characterized by a high level of food energy and more dependence on fruits, vegetables, and meats than grains.

Even with less nutritious food available in the east, the average European is not only stronger but better able to ward off disease. All over Europe, death from infectious diseases, both bacterial and viral, is now the lowest of any place in the world. Not only have the diseases that formerly took the lives of so great a proportion of the population in the past been checked, but another problem, infant mortality, has also been reduced to an all-time low. It is now less than 2 percent of all live births. Life expectancy has changed as well; an infant born in Great Britain in 1972 could expect to live seventy-six years. Across Europe, life expectancy has grown to seventy-two years for men and seventy-six for woman. After 1945, medical care was so advanced that health could be more easily protected than ever before. The Soviet Union alone in 1969 had 550,000 doctors; West Germany had 103,000, and Italy 97,000. Medical care, aided by the highest proportion of doctors to overall population anywhere, is now available to all levels of society under a system of socialized medicine. Contributing even further to public health are thousands upon thousands of clinics, mental hospitals, sanatoria, convalescent homes, and hospitals.

Not only is the general population better cared for than at any previous time, it is also better clothed. With the cost of food taking less and less of the family budget, most Europeans are now in a position to buy more and more clothing. Because incomes have been rising across the Continent, the actual percentage of total income being spent on food and clothing has been dropping throughout the postwar period.

In Sweden, the cost of food has fallen from 30 percent of family income to 26 percent. By the same token, the cost of clothing, as a percentage of overall family income, fell throughout western Europe from 1954 to 1964. The average family expenditure on clothing is around 10 percent. All levels of society can afford fashionable dress; in cities such as Paris, Brussels, and Warsaw, it is almost impossible to distinguish the various social classes on the basis of dress. Most Europeans now follow middle class patterns. Among affluent workers in Great Britain, skilled factory hands can easily be identified during the week, but on weekends it is virtually impossible to tell what they are. They have two different sets of clothing, only one of which sets them apart as members of the working class.

Europe's housing problems were increased by massive bombings during World War II. A number of cities, including London, Rotterdam, Berlin, Warsaw, and Leningrad, suffered extensive bomb damage and had to be rebuilt. Once this had been completed, the overwhelming majority of Europeans found themselves living in permanent dwellings, mostly apartments. All European governments are now dedicated to the total elimination of the housing problem. In Great Britain, where housing is more readily available than ever before, even members of the working class are in a position to buy cooperative apartments or small houses. After 1958, the Gaullist government in France actively encouraged private capital to invest in housing, and then followed up that plan with money of its own. The present rate of construction in France, 400,000 new dwellings a year, is still considered inadequate. In spite of insufficient housing, rents are low largely because of government-imposed ceilings. Most economists believe that the housing problem in France will not be solved until rent ceilings are removed. In the Soviet Union, there has been an even more determined effort to eliminate the housing shortage. In 1956, the Communist Party adopted a policy calling for the total elimination of housing problems within twenty years. During the 1959–65 Seven-Year Plan, the government planned to construct 15 million new dwellings. In 1961 alone, it was able to move half a million people in Moscow into entirely new dwellings.

The Growth of Affluence

If affluence can be defined as having resources beyond those necessary for food, clothing, and shelter and the leisure to enjoy them, then European society has known affluence in the past. The elites of the eighteenth century knew affluence, as did many levels of the middle class in the nineteenth century. But affluence has only touched the lower in the postwar period, increasing by 400 percent between the end of World War II and 1962. Yet, within the same bloc, Poland increased its industrial production sixfold and Czechoslovakia fivefold.

The growth of economic wealth within Comecon was based on certain deliberate policies. Total integration was not achieved, but trade was expanded, a common system of pricing was introduced, and technical knowledge was exchanged. Common policies in all three areas were enough to stimulate the economies of the six countries. Beginning in 1949, Comecon countries steadily began to reduce their volume of trade with western Europe and to increase the exchange of goods among themselves. As a result, trade within the Communist bloc increased seven times in the period between the late forties and early sixties. For the most part, the countries of Comecon traded raw materials, helping to overcome each other's deficiencies, particularly in fuels and metals. Even more stimulating to the economies of these east European states was the way in which they shared technical knowledge. A headquarters for technical information was established in Moscow. The data gathered here are translated into four languages and then disbursed to agencies planted throughout the Comecon states for even wider distribution. A common pricing policy has also helped to link the economies of eastern Europe. It took several years, but the six countries involved did establish equivalent prices for most of the major commodities that were being traded between them.

As successful as Comecon has been, it could not match the even higher rate of industrial growth that has been a feature of the European Economic Community. The most sophisticated of the post-World War II mergers, the Common Market has been Europe's most successful attempt at international economic cooperation. It is a conscious attempt to copy some of the natural economic relationships and practices that had grown up in Europe prior to 1914. The natural flow of men, money, and material that had been a part of Europe's growing economy in the nineteenth century and that had been lost between the wars was now to be re-created. The start came in 1951 when France, Italy, West Germany, and the Benelux countries joined in the European Coal and Steel Community. An international agency was thereby established to regulate on an integrated basis the production of coal and steel in all six countries. There were also other attempts at economic unions that were to pave the way, a few years later, to even greater economic integration in western Europe. The most conspicuous of these was the European Payments Union, which regulated credit as well as the flow of gold and dollars between various states.

All this, of course, was preparation for the eventual creation of the European Economic Community in 1957. The Common Market, with its

classes within recent decades. What would previously have been considered the privileges of the few have become commonplace for almost all levels of society. Education has become universal; so have vacations. Interest in sports, once considered to be an aristocratic or upper middle class concern, has become widespread. Beyond these, the masses have become involved in the consumer economy at yet another level. For many members of the lower middle class and the lower classes can, in contemporary Europe, afford televisions, radios, and cars, to say nothing of home appliances that make life easier. The deepening of affluence, unprecedented historically in Europe, has, of course, created an even greater contrast between the urban masses of the post-1945 period and the peasant masses that lived in Europe's poverty-stricken agricultural society.

University education in Europe, however, remains a prerogative of the few. Enrollment figures for Great Britain, Germany, and France in the 1960s were, relatively speaking, quite limited, ranging, respectively, from 347,000 to 431,000 to 620,000 in the three west European countries. The Soviet Union has the most extensive system of university training anywhere in Europe, with a student enrollment of almost 4.5 million. By contrast, the majority of students in Europe receive an elementary education up to the time when they are fifteen or sixteen. After this, education becomes the privilege of the few. For example, in Germany in 1970, 70 percent of the population received no education after the age of fifteen. In Italy, only one-third of the population went on to further education. Those who are not destined for high school, the lycée, or the gymnasium and thereafter the universities receive either two or four years of vocational and technical training. Both France and Italy have actively expanded their systems of secondary education since 1961—Italy, for example, doubling its enrollment. Those who have been taking advantage of the new educational opportunities in these two countries have largely been lower middle class elements.

Vacations, inconceivable in another age, have now become a part of life. Most European countries have become dedicated to the idea of providing virtually everyone with either a summer or winter holiday. With aid from the state, most French workmen are now able to take a vacation with their families. Tourist agencies, often functioning with financial assistance from the government, have sprung up all over the Continent. Foreign tours and excursions are usually offered at a wide variety of prices, so that factory workers in Vienna can easily vacation on the Black Sea during the summer months. And a chain of youth hostels has facilitated the increasing propensity of young Europeans to travel around their own continent.

With the growth of leisure time, sports activities of all types are becoming commonplace. Due in the main to modest costs, participation in such sports as swimming, soccer, fishing, horseback riding, and skiing, all once thought to the preserves of the aristocracy and upper middle class, has spread to the masses. The French are typical of the modern European tendency to emphasize sports and the physical side of life. France alone has some 66,000 sporting clubs with a combined membership of some 3 million individuals. Among the best known of these are the various soccer clubs, with 440,000 players at various levels, and a number of cycling clubs with 37,000 active racers. Spectator sports have also grown, with league soccer and car racing drawing the most fans. In the Soviet Union and Czechoslovakia, hockey games draw crowds in the tens of thousands, while Europe as a whole is dotted with soccer stadiums holding up to 75,000 and even 100,000 people. Leisure-time pursuits have also produced a market for outdoor equipment of all sorts. In France, the population now spends more money on camping and sporting equipment than it does for movie tickets.

Entertainment and leisure have spread to the masses in still other ways. The sale of radios and televisions has brought entertainment into most homes. The sale of automobiles has climbed to such a high that motoring has become a popular pastime. By 1965, radios were an almost universal feature of European homes. It is rare in countries like France, Italy, Czechoslovakia, and the Soviet Union to find a household without a radio. One of the very few exceptions to this rule is Spain, where only half of the households own a radio. Television viewing has become as much a part of everyday life as listening to the radio. In western Europe, by 1969, nearly 75 percent of all families had at least black and white television. The proportion in Czechoslovakia was about the same, but in the Soviet Union less than half of the households had a television set, although sales were expanding at a rate of nearly 3 million a year. The Soviet Union has, moreover, gone in for the mass production of automobiles and will soon have a motoring public. In time, the Soviets will catch up with western Europe, where automobiles are owned, on average, by about 80 percent of all families.

The overwhelming majority of Europeans are now in a position not only to satisfy their basic economic wants, but to begin to purchase luxury items as well. They have been able to operate at these levels because of constantly rising purchasing power. Over most of the period since 1945, wages have kept ahead of prices, just as they did during the nineteenth century up to 1914. The only break in that pattern was, of course, the interwar period, when purchasing power rose and declined depending on economic circumstances. From the previous history of Europe, it is abundantly evident that a rising standard of living and growing affluence for the masses are highly dependent on a healthy and expanding industrial economy. Most European governments in turn, concluded that a growing economy is more than ever the [uct of international cooperation.

The Appearance of Economic Blocs

The three distinct economic blocs that have appeared in Eu since 1945 all have had the same purpose: to facilitate the move of goods, people, and capital across national boundaries. The assump in each instance is the same, that economic growth and development best be accomplished on an international scale. The Council for M Economic Assistance, set up in 1948, was created in eastern Europe direct reaction to the Marshall Plan. Better known as Comecon, economic bloc was founded with Russian leadership after the S Union, fearful of American domination, had refused to participat an integrated European recovery plan. Rejecting Marshall Plan aid would have tied its economy to those of the west, the Soviet bloc bro into existence its own concerted plan for regional economic developm It took longer for France, Italy, West Germany, and the Benelux c tries to move closer together economically, but they finally did s the Treaty of Rome, which went into full effect in 1958 and fath the European Economic Community. The one major state to be out of these two economic blocs, Great Britain, combined two years with a number of smaller states to create the European Free Trade A ciation, still another victory for the idea of collective action.

Comecon began life as a Socialist alternative to the Marshall P The communiqué put out by the conferees at the time of its founda declared that its purpose was "to establish . . . wider economic operation between the countries of people's democracy and the USSF In spite of its strength and power, the Soviet Union has not domin this bloc. Most of the countries of eastern Europe have shown a str tendency to emphasize their own economic interests and not to giv to those of the Soviet colossus. With what sometimes amounted to ited and hesitant cooperation, the Soviet Union, Bulgaria, Hung Poland, Rumania, and Czechoslovakia nonetheless forged a bloc did spur economic growth in all six countries. By 1962, fourteen y after the foundation of Comecon, the union had increased its share world industrial production from 16 to 30 percent, and its percent of world trade from 7 to 11 percent. Industrial growth in the So Union, the second greatest industrial power in the world, was spectacu

[1] Michael Kaser, *Comecon: Integrated Problems of the Planned Economies* (ford, England: Oxford University Press, 1965), p. 12.

administration in Brussels, had as its chief aim the elimination, within a twelve-year period, of all barriers to the free flow of goods, capital, and labor. Economic integration was to be achieved first by means of progressive reduction of all tariff barriers among the member states of the Community. Simultaneously, there were to be deliberate efforts to encourage the movement of labor, largely Italian as it turned out, across national borders and to entice capital from one country into another. The EEC also set up a European Investment Bank with initial capital resources of $1 billion and an investment fund of $600 million for the overseas territories of member states, primarily those belonging to France. Other advantages were a common farm policy, common pricing for all major industrial and agricultural goods, and a common tariff policy.

Joint economic policies have turned the countries of the European Economic Community into the world's second most productive economic union, surpassed only by the United States. Once again, as in the case of Comecon, joint international effort has produced spectacular growth. The growth rate within the Common Market was a steady 5 percent right up to the early 1970s, so that both production and the standard of living within the market will have doubled by 1977. The growth rate has been so impressive that Great Britain, with a much slower pace of development, was finally forced to seek membership. Britain hoped that the move would encourage her own sluggish economy, a decision that the Irish and the Danes also took in the early 1970s. When the market recently expanded from six to nine members, it undermined the trading bloc that the British had originally established in 1960 to counter the influence of the Common Market, the European Free Trade Association.

Compared with the Common Market, the European Free Trade Association was a much more conventional approach to the idea of international economic cooperation. Lacking the intricacies that have welded together the various states in the Common Market, the association was more a simple union designed to benefit its members through a common tariff policy. Britain, shut off from the Common Market countries and feeling the loss of her traditional markets, tried to reestablish her economic connection with the Continent by taking the lead in the formation of the association. The European Free Trade Association joined Britain in an economic union with a number of smaller states—Austria, Denmark, Finland, Norway, Portugal, Sweden, and Switzerland. While it lived, the basic aim of the European Free Trade Association was to remove all existing tariff barriers. In the process, the association became a preferential area within which the goods of one country found a ready market in the others. Since it linked both industrial and agricultural states, the union turned out to be a very natural one.

The overall growth rate in the European Free Trade Association lagged behind both Comecon and the Common Market. This realization led Great Britain and some of the countries united with her in the association to seek membership in the Common Market. The move was especially important for Great Britain, since her standard of living, on a per capita basis, had begun to fall below those of France and West Germany. With the entry of Great Britain, Ireland, and Denmark into the Common Market, western Europe should be better able than ever to maintain a rising standard of living for those living within its boundaries. Comecon is likewise dedicated to the idea of economic improvement, and just like the Common Market sees international cooperation as the means by which even greater levels of affluence can be attained. The vehicle for continued development must be the city. For Europe is now an urban society, and it can hardly afford to allow the problems of the city to ruin the quality of life in an industrial society.

Urban Society

For almost a century and a half Europe has been progressively urbanized. In spite of wars and depressions, urbanization continued to the point where most Europeans now live in towns and cities. During this era, the population of Europe has grown from a pre-World War I total of 400 million to 750 million. The concentration of Europe's growing population into smaller and smaller geographic areas has itself created certain problems. Planning is today more important than ever before. Land use, public transportation, housing, and the emergence of new towns have all suddenly become the concern of urban planners. The cities of Europe threaten to grow to the point where they will become a hazard, both physically and psychologically. In 1930, Europe already had 270 cities with over 100,000 inhabitants, accounting for a full 27 percent of the population. By 1960, Europe had more than 420 cities with 100,000 residents, with a total of 41 percent of the population. The tendency toward overconcentration has been most dramatically revealed in the case of London, where the population of the total metropolitan area centered on the British capital reached more than 10 million in the 1960s.

Greater London is undoubtedly the most extreme example of the way in which Europe has concentrated its population in relatively small geographic areas, but there are others. The great industrial area of the Ruhr in western Germany has more than 5.5 million people concentrated in such major manufacturing centers as Essen, Dortmund, and Duisburg. In the Netherlands, the cities of Amsterdam, Rotterdam, The Hague, Haarlem, and a few smaller centers form a ring 40 miles in diameter. One third of the total Dutch population is contained within that circle.

These large cities are not, however, the urban areas with which most Europeans are familiar. Europe's urban population is concentrated in smaller cities, in urban areas that range in population from 250,000 to 500,000 inhabitants. In this sense, certain French cities such as Strasbourg, Toulouse, Nice, Nantes, and Rouen are, in fact, more representative than Paris. The contrast between the past and present is best illustrated by the fact that in the eighteenth century the average European lived in a village of some 700, while in the last half of the twentieth century, he lives in a medium-sized city of 375,000.

The city is the matrix of Europe's modern commercial and industrial society. Land is valuable in urban areas because it is used to support the banking, commercial, administrative, and industrial activities centered on the city. In this respect, London is a typical city. The central part of London is taken up by office buildings, financial and commercial headquarters, government offices, department stores, and expensive shops. Industry is not centrally located in London; it is to be found on the periphery of the city. Since land in the city is considered valuable because of its economic potential, housing in most European cities is crowded and, in a sense, limited. The average European still lives in relatively cramped quarters. Apartment houses, five, six, and seven stories high are typical of Birmingham, Leipzig, and Kiev, again because land is in such short supply that dwellings are built up, not out. Whatever land is left over is taken up by roads and boulevards. Laid down in a previous era, the side streets of Paris, to give one example, hardly seem fit to conduct car traffic, the job they are now expected to do. Parks and wide avenues sometimes break up the feeling that people and buildings are too close together in most European cities, but they are the exception in an otherwise rather cramped environment.

Moving large numbers of people to and from work has become a major concern of urban planners. In London, there is a growing conviction that the center of the city can no longer absorb any further increase in the volume of car and truck traffic. The problem is not passenger cars, which make up only 19 percent of the traffic entering the center of the city; it is commercial vehicles carrying goods. Most Londoners travel to and from work either by subway or train. Commuting by means of public transportation in London has in itself prevented a total collapse of traffic facilities. Traffic congestion plagues many areas. For example, the Paris region, as small as it is geographically, already has 1,850,000 registered vehicles, 85 percent of them passenger cars. To accommodate this traffic, the Paris Regional Planning Board has decided to create new motorways. New highways and interchanges may take care of existing traffic, but they also tend to compound the problem by encouraging further use of private vehicles. The government of West Germany, leading businesses, and the

Land authorities of Rhineland-Westphalia have joined to come up with a concerted plan for all future traffic and transportation in the obviously overcrowded area of the Ruhr. And the Russians, just entering the automotive age, have extensive plans for directing the increased car traffic that they expect in Moscow and elsewhere.

The standard response of urban planners to the problems created by overconcentration has been to create satellite cities. The satellite city is supposed to save the large metropolitan area from most of the pressures that now threaten it by drawing off a portion of the population, cutting down on transportation problems, relieving the demand for housing, and absorbing both new and old industry. These new towns are, according to the planners, to be built at a distance from the large metropolitan areas, usually beyond a green belt of trees and farmlands. They are to be self-contained units with their own supporting industry, schools, recreation facilities, and shopping centers. Four countries are already in the process of building satellite cities to relieve urban congestion—Great Britain, France, Sweden, and the Soviet Union. London is eventually to have twenty satellite cities, many of them 40 to 60 miles away. Liverpool's population is also to be reduced by seven new towns that are to draw off a part of that metropolis's extra population. As of 1959, the Soviet Union had plans for the construction of 319 satellite cities to relieve the pressure on such major metropolitan areas as Moscow, Leningrad, Kiev, Sverdlovsk, and Novosibirsk. As grandiose as these plans sound, they have, in fact, become little more than a means of removing the working class and industry from the larger metropolitan areas.

In spite of the fact that the cities of Europe are still faced with serious problems, the urban environment continues to offer opportunities. The standard of living is high and employment opportunities varied. Food and clothing are plentiful and housing adequate. Moreover, the amenities are there in the form of the theater, operas, and concerts. Recreational facilities could be better, but the automobile is solving this problem by giving people access to the seaside, the country, and the mountains. Even if problems still remain, the city in the last half of the twentieth century appears a much more satisfying and humane environment than that provided by rural Europe in the eighteenth century.

16

Conclusion:
Continuity and Change

Now that Europe has completed the transition from an agricultural to an industrial society, it is easier to look back at what has happened. With urbanization nearly complete and the social order stabilized, continuity rather than change is becoming more and more a feature of Europe's modern industrial society. The social stratification of the post-World War II period is not the castelike system of the preindustrial age. There is still room for peripheral mobility by individuals, even if massive social movement up and down the social scale has stopped. The growing stratification of the social classes, both west and east, differs in yet another respect from the rigid ordering of society in the eighteenth century. While Europe was an overwhelmingly agricultural society, there was no real economic advance for the masses. By comparison, in present-day society the standard of living keeps rising and carrying the various lower levels of modern mass society beyond basic concerns for food, clothing, and shelter to affluence.

The most striking feature of the transformation of European society between 1700 and now is the way in which the petty bourgeoisie, the working class, and the peasantry have fared under industrialization. Elites, whether aristocratic or bourgeois, have experienced affluence, luxury, and often good health on a more or less continuous basis. The artisan and peasant masses of the preindustrial period, of course, did not. They lived below the poverty line, often ignored by their more well-to-do contemporaries—and by the writers of history.

During the nineteenth century, Europe began to transform its illiterate, undernourished, and often unproductive peasant masses into a much more dynamic and productive group. They became the new elements in the cities. The key to this enormous change was industrialization. That change did not come instantly; Europe did not just jump from the poverty of the last half of eighteenth century to the affluence of the latter part of the twentieth century. It progressed step-by-step, raising up the rural population and then creating new social classes in the cities. This was true whether the society was capitalist or socialist. What really mattered was not ideology, but the growth of productivity. In sum, progressive improvement is one of the dominant characteristics of modern industrial society. Tracing the rise in real wages through the age of social transformation demonstrates this; so does the fact that life expectancy in Europe has nearly tripled since 1800. It has been raised decade by decade, just like the European standard of living.

It is little wonder that most underdeveloped agricultural societies would like to follow the example of the most advanced countries and industrialize, for Europe too was poorly developed in the eighteenth century, but in time grew prosperous. The Industrial Revolution may well be seen, especially from the point of view of social and economic history, as the only real revolution Europe has ever experienced. It is the only event that deserves that title because no other experience in European history produced the changes industrialization was able to bring about. This is particularly the case if one broadens the definition of the Industrial Revolution to include all the major economic changes that took place from the 1750s on.

The economic changes caused by industrialization worked a very subtle effect upon the European social order. As economic wealth shifted from the aristocracy to the upper middle class, investment for the purpose of economic growth became more of a reality. Capital at this level was put to use, with the result a major expansion of the economy. Between 1800 and 1900, Europe increased its production of agricultural and industrial goods by nearly 500 percent. All of this had a dramatic effect on the social order. The old society was literally dismantled within two generations of the coming of industrialization. It was almost as if an invisible hand was operating, reducing the prestige and significance of older social classes and reshaping and redesigning society to the point where it took on a modern complexion, with new classes and groups.

Economic changes, whether they took the form of savings, investment, profits, inflation, income, purchasing power, or taxes, helped reshape the European social order. A new elite arose, and a new elite-mass relationship. The masses were not, and never have been, unified. There was no consciousness on the part of the petty bourgeoisie, the working class, and the peasantry, once they took on their present social dimensions, of belonging to a common group. Quite often, in fact, they distrusted one another. Sometimes great social and economic differences separated the various levels in mass society. Yet the concessions to the masses came, first in the form of rising wages and then thereafter as political, educational, and welfare benefits. To a large extent, the elite not only gave in on these issues, but also helped to finance them. For it was the tax money of the upper reaches of the middle class that paid for public education and social security.

This does not mean that social tensions between the elite and the mass have vanished, but they have diminished. They were at a relatively low ebb before 1914 and after 1945, when the masses seemed to be benefitting from industrial society. Social tensions increased to the point of class conflict only in the interwar period. The elite was frankly unable to keep up the gains that the masses had known before World War I, and resulting severe social tension was relieved only in the post-World War II period by a renewal of major economic concessions to the masses.

Is the age of change over? The massive changes of the past have apparently come to an end. With industrial society essentially formed and the urban areas saturated, Europe seems to be reaching a state of equilibrium. As it does, it will undoubtedly grow more conservative. Continuity, in the form of social stratification and a certain immobility, is now evident. Habit is becoming dominant. Existing social patterns are again becoming hard and fast. The standard of living will undoubtedly still rise, but people are being improved where they are in the social order, not as a result of social mobility, though individual acts of mobility are still possible.

All of this raises the question whether change is or is not a permanent feature of society. Change, intense change, was certainly a characteristic of Europe while it was advancing from one stage of economic development to another. But now change is becoming less and less important. Continuity has reasserted itself as the European social order settles into place. It is possible that change may not be a continuous feature of society, but only of eras of transition like that Europe has just passed through.

Bibliography

The content of this book is largely based upon recent articles that have appeared in English, French, German and Russian journals. Social history is such a young area that a great deal of the basic material is not yet in book form. As a result, the books that have been written contain only a part of the information we now have. As social history matures, more studies about social class and the standard of living in the past will appear. But in the meantime, those interested in the basic history of Europe are dependent on the work of historians who have collected data and passed them on to us in the form of journal articles, of which there are literally hundreds in each of the basic European languages.

Books dealing with the various aspects of European social history are now being published with greater and greater frequency, as a glance at the works listed in the following bibliography will show. The bibliography presented here is not all-inclusive; it is a reasonable attempt to list most of the pertinent books available on various aspects of social history.

Because social history is so new, there are gaps in our knowledge. For some reason, just to give one example, preindustrial society seems to have drawn more attention than industrial society, so that we now know more about the aristocracy and the artisans than we do about the middle class and the factory working element. These areas of insufficient knowledge will undoubtedly soon be filled, but until that happens, the present bibliography should serve to advance the knowledge of those whose interest leads them beyond the information contained within this book.

General Works

ANDERSON, EUGENE, and PAULINE R. ANDERSON, *Political Institutions and Social Change in Continental Europe in the Nineteenth Century.* Berkeley: University of California Press, 1967.

BRUCK, WERNER F., *Social and Economic History of Germany from William II to Hitler, 1888–1938.* Cardiff: University Press Board, 1938.

COLE, G. D. H., *Studies in Class Structure.* London: Routledge and Paul, 1955.

CONZE, WERNER, *Staat und Gessellschaft im deutschen Vormärz, 1815–1848.* Stuttgart: E. Klett, 1962.

DUPEUX, GEORGES, *La Société Française, 1789–1960.* Paris: A. Colin, 1964.

ENGELSING, ROLF, *Zur Sozialgeschichte deutschen Mittel-lung Unterschichten.* Göttingen: Vandenhoeck & Ruprecht, 1973.

GREGG, PAULINE, *Social and Economic History of Britain, 1760–1960.* London: Harrap, 1962.

HAMEROW, THEODORE S., *Restoration, Revolution, Reaction: Economics and Politics in Germany, 1815–1871.* Princeton: Princeton University Press, 1958.

HAMPSON, NORMAN, *A Social History of the French Revolution.* Toronto: University of Toronto Press, 1963.

LEFEBVRE, GEORGES, *The Coming of the French Revolution,* tr. R. R. Palmer. Princeton: Princeton University Press, 1947.

LIPSET, SEYMOUR M., and REINHARD BENDIX, *Social Mobility in Industrial Society.* Berkeley: University of California Press, 1959.

PERKIN, HAROLD, *The Origins of Modern English Society, 1780–1880.* London: Routledge and Paul, 1969.

PIKE, E. ROYSTON, ed., *Human Documents of the Age of the Forsytes.* London: Allen & Unwin, 1969.

RYDER, JUDITH, and HAROLD SILVER, *Modern English Society: History and Structure.* New York: Barnes & Noble, 1970.

SOBOUL, ALBERT, *La Société Française dans la Seconda Moitié du XVIIIème Siècle.* Paris: Centre de Documentation Universitaire, 1969.

STADELMANN, RUDOLF, *Soziale und Politische Geschichte der Revolution von 1848.* Munich: Bruckmann, 1948.

STEARNS, PETER N., *European Society in Upheaval.* London: Macmillan, 1967.

Population Shifts
and Urban Development

ADAMS, WILLIAM, *Ireland and Irish Emigration to the New World.* New Haven: Yale University Press, 1932.

BERNARD, LEON, *The Emerging City: Paris in the Age of Louis XIV.* Durham, N.C.: Duke University Press, 1970.

CARROTHERS, W. A., *Emigration from the British Isles.* New York: A. M. Kelley, 1969.

CHEVALIER, LOUIS, *La Formation de la Population Parisienne au XIXe Siècle.* Paris: Presses Universitaires de France, 1950.

DICKINSON, ROBERT E., *The West European City: A Geographical Interpretation.* London: Routledge & Paul, 1961.

FORD, FRANKLIN L., *Strasbourg in Transition, 1648–1789.* Cambridge, Mass.: Harvard University Press, 1958.

HALL, PETER, *The World Cities.* New York: McGraw-Hill, 1966.

HANSEN, MARCUS L., *The Atlantic Migration, 1607–1860.* Cambridge, Mass.: Harvard University Press, 1941.

HAUSER, ALBERT, *Die wirtschaftliche und soziale Entwicklung eines Bauerndorfes zur Industrie Gemeinde.* Wädenswil: Buchdruckerei Stutz, 1956.

KÖLLMANN, WOLFGANG, *Sozialgeschichte der Stadt Barmen im 19. Jahrhundert.* Tübingen: Mohr, 1960.

MASUR, GERHARD, *Imperial Berlin.* New York: Basic Books, 1971.

MIDWINTER, E. C., *Social Administration in Lancashire, 1830–1860.* Manchester: Manchester University Press, 1969.

POLLARD, SIDNEY, *A History of Labour in Sheffield.* Liverpool: Liverpool University Press, 1959.

RUDÉ, GEORGE, *Hanoverian London, 1714–1808.* London: Secker & Warburg, 1970.

SHEPPARD, FRANCIS, *London 1808–1870: The Infernal Wen.* London: Secker & Warburg, 1971.

SHEPPERSON, W. S., *British Emigration to North America.* Minneapolis: University of Minnesota Press, 1957.

WALKER, MACK, *Germany and the Emigration, 1816–1885.* Cambridge, Mass.: Harvard University Press, 1964.

———, *German Home Towns.* Ithaca: Cornell University Press, 1971.

WEBER, ADNA F., *The Growth of Cities in the Nineteenth Century.* New York: Columbia University Press, 1899.

WRIGLEY, E. A., *Industrial Growth and Population Change: A Regional Study of North-West Europe in the Later Nineteenth Century.* Cambridge, England: Cambridge University Press, 1961.

————, *Population and History.* New York: McGraw-Hill, 1969.

The Aristocracy

BLUM, JEROME, *Noble Landowners and Agriculture in Austria.* Baltimore: Johns Hopkins Press, 1948.

————, *Lord and Peasant in Russia.* Princeton: Princeton University Press, 1961.

COHEN, EMMELINE, *The Growth of the British Civil Service, 1789–1939.* Hamden, Conn.: Archon Books, 1965.

EMMONS, TERENCE, *The Russian Landed Gentry and the Peasant Emancipation 1861.* Cambridge, England: Cambridge University Press, 1968.

FORD, FRANKLIN L., *Robe and Sword: The Regrouping of the French Aristocracy after Louis XIV.* Cambridge, Mass.: Harvard University Press, 1953.

GOODWIN, ALBERT, ed., *The European Nobility in the Eighteenth Century.* London: A. & C. Black, 1953.

HERTZ-EICHENRODE, DIETER, *Politik und Landwirtschaft in Ostpreussen, 1919–1930.* Cologne: Westdeutscher Verlag, 1969.

KOHN-BRAMSTEDT, ERNST, *Aristocracy and the Middle Classes in Germany.* Rev. ed., Chicago: University of Chicago Press, 1964.

MATHER, F. C., *After the Canal Duke: A Study of Industrial Estates.* Oxford: Clarendon Press, 1970.

MINGAY, G. E., *English Landed Society in the Eighteenth Century.* London: Routledge & Paul, 1963.

MUNCY, LYSBETH, *The Junker in the Prussian Administration under William the Second, 1888–1914.* New York: H. Fertig, 1944.

ROSENBERG, HANS, *Bureaucracy, Aristocracy and Autocracy: The Prussian Experience, 1660–1885.* Cambridge, Mass.: Harvard University Press, 1958.

SCHLINGENSIEPEN, GEORGE, *Der Strukturwandel des Baltischen Adels vor dem Ersten Weltkrieg.* Marburg: Johann Gottfried Herder-Institut, 1959.

THOMPSON, F. M. L., *English Landed Society in the Nineteenth Century.* London: Routledge & Paul, 1963.

The Middle Class

ALEXANDER, DAVID, *Retailing in England during the Industrial Revolution.* London: Athlone, 1970.

ARMYTAGE, W. H. G., *The Rise of the Technocrats: A Social History.* London: Routledge & Paul, 1965.

BAHRDT, HANS P., *Industriebürokratie: Versuch einer Soziologie des Industrialisierten Bürobetriebes und Seiner Angestellten.* Stuttgart: F. Enke, 1958.

BARBER, ELINOR G., *The Bourgeoisie in 18th Century France.* Princeton: Princeton University Press, 1955.

BAYER, HANS, ed., *Der Angestellte zwischen Arbeiterschaft und Management.* Berlin: Duncker & Hamblot, 1961.

BENDIX, REINHARD, *Work and Authority in Industry: Ideologies of Management in the Course of Industrialization.* New York: Wiley, 1956.

CLEMENTS, ROGER, *Managers: A Study of Their Careers in Industry.* London: Allen & Unwin, 1958.

CONYNGHAM, WILLIAM J., *Industrial Management in the Soviet Union.* Stanford: Hoover Institution Press, 1973.

CROWTHER, J. B., *Discoveries and Inventions of the 20th Century.* London: Routledge & Paul, 1955.

CROZIER, MICHEL, *The World of the Office Worker.* Chicago: University of Chicago Press. 1971.

DAUMARD, ADÉLINE, *La Bourgeoisie de Paris au 19e Siècle.* Paris: Flammarion, 1970.

DJILAS, MILOVAN, *The New Class.* New York: Praeger, 1957.

ELLUL. JACQUES, *Métamophose du Bourgeois.* Paris: Calmann-Lévy, 1967.

GUTTSMAN, W. L., *The British Political Elite.* New York: Basic Books, 1963.

HAMEROW, THEODORE, *The Social Foundations of German Unification* (2 vols.). Princeton: Princeton University Press, 1969–72.

KELSALL, R. K., *Higher Civil Servants in Britain from 1870 to the Present.* London: Routledge & Paul, 1955.

KOCKA, JÜRGEN, *Unternehmungsverwaltung und Angestelltenshaft am Beispiel Siemens, 1847–1914.* Stuttgart: E. Klett, 1969.

KRACAUER, SIEGFRIED, *Die Angestellten.* Frankfurt-am-Main: Frankfurter Societäts-Druckerei, 1930.

LEWIS, ROY, and ANGUS MAUDE, *The English Middle Classes.* New York: Knopf, 1950.

LHOMME, J., *La Grande Bourgeoisie au Pouvoir, 1830–1880.* Paris: A. Colin, 1960.

LOCKWOOD, DAVID, *The Blackcoated Worker: A Study in Class Consciousness.* London: Unwin University Books, 1966.

LOTZ, ALBERT, *Geschichte des Deutschen Beamtentums.* Falkenstein: Europa Verlag, 1970.

MARTÍ-IBAÑEZ, FELIX, *The Epic of Medicine.* New York: C. N. Potter, 1959.

MOHLER, WALTER, *Der Laborant: Entstehung und Entwicklung eines Berufes in der Basler chemischen Industrie.* Bern: Herbert Lang, 1970.

MORAZÉ, CHARLES, *La France Bourgeoisie.* Paris: A. Colin, 1952.

———, *The Triumph of the Middle Classes.* London: Weidenfeld & Nicholson, 1966.

PERROT, MARGUERITE, *La Mode de Vie des Familles Bourgeoises, 1873–1953.* Paris: A. Colin, 1961.

POLLARD, SIDNEY, *The Genesis of Modern Management.* Cambridge, Mass.: Harvard University Press, 1965.

READER, W. J., *Professional Men.* New York: Basic Books, 1966.

SINGER, CHARLES, and A. ASHWORTH UNDERWOOD, *A Short History of Medicine* (2nd ed.). New York: Oxford University Press, 1962.

STURMTHAL, ADOLF, ed., *White-Collar Trade Unions: Contemporary Developments in Industrialized Societies*. Urbana, Ill.: University of Illinois Press, 1966.

VAN DILLEN, J. G., *History of the Principal Public Banks*. The Hague: Nijhoff, 1934.

WILSON, R. G., *Gentlemen Merchants: The Merchant Community in Leeds, 1700–1830*. Manchester: Manchester University Press, 1971.

ZAPF, WOLFGANG, *Wandlungen der Deutschen Elite: Ein Zirkulationsmodell deutscher Führungsgruppen, 1919–1961*. Munich: Piper, 1965.

The Peasantry

CONZE, WERNER, ed., *Quellen zur Geschichte der deutschen Bauernbefreiung*. Göttingen: Musterschmidt, 1957.

DOVRING, FOLKE, *Land and Labour in Europe in the Twentieth Century: A Comparative Study of Recent Agrarian History* (3rd rev. ed.). The Hague: Nijhoff, 1965.

FEL, ANDRÉ, *Les Haute Terres du Massif Central: Tradition Paysanne et Economie Agricole*. Paris: Presses Universitaires de France, 1962.

FUSSELL, G. E., *The English Rural Labourer*. London: Batchworth, 1949.

GREEN, FREDERICK E., *A History of the English Agricultural Labourer, 1870–1920*. London: P. S. King, 1920.

HALPERN, J. M., *A Serbian Village*. New York: Holt, Rinehart & Winston, 1968.

HASBACH, W., *A History of the English Agricultural Labourer*. London: P. S. King, 1908.

HENNING, FRIEDRICH-WILHELM, *Dienste und Abgaben der Bauern im 18. Jahrhundert*. Stuttgart: G. Fisher, 1969.

HOSKINS, WILLIAM G., *The Midland Peasant: The Economic and Social History of a Leicestershire Village*. London: St. Martin's Press, 1957.

KIENIEWICZ, STEFAN, *The Emancipation of the Polish Peasantry*. Chicago: University of Chicago Press, 1969.

KNAPP, G. P., *Bauernfreiung und der Ursprung der Landarbeiter in den alteren Theilen Preussens* (2 vols.). Munich: Duncker & Humblot, 1927.

LEFEBVRE, GEORGES, *Les Paysans du Nord pendant la Révolution Française* (2 vols.). Paris: F. Rieder, 1924.

MAGER, FRIEDRICH, *Geschichte des Bauerntums und der Bodenkultur im Lande Mecklenburg*. Berlin: Akademie-Verlag, 1955.

MALEFAKIS, EDWARD E., *Agrarian Reform and Peasant Revolution in Spain: Origins of the Civil War*. New Haven: Yale University Press, 1970.

MITRANY, DAVID, *The Land and the Peasant in Rumania: The War and Agrarian Reform*. London: Oxford University Press, 1930.

ROBINSON, GEROID T., *Rural Russia under the Old Regime*. New York: Macmillan, 1932.

SHEPPARD, THOMAS, *Lourmarin in the Eighteenth Century*. Baltimore: Johns Hopkins Press, 1971.

SOLTA, JAN, *Die Bauern der Lausitz*. Bautzen: Domowing-Verlag, 1968.

TAVERNIER, JACQUES, *Le Syndicalisme Paysan*. Paris: A. Colin, 1969.

TILLY, CHARLES, *The Vendée*. Cambridge, Mass.: Harvard University Press, 1964.

VUCINICH, WAYNE, ed., *The Peasant in Nineteenth-century Russia*. Stanford: Stanford University Press, 1968.

WALTER, GÉRARD, *Histoire des Paysans de France*. Paris: Flammarion, 1963.

WINKEL, HARALD, *Die Ablosungskapitalien aus der Bauernfreiung im West- und Süddeutschland*. Stuttgart: G. Fisher, 1968.

WOODHAM-SMITH, CECIL, *The Great Hunger*. New York: Harper & Row, 1963.

WRIGHT, GORDON, *Rural Revolution in France: The Peasant in the Twentieth Century*. Stanford: Stanford University Press, 1964.

WUNDERLICH, FRIEDA, *Farm Labor in Germany, 1810–1945*. Princeton: Princeton University Press, 1961.

ZINK, ANNE, *Azereix: La Vie d'une Communauté Rurale à la Fin du XVIIIe Siècle*. Paris: S.E.V.P.E.N., 1969.

The Artisans

BYTHELL, DUNCAN, *The Handloom Weavers*. Cambridge, England: Cambridge University Press, 1969.

CHEVALIER, LOUIS, *Laboring Classes and Dangerous Classes*, tr. Frank Jellinek. New York: H. Fertig, 1973.

COORNAERT, ÉMILE, *Les Corporations en France avant 1789*. Paris: Les Editions Ouvrières, 1968.

FISCHER, WOLFRAM, *Handwerksrecht und Handwerkswirtschaft um 1800: Studien zur Sozial- und Wirtschaftsverfassung vor der industriellen Revolution*. Berlin: Duncker & Humblot, 1955.

GEORGE, M. DOROTHY, *London Life in the Eighteenth Century*. London: Paul, Trench, Trubner, 1925.

JOHNSON, L. G., *The Social Evolution of Industrial Britain*. Liverpool: Liverpool University Press, 1963.

SACK, FRITZ, *Integration und Anpassung des Handwerks in der Industriellen Gesellschaft*. Cologne: Westdeutscher Verlag, 1966.

THOMPSON, E. P., *The Making of the English Working Class*. New York: Pantheon Books, 1966.

The Working Class

AERNI, KURT, *Die Ermüdung des Maschinenarbeiters*. Bern: P. G. Keller, 1959.

BERGSON, ABRAHM, *The Structure of Soviet Wages*. Cambridge, Mass.: Harvard University Press, 1954.

CHOMBART DE LAUWE, P., *La Vie Quotidienne des Familles Ouvrières*. Paris: Centre National de la Recherche Scientifique, 1956.

COENEN, JACQUES, *Opinions Politiques en Milieu Ouvrier*. Paris: Fondation Louis de Brouckere, 1961.

COLLIER, FRANCES, *The Family Economy of the Working Class in the Cotton Industry*. Manchester: Manchester University Press, 1965.

DAWSON, WILLIAM H., *The German Workman*. London: P. S. King, 1906.

FAY, CHARLES R., *Life and Labour in the Nineteenth Century*. Cambridge, England: The University Press, 1947.

FURSTENBERG, FRIEDRICH, et al., *Die Sociallage der Chemiearbeiter*. Berlin: Luchterhand, 1969.

GREBING, HELGA, *The History of the German Labor Movement: A Survey*. London: Wolff, 1969.

GRUNER, ERICH, *Die Arbeiter in der Schweiz im 19. Jahrhundert*. Bern: Francke, 1968.

HOROWITZ, DANIEL, *The Italian Labor Movement*. Cambridge, Mass.: Harvard University Press, 1963.

KLENNER, FRITZ, *Die österreichischen Gewerkschaften* (2 vols.). Vienna: Verlag des Oesterreichischen Gewerkschaftsbundes, 1951–53.

LORWIN, VAL R., *The French Labor Movement*. Cambridge, Mass.: Harvard University Press, 1954.

RAINVILLE, JEAN-MARIE, *Condition Ouvrière et Integration Sociale*. Paris: Les Editions Ouvrières, 1967.

REDFORD, ARTHUR, *Labour Migration in England, 1800–1850*. London: Longmans, Green, 1926.

RITTER, GERHARD, *Die Arbeiterbewegung in Wilhelmischen Reich*. Berlin: Colloquium Verlag, 1963.

SMELSER, NEIL J., *Social Change in the Industrial Revolution: An Application of Theory to the Lancashire Cotton Industry, 1770–1840*. London: Routledge & Paul, 1960.

STRAUSS, RUDOLPH, *Die Lage und die Bewegung der Chemnitzer Arbeiter in der ersten Halfte des 19. Jahrhunderts*. Berlin: Akademie Verlag, 1960.

ZWEIG, FERDYNAND, *The Worker in an Affluent Society*. New York: Free Press of Glencoe, 1961.

Specialized Topics

Popular Protest

BROEKER, GALEN, *Rural Disorder and Police Reform in Ireland, 1812–1836*. London: Routledge & Paul, 1970.

COBB, RICHARD, *The Police and the People: French Popular Protest, 1789–1820*. Oxford: Clarendon Press, 1970.

GODECHOT, JACQUES, *The Taking of the Bastille, July 4, 1789*. New York: Scribner's, 1970.

HOBSBAUM, E. J., and GEORGE RUDÉ, *Captain Swing*. New York: Pantheon Books, 1968.

LEFEBVRE, GEORGES, *The Great Fear of 1789*, tr. Joan White. New York: Pantheon Books, 1973.

MATHER, F. C., *Public Order in the Age of the Chartists*. Manchester: Manchester University Press, 1959.

RUDÉ, GEORGE, *The Crowd in the French Revolution*. Oxford: Oxford University Press, 1959.

———, *The Crowd in History, 1730–1848*. New York: Clarendon Press, 1964.

SOBOUL, ALBERT, *The Parisian Sans-Culottes and the French Revolution*. Oxford: Clarendon Press, 1964.

WILLIAMS, DAVID, *The Rebecca Riots: A Study in Agrarian Discontent*. Cardiff: University of Wales Press, 1955.

The Standard of Living

ATKINSON, A. B., *Poverty in Britain and the Reform of Social Security*. Cambridge, England: Cambridge University Press, 1969.

BRUCE, MAURICE, *The Coming of the Welfare State* (3rd ed.). London: Batsford, 1966.

BRY, GERHARD, *Wages in Germany, 1871–1945*. Princeton: Princeton University Press, 1960.

BURNETT, JOHN, *A History of the Cost of Living*. Hammondsworth: Penguin, 1969.

CHESNEY, KELLOW, *The Anti-society: An Account of the Victorian Under-world*. Boston: Gambit, 1970.

COLLINET, MICHEL, *L'Ouvrier Française; Essai sur la Condition Ouvrière, 1900–1950*. Paris: Éditions Ouvrières, 1951.

DESAI, ASHOK V., *Real Wages in Germany, 1871–1913*. Oxford: Clarendon Press, 1968.

DUVEAU, GEORGES, *La Vie Ouvrière en France sous le Second Empire*. Paris: Gallimard, 1946.

FRIED, ALBERT, and RICHARD M. ELAM, eds., *Charles Booth's London: A Portrait of the Poor at the Turn of the Century*. New York: Pantheon Books, 1967.

GEORGE, V. M., *Social Security: Beveridge and After*. London: Routledge & Paul, 1968.

GILBERT, BENTLEY, *The Evolution of National Insurance in Great Britain: The Origins of the Welfare State*. London: Joseph, 1966.

HALBWACHS, MAURICE, *L'Evolution des Besoins dans les Classes Ouvrières*. Paris: F. Alcan, 1933.

HANSON, PHILIP, *The Consumer in the Soviet Economy*. Evanston, Ill.: Northwestern University Press, 1968.

KEENE, NANCY, *The Employment of Young Workers*. London: Batsford, 1969.

MADISON, BERNICE Q., *Social Welfare in the Soviet Union*. Stanford: Stanford University Press, 1968.

ROBERTS, DAVID, *Victorian Origins of the British Welfare State*. New Haven: Yale University Press, 1960.

ROSENTHAL, ALBERT H., *The Social Programs of Sweden: A Search for Security in a Free Society.* Minneapolis: University of Minnesota Press, 1967.

ROUTH, GUY, *Occupation and Pay in Great Britain, 1906–1960.* Cambridge, England: Cambridge University Press, 1965.

SCHEWE, DIETER, et al., *Survey of Social Security in the Federal Republic of Germany,* tr. Frank Kenny. Bonn: Federal Ministry for Labour and Social Affairs, 1972.

SCHORR, ALVIN L., *Social Security and Social Services in France.* Washington, D.C.: U.S. Department of Social Security, 1955.

VON TYSKA, CARL, *Löhne und Lebenskosten in Westeuropa im 19. Jahrhundert.* Munich: Duncker & Humblot, 1914.

YOUNG, A. F., *Social Services in British Industry.* London: Routledge & Paul, 1968.

Contemporary Society

ARCHER, MARGARET S., and SALVADOR GINER, eds., *Contemporary Europe: Class, Status and Power.* New York: St. Martin's Press, 1971.

ARDAGH, JOHN, *The New French Revolution.* New York: Harper & Row, 1968.

BALDWIN, HANSON W., *World War I: An Outline History.* New York: Harper & Row, 1962.

BECK, ROBERT H., et al., *The Changing Structure of Europe.* Minneapolis: University of Minnesota Press, 1970.

BLACK, CYRIL E., ed., *The Transformation of Russian Society.* Cambridge, Mass.: Harvard University Press, 1960.

BOUVIER-AJAM, MAURICE, *Les Classes Sociales en France.* Paris: Éditions Sociales, 1963.

CROUZET, MAURICE, *The European Renaissance since 1945.* London: Thames & Hudson, 1970.

DAHRENDORF, RALF, *Society and Democracy in Germany.* Garden City, N.Y.: Doubleday, 1971.

FALLS, CYRIL B., *The Great War.* New York: Putnam, 1959.

FERRÉ, LOUISE, *Les Classes Sociales dans la France Contemporaine.* Paris: J. Vrin, 1934.

FISCHER-GALATI, STEPHEN, ed., *Eastern Europe in the Sixties.* New York: Praeger, 1963.

FRUMKIN, GREGORY, *Population Changes in Europe since 1939.* New York: A. M. Kelley, 1951.

GEIGER, THEODOR, *Soziale Schichtung des deutschen Volkes.* Stuttgart: F. Enke, 1932.

GLASS, D. V., ed., *Social Mobility in Britain.* London: Routledge & Paul, 1954.

GRAUBARD, STEPHEN, ed., *A New Europe?* Boston: Houghton Mifflin, 1964.

GRAVES, ROBERT, and ALAN HODGE, *The Long-Weekend: A British Social History, 1918–1939.* New York: Macmillan, 1941.

HOFFMANN, STANLEY, et al., *In Search of France.* Cambridge, Mass.: Harvard University Press, 1963.

INKELES, ALEX, *Social Change in Soviet Russia*. New York: Simon and Schuster, 1971.

KNAPP, WILFRID, *A History of War and Peace, 1939–1965*. London: Oxford University Press, 1967.

LIDDELL-HART, BASIL HENRY, *History of the Second World War*. New York: Putnam, 1970.

LUXENBURG, NORMAN, *Europe since World War II: The Big Change*. Carbondale, Ill.: Southern Illinois University Press, 1973.

REED, JOHN, *The War in Eastern Europe*. New York: Scribner's, 1916.

SCHOENBAUM, DAVID, *Hitler's Social Revolution*. New York: Doubleday, 1966.

Economic History

ABEL, WILHELM, *Agrarkrisen und Agrarkonjunktur*. Hamburg: Parey, 1966.

ALPERT, PAUL, *Twentieth Century Economic History of Europe*. New York: Schuman, 1951.

AUGE-LARIBÉ, MICHEL, *L'Evolution de la France Agricole*. Paris: A. Colin, 1912.

BLACKWELL, WILLIAM L., *The Industrialization of Russia*. New York: Crowell, 1970.

CAMERON, RONDO, *France and the Economic Development of Europe, 1800–1914*. Princeton: Princeton University Press, 1961.

CLAPHAM, J. H., *An Economic History of Modern Britain* (3 vols.). Cambridge, England: Cambridge University Press, 1930–38.

———, *The Economic Development of France and Germany* (4th ed.). Cambridge, England: Cambridge University Press, 1966.

CLOUGH, SHEPARD B., *Economic History of Europe* (3rd ed.). Boston: Heath, 1952.

———, *France: A History of National Economics, 1789–1939*. New York: Octagon Books, 1964.

———, *The Economic History of Modern Italy*. New York: Columbia University Press, 1964.

CURZON, VICTOR, et al., *The European Free Trade Association and the Crisis of European Integration*. Geneva: Institute of International Studies, 1968.

DUNHAM, ARTHUR L., *The Industrial Revolution in France, 1815–1858*. New York: Exposition Press, 1955.

GROSS, REINER, *Die bürgerliche Agrarreform in Sachsen in den ersten Hälfte 19. Jahrhunderts*. Dresden: Böklau, 1968.

HAUSHOFER, HEINZ, *Die deutsche Landwirtschaft im technischen Zeitalter*. Stuttgart: E. Ulmer, 1963.

HEATON, HERBERT, *Economic History of Europe* (rev. ed.). New York: Harper, 1936.

HENDERSON, WILLIAM O., *Britain and Industrial Europe, 1750–1870*. Liverpool: Liverpool University Press, 1954.

———, *The Industrial Revolution on the Continent*. London: F. Cass, 1961.

———, *The Industrialization of Europe, 1780–1914*. London: Thames & Hudson, 1969.

HODSON, H. V., *Slump and Recovery, 1929–1937*. London: Oxford University Press, 1938.

KASER, MICHAEL, *Comecon: Integrated Problems of the Planned Economies*. Oxford: Oxford University Press, 1965.

POLLARD, SIDNEY, *European Economic Integration, 1815–1970*. London: Thames & Hudson, 1974.

———, and COLIN HOLMES, *Documents of European Economic History* (3 vols.). New York: St. Martin's Press, 1968–73.

POSTAN, M. M., *An Economic History of Western Europe, 1945–1964*. London: Methuen, 1967.

READER, W. J., *Imperial Chemical Industries, 1870–1926*. Oxford: Oxford University Press, 1970.

SLICHER VON BATH, BERNARD H., *The Agrarian History of Western Europe, 500–1840*, tr. Olive Ordish. New York: St. Martin's Press, 1963.

TRACY, MICHAEL, *Agriculture in Western Europe*. New York: Praeger, 1964.

WALSH, A. E., and JOHN PAXTON, *The Structure and Development of the Common Market*. New York: Taplinger, 1969.

ZAUBERMAN, ALFRED, *Industrial Progress in Poland, Czechoslovakia and East Germany, 1937–1962*. Oxford: Oxford University Press, 1964.

Index